The I in We

The I in We

Studies in the Theory of Recognition

Axel Honneth

Translated by Joseph Ganahl

polity

First published in German as *Das Ich im Wir* © Suhrkamp Verlag Berlin, 2010

This English edition © Polity Press, 2014

Reprinted 2014 (twice), 2015, 2016

Polity Press
65 Bridge Street
Cambridge CB2 1UR, UK

Polity Press
350 Main Street
Malden, MA 02148, USA

ISBN-13: 978-0-7456-5232-0
ISBN-13: 978-0-7456-5233-7(pb)

A catalogue record for this book is available from the British Library.

Typeset in 10.5 on 12 pt Palatino
by Toppan Best-set Premedia Limited
Printed and bound in Great Britain by Clays Ltd, St Ives plc

The publisher has used its best endeavours to ensure that the URLs for external websites referred to in this book are correct and active at the time of going to press. However, the publisher has no responsibility for the websites and can make no guarantee that a site will remain live or that the content is or will remain appropriate.

Every effort has been made to trace all copyright holders, but if any have been inadvertently overlooked the publisher will be pleased to include any necessary credits in any subsequent reprint or edition.

For further information on Polity, visit our website: www.politybooks.com

Contents

Preface

This volume brings together a number of contributions to discussions over recent years on how to build upon the basic assumptions of a Hegelian theory of recognition. After initially outlining my interpretation of Hegel's approach in *The Struggle for Recognition*, I had my hands full correcting or further elucidating my position in response to various objections. In particular, a debate with Nancy Fraser and the Tanner Lectures at the University of California, Berkeley, offered welcome opportunities to give a more precise account of what were still vague considerations.[1] But in going down this path and attempting to deal with various impulses from alternative theories of intersubjectivity,[2] many questions still remained unsolved. After all, the reason I had sought to reconstruct Hegel's theory of recognition was to garner insights that would not only allow a rethinking of the concept of justice, but also lead to a better account of the relationship between socialization and individuation, between social reproduction and individual identity formation. My diverse efforts to clarify this relationship over recent years are gathered in this volume. Apart from a few exceptions, the essays move along the margins of social philosophy, where normative questions can only be answered by taking into account the empirical undertakings of other, neighbouring disciplines.

Part I, however, contains two essays in which I return to essential elements of Hegel's practical philosophy. Whereas in *The Struggle for Recognition* I had still assumed that only Hegel's Jena lectures contained coherent elements of a theory of recognition, after more intensive study of his mature writings I came to realize how wrong I had been. I no longer believe that Hegel sacrificed his initial intersubjectivism in the course of developing a monological concept of spirit; rather, Hegel sought throughout his life to interpret objective spirit, i.e. social reality, as a set of layered relations of recognition. On the basis of this reassessment I sought to make Hegel's *Philosophy of Right* fruitful for the development of a theory of recognition. Expressed much more strongly than in his early writings is the groundbreaking notion that social justice is to be defined in terms of the requirements of mutual recognition, and that we must take our point of departure in historically developed and already institutionalized relations of recognition.[3] In the essay on Hegel's concept of self-consciousness (Chapter 1), which deals with a key chapter from *Phenomenology of Spirit*, I attempt to clarify the systematic meaning of recognition in this context; for the mature Hegel, recognition refers to an act of moral self-restriction, which we must be able to perform on ourselves in the face of others if we are to arrive at a consciousness of our self. By contrast, the essay on Hegel's *Philosophy of Right* (Chapter 2) attempts to answer the difficult question of how we are to conceive of the internal connection between recognition and human freedom. According to my interpretation, Hegel creates this link by attempting to demonstrate to contemporary proponents of liberalism that it is only by taking part in institutionalized practices of individual self-restriction that we can experience our own will as being completely free.

In the essays that make up Part II, I attempt to further develop these Hegelian ideas in order to solve some central problems of contemporary theories of justice. The systematic framework for these approaches can be found in the first essay (Chapter 3), which is meant to correct our customary conception of social justice by redirecting it from a fixation on the principles of distributing goods towards measures for creating symmetrical relations of recognition. However, and as I attempt to show in the subsequent chapters, such a theoretical reversal must not shy away from problematizing the current organization of labour (Chapter 4), or from the difficult question of which forms of social recognition currently contribute indirectly to reinforcing social domination (Chapter 5). Theoretical predeterminations can exclude neither the sphere of societal labour nor ideologies that serve to stabilize domination from the corpus of a theory of justice. In a discussion of the highly instructive study *On Justification* by Luc Boltanski and Laurent Thévenot (Chapter 6), I combine some of the already developed ideas by arguing against the authors' tendency to de-structure social morality, instead emphasizing the normative weight of already institutionalized spheres of recognition. I undertake a similar endeavour in the chapter on David Miller's theory of justice (Chapter 7), which was originally published as a preface to the German edition of his now classic monograph, *The Principles of Social Justice*. Here as well, I argue that if a theory of justice is to establish stronger ties to social reality, a Hegelian 'reconstruction' of already established principles of recognition is crucial.

In Part III, which bears the relatively vague title 'Social and Theoretical Applications', I take the ideas described in the first two parts of the book and attempt to make them useful for explanatory purposes. Therefore, problems of sociological explanation, rather than normative questions, stand at the centre of these individual essays. It will soon become apparent, however, that when it comes to 'applying' these ideas, there is no way of cleanly separating social facts from normative claims to validity. As soon as we follow Hegel and interpret relations of recognition as being constitutive for all of social reality, we must recognize that any explanation of social processes necessarily invokes prevailing norms and principles. Claims and demands, obligations and beliefs are just as much a part of reality as supposedly purely 'objective' matters. The first chapter in this part (Chapter 8) represents what is still a very tentative response to recent attempts within political science to employ the concept of recognition to explain tensions and dynamics within the field of international relations. My sole aim in this chapter is to clarify the extent to which it makes sense to conceive of relations between states as being regulated by expectations of recognition. The other two chapters in this part are dedicated to theoretical explorations undertaken at the Institute of Social Research in Frankfurt (Chapters 9 and 10). Together with Martin Hartmann, I attempt to give a more detailed explanation of our interdisciplinary research on 'paradoxes' in the development of contemporary capitalism. I do so by empirically illustrating the extent to which structural economic changes have transformed historically developed recognitional expectations into disciplinary demands on subjects. In the context of this book, however, both of these more sociological essays can only give some initial indications of what a recognition-theoretical diagnosis of the present would have to look like.

Part IV picks up a theoretical issue that I have left almost entirely untouched since the publication of *The Struggle for Recognition*.[4] I have always been convinced that social relations of recognition can only develop under the precondition of corresponding structural

developments within the human psyche, such as have been investigated in exemplary fashion by object relations theory. Although
my recourse to psychoanalysis has occasionally provoked the
accusation that I make the theory of recognition altogether 'too
psychological', even today I see no reason to abandon my plan to
draw a connection between external social recognition and structural psychological formation. Of course, one could draw a false
genetic conclusion and justify claims to recognition with reference
to the danger of psychological injury, but apart from that, dovetail-
ing the theory of recognition with psychoanalysis seems to me to
be an entirely advantageous endeavour. I have sought to further
develop some of these insights in two essays in which I address the
significance of social groups (Chapter 12) and the role of psychological 'dedifferentiations' (*Entgrenzungen*) (Chapter 14). The other
two chapters in the final part of the volume (Chapters 11 and 13),
especially the discussion of the work of my friend Joel Whitebook,
represent attempts to defend my own, recognition-theoretical interpretation of psychoanalysis against the obvious objection that I
have neglected destructive, antisocial drives.

I wish to thank Stephan Altemeier and Frauke Köhler for technical
assistance in completing the book. Their calm and care ensured that
the scattered essays could be put into a unified and systematic
form. Eva Gilmer at Suhrkamp once again provided excellent
advice in compiling the various chapters. Finally, I wish to thank
the translator, Joseph Ganahl, for his loyal service over the years
and for ensuring that this volume could appear in English that is
both readable and true to the content.

Notes

1   Nancy Fraser and Axel Honneth, *Redistribution or Recognition?
    A Political–Philosophical Exchange* (London and New York: Verso,
    2003).
2   Axel Honneth, *Unsichtbarkeit: Stationen einer Theorie der Intersubjek-
    tivität* (Frankfurt: Suhrkamp, 2003).
3   Axel Honneth, *Suffering from Indeterminacy: An Attempt at a Reactu-
    alization of Hegel's Philosophy of Right*, trans. Jack Ben-Levi (Amster-
    dam: Van Gorcum Ltd, 2000).
4   The following essays represent the few exceptions: Axel Honneth,
    'Objektbeziehungstheorie und postmoderne Identität: Über das

vermeintliche Veralten der Psychoanalyse', in *Unsichtbarkeit*, pp. 138–61; Honneth, 'Appropriating Freedom: Freud's Conception of Individual Self-Relation', in *Pathologies of Reason: On the Legacy of Critical Theory*, trans. James Ingram (New York: Columbia University Press, 2009), pp. 126–45.

Part I

Hegelian Roots

1

From Desire to Recognition: Hegel's Grounding of Self-Consciousness

Hardly any of Hegel's works have attracted as much attention as the chapter on 'Self-Consciousness' in the *Phenomenology of Spirit*. As difficult and inaccessible as the book may be on the whole, this chapter, in which consciousness exits 'the nightlike void of the super-sensible beyond, and steps out into the spiritual daylight of the present'[1] (111), finally offers something that we can understand. All of a sudden, his account of the mind's experience of itself takes on more striking colours, the lonely self-consciousness unsuspectingly encounters other subjects, and what was previously a merely cognitive matter is transformed into a social drama consisting of a 'struggle for life and death'. In short, this chapter brings together all the elements capable of supplying post-idealistic philosophy's hunger for reality with material for concretion and elaboration. Hegel's first students seized the opportunity offered by this chapter and took his speculative philosophy out of the ethereal sphere of ideas and notions, pulling it back down to the earth of social reality. And ever since, authors from Lukács and Brecht to Kojève have sought unceasingly to uncover in the succession of desire, recognition and struggle the outlines of a historically situatable, political course of events.

However, by sharpening Hegel's considerations into concrete and tangible concepts, we risk losing sight of this chapter's argumentative core in the face of all this conflictual interaction. After all, Hegel intended to do much more than merely prove that subjects must necessarily enter into a struggle once they have realized their mutual dependence. By employing his phenomenological method, he sought to demonstrate that a subject can only arrive at a 'consciousness' of its own 'self' if it enters into a relationship of 'recognition' with another subject. Hegel's aims were much more fundamental than historicizing or sociological interpretations cared to realize; he was primarily interested in elucidating not an historical event or instance of conflict, but a transcendental fact that should prove to be a prerequisite of all human sociality. If any description of an historical event is to be found at all in the chapter on 'Self-Consciousness', then it is only after the event that Hegel is truly interested in has already occurred: that is, after the subject has emerged from the self-referentiality of mere desire and become aware of its dependence on its fellow human subjects. Hegel thus seeks to do nothing less than explain the transition from natural to conscious (*geistig*) being, from the human animal to the rational subject. The social conflicts that follow in this chapter are merely intended as a processual articulation of the implications this consciousness (*Geistigkeit*) has for human beings.

In what follows I will attempt to reconstruct the decisive step in Hegel's line of argumentation: the transition from 'Desire' to 'Recognition'. The difficulty of this endeavour is clearly demonstrated by the long list of interpretations that, by failing to pay any real attention to Hegel's own formulations, have arrived at quite wilful and even absurd understandings of his text.[2] One reason for this tendency might lie in the quantitative imbalance between the length of the chapter on 'Self-Consciousness' and its central line of argumentation. Of the nearly forty pages comprising the chapter, Hegel dedicates only one and a half pages to his claim that self-consciousness requires the recognition of another self. I want to place these few pages at the centre of my reconstruction by first of all clarifying Hegel's concept of desire (I), in order to then elucidate his internal transition to the concept of recognition (II). My interpretation, which focuses strongly on Hegel's precise wording, will demonstrate that Hegel provides us with more than one argument as to why intersubjective recognition constitutes a necessary prerequisite for attaining self-consciousness.

I

In the *Phenomenology of Spirit*, Hegel describes the process by which we arrive at an understanding of the presuppositions of all our knowledge from the perspective of both an observing philosopher and the subjects involved. He seeks to portray every step in the consummation of this understanding so as to make them intelligible not only to the reflective observer, but also to the agents involved. The chapter begins with the observation that both parties have already learned, through the previously described steps, that the object of their cognition is dependent on their own actions. The world of objects no longer faces them as a merely external 'given' about which they must attain certainty; rather, this world proves to be a 'mode' of their own relation to it: 'But now there has arisen what did not emerge in these previous relationships [of sense certainty, perception and understanding], viz. a certainty which is identical with its truth; for the certainty is to itself its own object, and consciousness is to itself the truth' (104). Hegel means that the subject is now capable of perceiving itself as an authoritative source of its own knowledge about the world. Whatever 'truth' about reality it is capable of calling to mind is due not to its passive perception of reality, but to an active act of consciousness that has already constituted the alleged 'object'. In a certain sense, both the observer and the observed have advanced to an epistemological standpoint already characterized by Kant's transcendental philosophy. As a result, both parties are faced with the question as to the nature of the knowledge that subjects can have of themselves as originators of true claims. The 'self', whose consciousness of itself forms the object of Hegel's subsequent considerations, is therefore the rational individual, who is already abstractly aware of its constitutive, world-creating cognitive acts.

Hegel then attempts to solve this problem by first having the phenomenological observer anticipate the steps of experience that the involved subject will then have to take. From the perspective of the observer, it is easy to see the kind of difficulty or insufficiency that marks the beginning of each new stage, such that the observed subject sees itself compelled to proceed to the subsequent process of experience. What this subject would need to perceive itself as in order to truly possess self-consciousness is its own active role as an originator of reality. But as long as it is only aware of itself as the 'consciousness' that, according to Kant, must be able to accompany all 'ideas', the subject does not experience itself as constituting objects of experience. My awareness of the fact that reality is ultimately the content of my mental states is not enough to assure myself of my synthesizing and determining activity; rather, I perceive my consciousness just as selectively (*punktuell*) and passively as I perceive the mental attention I pay to it in that moment.[3] For this reason, Hegel explicitly criticizes Kant and Fichte in speaking of a mere duplication of consciousness: 'But since what it [self-consciousness] distinguishes from itself is *only itself as* itself, the difference, as an otherness, is *immediately superseded* for it; the difference *is not*, and *it* [self-consciousness] is only the motionless tautology of: 'I am I'; but since for it the difference does not have the form of *being*, it is *not* self-consciousness' (105).

There must be a difference between the type of consciousness I have of my mental activities and these activities themselves, one that is not yet present in the initial stage of self-consciousness. After all, I lack the experience that would make me aware of the fact that, unlike my accompanying and floating attention, the activities of my consciousness are active and modify reality. The philosophical observer, who is aware of this insufficiency at the first stage of self-consciousness, thus sketches in advance the type of experience needed in order to become conscious of this difference. At this very early point, Hegel surprisingly uses the notion of 'Desire' to describe this second stage. He thus chooses a term that refers not to a mental but to a corporeal activity. However, before the involved subject can take up such a stance, one that Robert Brandom terms 'erotic',[4] it must first learn to grasp reality as something it can relate to in its efforts to satisfy elementary needs. Hegel uses the notion of 'Life' to elucidate this intermediate step, which is meant to explain why observing subjects are motivated to take up a stance of 'Desire'. This notion consequently occupies a key position in his argumentation, for otherwise we would not be capable of understanding the transition that compels individuals to continue the process of exploring their self-consciousness.

Hegel already speaks of 'Life' in the previous chapter, in which he introduces 'Understanding' (*Verstand*) as a form of knowledge of objects that is superior to 'perception' (A.III). To understand reality in its totality with the help of Understanding as 'Life' not only means ascribing to the disassociated elements of perception a unified principle in the form of 'Force' (*Kraft*), but, more importantly, it also means learning how to grasp the synthesizing capacity of one's own consciousness in relation to this sort of knowledge. The category of 'Life' therefore represents the turning point that provides the prerequisites for the chapter on self-consciousness, because the subject here starts to interpret the world as being dependent on its own cognition, thereby beginning to develop 'self-consciousness'. But surprisingly, the same category of 'Life' reappears in this new context precisely at the point of transition from the initial, empty or merely duplicated form of self-consciousness to a second, superior form. After the observer has finished the act of anticipation (*Vorausschau*), which means that it is only through the stance of 'Desire' that the subject can arrive at a better consciousness of its 'Self', Hegel provides an account of all the implications of the notion of Life, one that is clearly described as an act of reflection on the part of the involved subject: 'What self-consciousness distinguishes from itself as having *being*, also has in it, in so far as it is posited as being, not merely the character of sense-certainty and perception, but it is being that is reflected into itself, and the object of immediate desire is a *living thing*' (106). We can conclude that at this point, Hegel has begun to demonstrate how the observing subject begins to draw consequences from the previously developed notion of 'Life' for its own understanding of self. While previously it could only conceive of this 'Self' in accordance with the passive observation of its mental activities, thereby envisioning this 'Self' as a worldless, non-corporeal and non-situated 'I', it now begins to perceive itself in opposition to the concept of the 'living thing', a concept of which it is already in cognitive possession. What the observer already knows – i.e. that the subject must take up a stance of desire in order to arrive at a better and more complete self-consciousness – is something that this subject only gradually calls to mind by applying the notion of Life reflexively to its own stance towards the world. It learns that its self is not a placeless, selective consciousness, but always related to organic reality in active praxis; it can no longer behave actively, i.e. as a naturally self-reproducing being, towards a world that is full of liveliness. In this sense, we could follow Fred Neuhouser and claim that the subject has had a transcendental experience, because it recalls that it was only capable of conceiving of the notion of 'Life' because it had encountered this object in the practical stance of active access.[5]

Of course, before Hegel can ascribe this kind of experience to the subject, he must develop categorically the concept of 'Life' up to the point at which its consequences for the individual's relation-to-world arise automatically. After all, the change that occurs in the subject's reflection on the notion of Life is intended not as a mere change in the external determination of the observer, but as a conclusion that the observed subject itself draws. In reflecting on what it encounters in the unity of reality it has created with the help of the category of 'Life', the individual cannot avoid having two simultaneous realizations. It observes that the world it has constructed is a totality, preserved through permanent transformation, i.e. a totality of genii whose generic qualities are constantly reproduced through the life cycle of its individual members. 'It is the whole round of this activity that constitutes Life . . . the self-developing whole which dissolves its development and in this movement simply preserves itself' (108). Yet because only the individual consciousness can perceive this particularity of the living being, of its genus character, the subject must realize at the same time that it is partially excluded from this life process. As a bearer of consciousness, it seems to belong to a different category from the quality it is conscious of as a living genus: '. . . in this *result*, Life points to something other than itself, viz. to consciousness, for which Life exists as this unity, or as genus' (109). At this point, at which we see the preliminary result of the involved subject's self-application of the notion of Life, Hegel's text is especially difficult to understand. The well-known difficulty of not being able to determine precisely whether the determinations he chooses are merely characterizations of the observer or results of the observed subject's experiences becomes even more acute. Hegel formulates the issue as follows:

> This other Life, however, for which the *genus* as such exists, and which is genus on its own account, viz. self-consciousness, exists in the first instance for self-consciousness only as this simple essence, and has itself as pure 'I' for object. In the course of its experience which we are now to consider, this abstract object will enrich itself for the 'I' and undergo the unfolding which we have seen in the sphere of Life. (109)

I take the first part of the first sentence of this compact statement to be an anticipation of the desired result of the observed subject's experience, while the second part of the sentence, which begins with 'in the first instance', points out the momentary state of its self-consciousness. Involved individuals still conceive of their own 'self' as pure, non-situated consciousness, but from the perspective of the observer, the subject must understand itself as an individual member of a living genus. Hegel means that the subject is compelled to make such a transition from pure self-consciousness to 'living' (*lebendig*) self-consciousness in that it must recognize its own liveliness (*Lebendigkeit*) in the liveliness of the reality it constitutes. In a certain sense, it cannot help but discover retrospectively in its own self, through reflection on its own notion of the organic life process, the natural features it shares with the reality that is dependent on it. Yet, Hegel skips this step – at which the subject's own naturalness is discovered in the liveliness of the self-created object – and immediately moves to the stance in which the observed subject reaffirms its newly gained understanding. In the stance of 'Desire', the individual assures itself of itself as a living consciousness, which, although it shares the features of life with all of reality, is still superior to reality in that the latter remains dependent on it as consciousness. Therefore, Desire is a corporeal form of expression in which the subject assures itself that it, as consciousness, possesses living, natural features: '. . . and self-consciousness is thus certain of itself only by superseding this other that presents itself to self-consciousness as an independent life; self-consciousness is Desire' (109).

Hegel's notion of 'Desire', which outlines the second stage of self-consciousness, is also clearly intended as a far-reaching critique of the philosophy of consciousness prevalent in his time. He points out that when Kant and Fichte conceive of self-consciousness as the activity by which consciousness merely observes itself, they lose sight of more than just the active, synthesizing side of consciousness. Or in other words, this conception not only robs the subject of the chance to recall its own activity of guaranteeing truth (*wahrheitsverbürgende Aktivität*), but it also suggests that the rational self, of which the subject is seen as possessing knowledge, is free of all natural determinations and thus lacks any kind of organic liveliness. Hegel appears to claim that the philosophy of consciousness denies the subject any kind of direct, unmediated experience of its own corporeality. Not least for the purpose of countering the anti-naturalism of his contemporaries, Hegel builds a second stage of 'Desire' into the process of acquiring self-consciousness. In this stance the subject assures itself of its own biological nature in such a way that it expresses its superiority over all other beings. By virtue of its capacity to differentiate between what is good or bad for it, the subject is always certain of the element of its consciousness that makes it unique. For Hegel, the confirmation of desires, i.e. the satisfaction of elementary, organic needs, plays a double role with regard to self-consciousness. The subject experiences itself both as a part of nature, because it is involved in the determining and heteronomous 'movement of Life', and as the active organizing centre of this life, because it can make essential differentiations in Life by virtue of its consciousness. We might even say that Hegel's conception of desire is intended as a demonstration of just how much humans are always antecedently aware of their 'excentric position' (Plessner). As long as humans view themselves as need-fulfilling beings and are active in the framework of their desires, they have unmediated knowledge of their double nature, which allows them to stand both inside and outside nature at the same time.

It is important that we attain some clarity about the role played by 'Desire', because the literature on Hegel often tends to dismiss this stage merely as something negative, as something to be overcome. But to me, Hegel appears to insist that the experience associated with the satisfaction of our most basic drives gives rise to a kind of self-consciousness that goes far beyond the first form of self-consciousness in terms of content and complexity. Instead of having the subject merely experience itself as selective (*punktuell*) consciousness, which always remains present in all its mental activities, the satisfaction of its desires provides it with the unmediated certainty of a self that has been placed excentrically, along with its mental activity, within nature. Because this self-consciousness does justice to humans' biological nature, Hegel is also convinced that we cannot give up the fundamental achievement of this stage of self-consciousness. Whatever other prerequisites are necessary in order to allow the subject to attain a proper awareness of its self, these prerequisites must be contained in our awareness of being involved as a 'living member' in nature. However, the more we emphasize the achievement of 'Desire', the more urgent becomes our search for why Hegel regards this stage of 'self-consciousness' as insufficient. He needs but a single brief passage in order to demonstrate the necessity of a further transition. This passage constitutes the next step of our reconstruction.

II

Hardly has Hegel described the essential importance of desires for self-consciousness than he outlines the reasons for the failure of the associated kind of experience. Unlike in his elucidation of the transition from the first stage of self-consciousness to Desire, Hegel does not make a clear distinction between the perspective of the observer and that of the participant. He does not take up the philosophical standpoint and sketch in advance the aim of the next step of experience in order to then have the subject itself go through this learning process; rather, both processes appear to be joined somehow. The starting point for this accelerated, almost rushed description is a summary of the achievement of Desire. In this stance the subject is certain of the 'nothingness' or 'nullity' of living reality; it views itself in its excentric position as superior to the rest of nature. As a human animal, the appropriate way to express this superiority is to consume the objects of nature in the satisfaction of its desires. Hegel thus remarks that in its desires, the subject 'gives itself the certainty of itself as a *true* certainty, a certainty which has become explicit for self-consciousness itself *in an objective manner*' (109). The transition follows immediately in the next sentence, in which Hegel remarks laconically: 'In this satisfaction, however, experience makes it aware that the object has its own independence' (Ibid.). A few lines further on, Hegel asserts even more explicitly that self-consciousness is unable to 'supersede' its object 'by its negative relation' to this object; rather, 'it produces the object again, and the desire as well' (Ibid.). Hegel is therefore convinced of having uncovered an element of self-deception in the stance of Desire. The subject deceives itself about itself. By believing itself capable of destroying its object through the satisfaction of its needs, through the fulfilment of its desires, it entertains false ideas about its relation to the world. It is much more difficult, however, to determine why this sort of self-deception should motivate a transition to a new stage of self-consciousness. It is unclear why disappointment over the independence of the object should lead to an encounter with the other and to recognition. Nearly all the interpretations of this passage I have seen resort either to metaphorical bridges over this divide or to additional constructions not found in the text itself.[6]

First of all, we need to clarify more precisely what Hegel takes to be the deficit of desire in relation to self-consciousness. His reference to self-deception can only be seen as a first indication of the direction we must go in, not as the solution itself. As readers who follow the directions of the philosophical observer, we already know what kind of self the observed subject is to attain consciousness of after having gone through the previously analysed stages: this subject must truly realize that it itself is the rational, reality-constructing actor of which it is only abstractly and generally aware at the beginning of the chapter. We could also say that the 'I' must arrive at a point at which it understands itself in the constructive activity through which it produces an objective world. In the wake of this process of experience, however, a new demand is made on self-consciousness, one that the subject could not at all have been aware of at the first stage. By placing itself, as a 'transcendental' consequence of its own notion of living reality, within nature as a consuming being, the subject must realize that its reality-creating activity is not merely a particularity of its own self, but a fundamental property of human beings in general. By recognizing the genus-character of Life, i.e. the fact that natural reality exists independent of the continued existence of its individual specimens, the subject is compelled to grasp its own self as an instantiation of an entire genus – the human genus. At the first stage of self-consciousness, self-accompanying observant consciousness, the subject was still very far away from this form of self-consciousness. But at the second stage, rationally compelled by the implications of its own notion of 'Life', it attained the threshold at which it views itself and its consciousness as being placed within nature as a superior being. Here it conceives of itself as a natural, organic self that has acquired the certainty of its ability to destroy the rest of nature by consuming its objects in the process of satisfying desires. Hegel now abruptly claims that this ontological assumption is bound to be false, because natural reality continues to exist despite humans' consumptive acts. However restlessly the subject satisfies its desires, the 'process of life' as a whole continues despite the destruction of its individual elements. As a result, nature's objects retain their 'independence'. Therefore, the insufficiency of the experience of 'Desire' is, strictly speaking, twofold: first of all, this experience provides the subject with a 'delusion of omnipotence', leading it to believe that all of reality is but a product of its own individual conscious activity; second, this prevents the subject from conceiving of itself as a member of a genus. So despite all the advantages this stage has for self-consciousness, it must fail owing to the fact that it creates a false conception of an omnipotent self. Within the framework of desire, the subject can grasp neither its reality-producing activity nor its own genus-character, because reality in its living totality remains untouched by the activity through which the subject merely satisfies its individual needs.

I have chosen the expressions 'delusion of omnipotence' (*Allmachtsphantasie*) and 'omnipotence' (*Omnipotenz*) with caution in order to enable comparison with ontogenesis, a comparison that could be helpful at this point. The ingenious psychoanalyst Donald Winnicott has described children's world of experience as a state in which they follow a nearly ontological need to prove to themselves that their environment is dependent on their own intentions. By destroying the objects they possess, children intend to prove that reality obeys their all-encompassing power.[7] What is important for our purposes is not the empirical accuracy of these observations, but their potential usefulness in elucidating Hegel's claims. Hegel seems to want to say the same thing as Winnicott – not in relation to ontogenesis, but certainly with regard to the observed subject's experiences. Both seem to claim that this subject strives, through the need-driven consumption of its environment, to assure itself that the entirety of reality it encounters is a product of its own mental activity. In the course of this striving, however, it is faced with the fact that, as Hegel puts it, the world retains its 'independence' (*Selbstständigkeit*), since the existence of reality is not dependent on the survival of its individual elements. According to Winnicott, children exit this omnipotent stage by learning to discover, in the form of the mother or some other attachment figure, a being that reacts to their destructive acts in different ways. Depending on the situation and her own feelings, a mother will sometimes react to a child's attacks by showing understanding, and sometimes disapproval, such that the child eventually learns to accept another source of intentionality besides his or her own, one to which the child must subordinate his or her conception of the world. Winnicott's line of argumentation can serve as a key for understanding the considerations with which Hegel attempts to motivate a transition from the second to the third stage of self-consciousness.

The sentence immediately following Hegel's description of the failure of 'Desire' is quite possibly the most difficult sentence in the chapter on self-consciousness. Without any warning from the knowing observer, Hegel claims that in order for the subject to consummate its self-consciousness, it requires another subject that carries out the same negation 'within itself' (*an ihm*) that the former had only performed upon natural reality: 'On account of the independence of the object, therefore, it can achieve satisfaction only when the object itself effects the negation within itself (*an ihm*); and it must carry out this negation of itself in itself, for it is *in itself* the negative, and must be for the other what it *is*' (109). Perhaps we should ask what need Hegel is referring to – which he claims can only be satisfied by mutual negation. He cannot have in mind the organic drive previously expressed in the notion of 'Desire', because this need has already attained fulfilment in the consumption of the natural world. Despite all the disappointment the subject brought upon itself in this stage, it did succeed in appropriating from reality, according to its own discriminations, the materials that could satisfy its animal or 'erotic' needs. So the need that Hegel has in mind must lie deeper and be likewise contained in 'Desire', a need we could call 'ontological' because it seeks confirmation of a certain specific conception of the ontological character of reality. In the destructive activity of the subject for the purpose of satisfying its desires, the subject seeks to assure itself of the 'nothingness' or 'nullity' of the world, of its existence as a mere product of its own mental activity. Hegel now claims that this previously unfulfilled ontological need can only be fulfilled under the two following conditions: first, the subject must encounter an element of reality that performs this same act of negation on it in return; second, the subject must perform the same kind of negation on itself.[8]

Despite the complexity of Hegel's line of argumentation, it is easy to ascertain a reference to the necessity that the observed subject encounter another subject, a second consciousness. After all, the only 'object' capable of such a negation is a being that likewise possesses consciousness. In this sense the sentence with which Hegel begins his characterization of the third stage of self-consciousness clearly opens up a new sphere in the subject's experience. The subject not only sees itself confronted with living reality, but encounters in reality an actor that is likewise capable of conscious negation. What is more difficult to understand, however, is Hegel's remark that this second subject must apparently be capable of performing a negation *an ihm*, i.e. upon the first, observed subject, in order that the desired satisfaction of the ontological need can come about – at least this is the customary interpretation of the formulation according to which the new 'object' carries out a 'negation within itself (*an ihm*)'. We shouldn't, however, take this thought literally as indicating an act of destruction or need-driven consumption. Instead we should take this '*an ihm*' to mean '*an sich selbst*'. This would mean that the second subject performs an act of negation directed at itself, a type of self-negation. Therefore, the first subject encounters the second subject as a being that, in the face of the first subject, performs a negation upon itself. In any case, this interpretation would explain why the observed subject's ontological need can only be satisfied in an encounter with the other: if this second subject carries out a self-negation, a decentring, only because it becomes aware of the first subject, then the first subject is thereby confronted with an element of reality that can only change its own state on the basis of the first subject's presence. If we refer back to our comparison with Winnicott's thesis, we could say that the subject encounters in the other a being which, through an act of self-restriction, makes the subject aware of its own 'ontological' dependency.

Hegel, however, is not content to merely mention this first movement of negation, but adds to it a complementary movement of negation on the part of the observed subject. Not only does the alter ego carry out a kind of self-negation, but so does the ego. Yet, with this second step, Hegel merely draws the necessary conclusions from the argument he has already developed, for if the second subject only performs a negation on itself because it encounters the first subject as a being of the same type, then the first subject must also carry out the same kind of self-negation as soon as it encounters this fellow human being. Hegel, therefore, claims that this type of intersubjective encounter, which he claims to be a necessary condition of self-consciousness, is strictly reciprocal. The moment these two subjects encounter each other, both must perform a negation upon themselves in which they distance themselves from what is their own (*Eigenen*). If we add to this thought Kant's definition of 'respect' (*Achtung*), which he views as 'thwarting' (*Abbruch*) or negating self-love,[9] then for the first time we see clearly what Hegel sought to prove by introducing the intersubjective relation. In the encounter between two subjects, a new sphere of action is opened in the sense that both sides are compelled to restrict their self-seeking drives as soon as they encounter each other.[10] Unlike the act of satisfying needs, in which living reality ultimately remains unchanged, in the process of interaction both subjects undergo a transformation. Ego and alter ego react to each other by restricting or negating their own respective, egocentric desires; they can then encounter each other without having the purpose of mere consumption. If we assume further that Hegel was thoroughly aware of the link between his idea of self-negation and Kant's definition of respect, we might even ascribe to him a more far-reaching intention. He appears to argue that the observed subject can attain self-consciousness only with the aid of an experience that is moral in an elementary sense. It is not only in the chapter on 'Spirit', in which he explicitly deals with 'morality', that Hegel posits self-restriction as a necessary condition of all morality, but already in connection with the conditions of self-consciousness. However, this step in Hegel's description takes on a peculiarly automatic, even mechanical character, for it is not the case that both subjects limit their respective desires by free decision; rather, the act of decentring almost appears to be a reflexive reaction to the perception of the other. Hegel apparently maintains that the specific morality of human intersubjectivity begins at this early stage, if only in the form of reciprocal, reactive behaviour. Ego and alter ego react to each other by limiting their respective egocentric needs, making their further actions dependent on each other's comportment. From here it is only a small step to an understanding of why Hegel regards this kind of proto-morality as a condition on self-consciousness.

We have already seen that Hegel views the observed subject's ontological need as being satisfied in the intersubjective encounter. As soon as this subject encounters another human being, it can see in the latter's act of self-negation that a relevant element of reality reacts to its mere presence. The observed subject is capable of ascertaining its own dependence on its own consciousness in the quasi-moral reaction of the other. But for Hegel, self-consciousness goes beyond the ontological insight that reality is a product of one's own conscious self. The observed subject should be able to perceive itself in the activity through which it produces reality. At this point Hegel makes use of the reciprocity of the interaction he has described in order to explain the possibility of perceiving one's own activity. It is the self-restricting act of the alter ego that allows the ego to observe first hand the type of activity through which it effects a real change in another subject. Both subjects perceive in the other the negative activity through which they themselves produce a reality they can grasp as their own product. Therefore, we can conclude along with Hegel that the possibility of self-consciousness requires a kind of proto-morality, because only in the moral self-restriction of the other can we recognize the activity by which our own self instantaneously effects a permanent change in the world and even produces a new reality.

For Hegel, however, this consummation of the process of self-consciousness does not lead immediately to a world of commonly shared reason. The creation of this kind of 'space of reasons' is instead the result of the struggle that subjects must engage in once they realize their mutual dependency. Almost naturalistically, Hegel formulates what the subject has learned in terms of the notion of Life so decisive for the stage of 'Desire'. After the subject has attained self-consciousness through the experience of moral reciprocity, the individual is capable of understanding itself as a living member of the human genus. This subject has become *'for itself* a genus' (110). At this point, therefore, the three demands Hegel makes on self-consciousness have been fulfilled. In the self-restriction of the other, the subject simultaneously perceives the activity through which it produces (social) reality, and it thereby understands itself as a member of a genus whose existence is maintained by precisely this type of reciprocity. So it cannot surprise us that Hegel ultimately reserves a single expression for the particularity of this genus: 'recognition' – the reciprocal limitation of one's own, egocentric desires for the benefit of the other.

Notes

1   All page numbers in parentheses refer to G.W.F. Hegel, *Phenomenology of Spirit*, trans. A.V. Miller (Oxford: Oxford University Press, 1977).

2   This tendency can even be found in the otherwise impressive interpretation offered by Terry Pinkard in *Hegel's Phenomenology: The Sociality of Reason* (Cambridge: Cambridge University Press, 1994). My impression is that in his interpretation of this central point in the *Phenomenology*, the transition from 'Desire' to 'Recognition', he resorts to various lines of argumentation in Hegel's *Philosophy of Right* as a kind of interpretive crutch.

3   Hans-Georg Gadamer offers a very plausible and clear interpretation of this issue in his essay 'Hegel's Dialectic of Self-Consciousness', in *Hegel's Dialectic: Five Hermeneutical Studies*, trans. P. Christopher Smith (New Haven: Yale University Press, 1976), pp. 54–74.

4   Robert Brandom, 'Selbstbewusstsein und Selbst-Konstitution', in Christoph Halbig, Michael Quante and Ludwig Siep, eds, *Hegels Erbe* (Frankfurt/Main: Suhrkamp, 2004), pp. 46–77.

5   Frederick Neuhouser, 'Deducing Desire and Recognition in the *Phenomenology of Spirit*', *Journal of the History of Philosophy*, vol. 24 (1986), pp. 243–62.

6   The interpretation offered by Neuhouser in 'Deducing Desire and Recognition in the *Phenomenology of Spirit*', which I also followed in an essential point in my first step, is the exception.

7   Donald W. Winnicott, 'From Dependence towards Independence in the Development of the Individual', in *The Maturational Processes and the Facilitating Environment* (London: Hogarth Press, 1965), pp. 83–92.

8   It is thus false to speak of a 'need for recognition' at this point, as is often done in the works of Kojève and his disciples. The need that Hegel really does seem to assume here by speaking of its 'satisfaction' through the subsequently described reciprocal negation is instead the demand of the observed subject to be able to change reality through the activity of its consciousness. In my words, this would be an 'ontological' need. For a critique of Kojève's

interpretation, see Gadamer, 'Hegel's Dialectic of Self-Consciousness'. For Hegel, 'recognition' is not the intentional content of
a desire or need, but the (social) means that satisfies a subject's
desire to experience its own capacity to modify reality.

9   Immanuel Kant, *Groundwork for the Metaphysics of Morals*, trans.
     H.J. Paton (New York: Harper, 1964), p. 69.

10 G.W.F. Hegel, *Encyclopedia of the Philosophical Sciences*, vol. III,
     trans. William Wallace (Oxford: Oxford University Press, 1971),
     § 408.

2

The Realm of Actualized Freedom: Hegel's Notion of a 'Philosophy of Right'

Unlike Kant or Fichte, when it comes to political philosophy, Hegel was not a master of the small form. Although he composed a number of short, even journalistic essays on the political events of his time,[1] neither their weight nor their style measures up to the great essays of these two other philosophers.[2] Our knowledge of the basic outlines of Hegel's political philosophy thus largely derives from the one book in which he, after a fashion, summarized his central ideas: the *Philosophy of Right*, published in 1820 in Berlin.[3]

I The context of the book

The form of the book as it exists today betrays its origins in regularly repeated lectures. It is mostly organized in short paragraphs, which Hegel later supplemented with written commentaries for the sake of easier comprehension. With graceful and prim language, along with metaphorical images that are occasionally overwhelming, he develops his views on the basic principles of a liberal political order. Already during his tenure as a professor in Heidelberg (1816/1817), Hegel gave public lectures on political philosophy in which he sought to substantiate the outlines of his doctrine of an 'objective', institutional stage of actualizing freedom in the *Encyclopedia*, published in 1817. After answering a call to the University of Berlin in 1818, which was modelled on the the ideas of Wilhelm von Humboldt, he continued his routine in new surroundings. Already during his first semester (the winter of 1818/1819), in which he also gave lectures on the *Encyclopedia*, he offered a series of lectures on 'natural law and the science of the state', which did not cause much of a sensation.[4] During this time, in which Hegel could finally enjoy a measure of peace, stable recognition and a more tranquil family life, he decided to turn his diverse lecture manuscripts into a self-contained book. Like the *Encyclopedia* he had published in Heidelberg, this new book was to be a 'manual' that could, if necessary, be supplemented with additional oral commentaries during the lectures. Despite the great disturbances caused by the Counter-Reform in Prussia, Hegel managed to complete the manuscript by June 1820. By October of that same year – though the cover page reads '1821' – Hegel's *Philosophy of Right* appeared in the Nicolai bookshop. For a long time, the title of the book and the circumstances surrounding the Counter-Reform prevented an adequate reception of his basic intentions. Hegel intended to provide not merely a more profound justification of modern law, but a revolutionary reformulation of our conception of the principles and prerequisites of a liberal social order.

II   The basic concept and structure of the text

Anyone who picks up Hegel's *Philosophy of Right* today and is only accustomed to customary, either Kantian or Lockian, attempts to justify the liberal political order will be confused by the outline and structure of the book. Unlike other treatments of the issue, at the centre of Hegel's investigation are not observations on constitutive legal principles and corresponding moral axioms, but reflections on institutional circumstances, summarized under the heading of 'ethical life'. Not only that, Hegel's subheadings and the way he organizes the text suggest that the notion of ethical life represents an overcoming of the deficits inherent in the principles of law and morality. On the whole the book gives the highly confusing impression of defending the bold claim that when it comes to the core of a liberal social order, certain 'ethical' institutions are superior to a series of legal or moral principles.

The key to understanding these theoretical novelties is found in the extensive 'Introduction' that Hegel places at the beginning of his treatment of the spheres of a liberal political order. Here we find all the conceptual elements of the philosophy of right, developed up to the point at which it becomes clear why a modern theory of politics and law must ultimately elucidate the institutions that are to guarantee freedom. The point of departure for Hegel's line of argumentation is the same idea that guided Rousseau, Kant and Fichte in their attempts to justify the principles of state order. Under modern and enlightened conditions, a state, i.e. a legally constituted social system, can be regarded as legitimate only if it is generally capable of protecting the individual freedom of each of its members. Therefore, as Hegel writes in § 4, 'The basis [*Boden*] of right . . . is the *will*; the will is *free*, so . . . the system of right is the realm of actualized freedom.' Hegel thus makes apparent that he intends to do more than define law as an institution that permits, protects and guarantees individual freedom. The system of law must instead create a 'realm' in which each individual's freedom can be actualized, which means that this freedom must contain determinations or elements that can count as goals of this kind of free self-actualization. In this very early formulation, we can see a first indication that Hegel does not intend to restrict his philosophy of right to the customary scope of the concept of law. If 'right' refers not only to the framework but to the 'realm' of individual self-actualization, then it cannot be reduced to the general, state-guaranteed and merely negatively formulated principles envisioned by Kant, Fichte and Rousseau.[5] That Hegel's intention is much more comprehensive than that of his predecessors becomes even clearer once he begins to elucidate the concept of the free will in the 'Introduction'. In a certain sense the extremely complicated and multi-layered determination that he gives to this concept represents the linchpin of his entire political philosophy.[6] The theoretical procedure that he employs derives largely from the dialectical operations with which he attempts to describe the process by which the mind (*Geist*) becomes conscious of itself (*Selbstwerdung*). The secondary literature has since shown that Hegel's determinations of the freedom of the will, as well as his further elucidations in the *Philosophy of Right*, can be made plausible even without taking into account the ontological premises anchoring his systematic account.[7]

Hegel begins by contrasting two models of the freedom of the will, both of which he views as incomplete or one-sided. On the one hand, individual self-determination is defined as humans' capacity to distance themselves, by an act of the will, from 'needs, desires, and drives' (§ 5), which can be experienced as restrictions on the independence of the 'I'. Although Hegel believes that this definition captures an elementary component of individual freedom, as can be seen in humans' characteristic capacity to commit suicide, it ultimately leads to a complete lack of freedom to act, because action is bound to the setting of goals that restrict the will (§ 5). The second model of the freedom of the will addresses this deficit of the first model by grasping the exercise of individual freedom as a rational decision for a certain 'content', which provides aim to our actions (§ 6). For Hegel, who at this point has Kant in mind (§ 15), this idea amounts to 'arbitrary freedom' or 'caprice' (*Willkürfreiheit*). This is a kind of will whose self-determination consists in deciding which of its inclinations or impulses it prefers to act upon. The deficit that Hegel sees in this second model is the fact that individual freedom does not extend to the material about which the will decides, but remains dependent on its 'finitude': 'It is inherent in arbitrariness that the content is not determined as mine by the nature of my will, but by *contingency*; thus I am also dependent on this content, and this is the contradiction which underlies arbitrariness' (§ 15, Addition).

If arbitrariness is incomplete or one-sided, because the act of decision refers to 'impulses' that remain heteronomous and factically given, then an adequate model of individual freedom must allow us to avoid this decisive flaw. In his 'Introduction', Hegel tries out various formulations in order to characterize such a third concept of the freedom of the will. He relies heavily upon the dialectical precept according to which the correct determination of a given object is to be achieved through a synthesis of two complementary one-sided determinations (e.g. § 7). But the concept that is most appropriate for understanding his intention is free of such formal elements and derives from his early writings. There, the will is free when it is 'with itself' 'in this other' (§ 7, Addition). Recently there have been a series of useful attempts to clarify the conception of freedom contained in this formulation.[8] We could briefly summarize the results of these efforts as follows: as long as a subject relates, through an act of its will, to an object in the world that remains foreign because the subject cannot recognize it as an extension of its own self, the subject is not yet truly free. It only finds its way to true freedom by being 'with itself' in this 'other' in such a way that it experiences the other's characteristics or particularities as something with which it can 'identify'. Here it might help to recall that in his early writings, Hegel always elucidated this form of freedom with reference to love. And in the *Philosophy of Right* as well, he refers to friendship and love as the feelings in which the structure of this 'being-with-itself-in-the-other' can be discerned most easily (§ 7, Addition). Therefore, it is according to this pattern, which strongly resembles the structure of the relationship of recognition, that Hegel conceives of that type of freedom whose actualization is the topic of his philosophy of right. Apparently he set himself the goal of outlining the legal or social circumstances that allow subjects to restrict their wills to activities or objects that they can grasp as expressions of their own self.

There is a second formulation in the 'Introduction' that is often used to explain Hegel's third model of individual freedom.[9] At the end of his reflections, which span over twenty-three paragraphs, just before he returns to the general aims of his philosophy of right, Hegel states that the free will is a 'will which wills the free will' (§ 27). Aside from the fact that he uses a reflexive formulation that recalls the two-stage model of the will developed by Harry Frankfurt,[10] this line of thought is hardly any different from what was already demonstrated in the previous determination: a subject is only truly free if it directs all its efforts towards finding itself in a world whose structure is an expression of the subject's own will. The extent to which these two formulations complement each other becomes apparent in the concluding determination, in which Hegel summarizes his elucidations on individual freedom. Here he writes that the 'substantial content of the Idea', of the freedom of the will, consists in the will's 'activity' of 'cancelling [*aufzuheben*] the contradiction between subjectivity and objectivity and in translating its ends from their subjective determination into an objective one, while at the same time remaining *with itself* in this objectivity' (§ 28).

From this last, summarizing formulation, we only need to take one more step in order to get a complete overview of Hegel's plan in the *Philosophy of Right*. If right is 'the realm of actualized freedom', then, as we have already seen, this requires an extension of the concept of right beyond the limits drawn by the modern tradition. It captures not only all the general principles that delimit the sphere of individual freedom, but also those conditions or circumstances presupposed by the individual's aim of actualizing its freedom. After clarifying the concept of the freedom of the will that Hegel takes to be the right one, we now have a more precise notion of what such a positive sphere of individual self-actualization is all about. It must consist in the 'objective' circumstances of an external, social world in which individuals can grasp its features as an expression of their own personality. This intermediate result is what Hegel emphasizes when he writes, in the famous § 29 of the 'Introduction', that right is 'any existence [*Dasein*] in general which is the existence of the *free will*'. If everyone has a right, a claim to existence (guaranteed by the state) within a social world, which is in turn the condition for the actualization of individual freedom, then this also comprises those objective institutions with which individuals can identify as the 'other' of their self. Therefore, Hegel clearly expands his philosophy of right to cover the field of the institutional reality of modern societies. He wants to include concrete institutions, not just general, formal principles of law, in that sphere about which a philosophical theory of political orders must make universally valid claims. He thereby departs from the mainstream of modern liberalism and opens up a path for another philosophical camp, which nowadays is termed either 'perfectionist liberalism' or, and perhaps misleadingly, 'communitarianism'.

But this rough account of Hegel's argument has not yet adequately outlined the actual, and much more sophisticated, intention of his philosophy of right. Already in the subsequent paragraphs (§§ 30 and 31), Hegel makes apparent that he is not content to merely add a few freedom-securing institutions to the already familiar principles of formal law. Instead he seeks to deliver a merely 'observational' description or representation of objective 'shapes' (§ 32) in which social reality already contains the 'stages' that the subject must pass through in order to arrive at the complete actualization of its individual freedom. In terms of both method and content, this formulation – recapitulated here in stylized form – is absolutely crucial, because it allows us for the first time to get an overview of the entirety of what Hegel intends to prove in the *Philosophy of Right*. His methodological procedure does not consist in mentally constructing, so to speak, what are considered the necessary conditions of individual freedom, in order to then critically apply them to social reality. Instead he intends to normatively reconstruct these prerequisites; in other words, he seeks to identify those structures in the social reality of modern societies in which these prerequisites are already normatively embodied. This method, which is based on a certain amount of – theoretically founded – trust in the rationality of social institutions,[11] could be termed a procedure of normative reconstruction.

Yet, Hegel does not merely intend to apply this procedure of normative reconstruction to the social reality of his time as a way of uncovering all the institutional complexes that could count as conditions for actualizing this third form of freedom. Instead he assumes that the other two incomplete and one-sided models of freedom must be embodied objectively in social reality, because they represent necessary stages in the process of actualizing individual freedom: 'Each stage in the development of the Idea of freedom has its distinctive right, because it is the existence of freedom in one of its own determinations' (§ 30). Therefore, the object of this normative reconstruction, which constitutes the aim of the *Philosophy of Right*, is a sequence of three increasingly complex spheres of freedom, which must have achieved enough objective significance in social reality to form either stable institutions or at least habitual attitudes. In any case, they must represent powers that have some effect on our actions. From this we must conclude that it is not until this entire, three-stage network of institutionalized practices and structures has been completely travelled through that the 'realm of actualized freedom', characterized by the modern liberal constitutional state, will be presented in its entirety.

Once we have arrived at this point of the 'Introduction', the initially confusing intention and outline of the *Philosophy of Right* is no longer so difficult to decode. With the help of the conceptual differentiations suggested by Frederick Neuhouser,[12] we could say that Hegel's text seeks to present sequentially the spheres of personal, moral and social freedom. In each of these three spheres, whose arrangement forms the thread of his entire investigation, we must be able to find the central determinations that have already been developed in the 'Introduction' as particularities of the various models of freedom (indeterminacy, determinacy, particularity). Hegel must elucidate in the reconstruction of each of these three spheres how they have already been actualized in social reality as objective structures, practices or institutions. Furthermore, he must present the first two spheres of freedom in such a way that it seems rational to individuals to not place one-sided trust in what these spheres promise, but instead to integrate the next, higher sphere into their self-understanding. Without going into this topic any further, I will only mention that Hegel accomplishes this task by offering a virtually sociological diagnosis, in which he seeks to flag up the social pathologies that arise when a society restricts itself to only one of these deficient concepts of freedom.[13] In these brief passages, Hegel anticipates the pathology diagnoses later developed by Max Weber and Émile Durkheim in the field of sociology.[14] His *Philosophy of Right* is therefore not merely a normative theory of the liberal constitutional state, but at the same time a diagnosis of the danger of social misdevelopments.

Hegel begins the main part of his investigation – the paragraphs that follow his long 'Introduction' (§§ 34ff.) – with an account of 'abstract right'. After what has already been said above, the reason for this starting point is obvious. Hegel was convinced that the first

and most 'primitive' form of individual freedom is objectified in a
formal-legal sphere. However, in order to understand this section,
which comprises seventy paragraphs (§§ 34–104), it is important
that we recognize that Hegel does not begin with the first type of
freedom he lists in the 'Introduction'. The prerequisite of self-determination that he there calls 'pure indeterminacy' (§ 5) is in his eyes
far too general, almost anthropological, to deserve being included
in the modern system of the various aspects of freedom. Instead,
what 'abstract right' refers to and what it must bring to objective
validity is the second form of freedom: 'arbitrariness' or 'caprice'.
As we saw above, this refers to that type of contingent, not yet
rational freedom which consists in choosing between various given
inclinations and selecting one that will guide the subject's action.
Hegel now arrives at the determination of the first sphere by asking
how a social order must be constituted so as to allow subjects to
make actual use of this 'personal freedom'.[15]

In answering this question, Hegel mostly keeps to the classical
doctrines of private property and elementary liberties. Just like
Locke and Kant, he claims that individuals must be able to possess
an exclusive portion of the external world, objects or 'things'
(*Sachen*) (§ 42), in order to be able to actualize the preferences they
have chosen without restrictions and according to their own calculations. Such a material free-space of subjective arbitrariness must
above all be protected from interference by other subjects who
contest their possession of the objects that guarantee their freedom.
For Hegel, therefore, the task of the sphere of 'abstract right' is to
constitute an area of exclusive power of ownership over material
things. The principles that, in his view, summarily define 'abstract
right' achieve this goal by defining the subjective rights that permanently guarantee an individual's zone of private property. In possession of such exclusively owned objects, among which Hegel counts
one's own life, body and private possessions, individuals can enjoy
the freedom that derives from their ability to determine the aims
of their own actions. Of course, in order to enjoy such rights, the
subject must be willing to concede other subjects the same claim to
the unhindered actualization of their personal freedom. For Hegel,
therefore, the basis of abstract right is an intersubjective form of recognition, which consists in mutual adherence to the demand that
they each 'be a person and respect others as persons' (§ 36). In the
same chapters in which Hegel develops the value of 'abstract right'
for individual freedom, he must now also present arguments that
reveal the limits of this particular embodiment of freedom. Apart

from the appearance of the previously mentioned social diagnosis, which Hegel uses to point out the pathological consequences of making this merely legal form of freedom absolute,[16] he explains why subjects must make the transition to a second, more complex stage: as long as subjects are only guided by the form of freedom permitted by the sphere of abstract right, they will only make the content of their will dependent on their own given, contingent preferences. But in this arbitrary, wholly unregulated type of decision-making, the intersubjective demands made by the law of property and contract will appear to them wholly external, as pure coercion. Yet because this remainder of heteronomy is ultimately irreconcilable with their claim to self-determination, they cannot avoid entering into a new stage of freedom at which they understand the rational purpose of legal principles and learn to grasp them as something they themselves desire.[17] Of course, we would need to deal with this issue in more detail in order to determine whether this argument is intended as a transcendental, conceptual or even empirical proof. In any case, Hegel wants to show that it is irreconcilable with the modern principle of self-determination for an individual will to feel itself bound by external constraints. The necessity of proceeding to a further, more complex stage of the actualization of freedom is for him not only an abstract, intellectually constructed demand, but also the result of the internal contradictions that the demand for self-determination is bound to confront in the sphere of abstract right.

After what has been said here, it is not difficult to guess what Hegel regards as the particularity of this second sphere of freedom: if the deficit of abstract right was that persons cannot make its intersubjective principles their own and grasp them as autonomously given, then the new form of freedom must be characterized by the capacity to link one's own will to a conception of universal good. Because this kind of individual self-determination presupposes the ability to adhere to universal rules accepted as rational, Hegel terms it – with clear reference to Kant – 'morality'. As for the social embodiment of 'freedom' that accompanies the 'point of view of the will' (§ 105), this we can term 'moral freedom'. If we relate this form of self-determination back to the differentiations Hegel makes in the 'Introduction', then it represents a new, previously unaccounted for phenomenon. It is as if Hegel once more subdivides the stage of 'determinate freedom' in order to get sight of the Kantian notion of autonomy, alongside arbitrariness, as a central, indispensable form of freedom in modernity. Be that as it may, Hegel's discussion of morality (§§ 105–41) is largely guided by the determinations Kant presents in his moral philosophy in order to explain the concept of the 'good will'. Consequently, in the second sphere, individuals exercise their freedom while examining whether the principles of their actions are reconcilable with the generally acceptable idea of the good – the categorical imperative. In terms of complexity, this form of self-determination is superior to that of 'personal freedom' because it implies a determination of the will in agreement with normative principles, which the individual – who has now become a moral 'subject' (§ 105) – can grasp as self-given, as its own. Therefore, the element of external coercion facing the 'person', once he or she is confronted with the intersubjective behavioural demands of abstract right, now disappears.

However, Hegel obviously runs into greater difficulties when it comes to determining why and in what sense morality should already be embodied in the external world of social reality. Unlike the principles of abstract right, which always require institutional anchoring in the authority of the state, the moral standpoint seems to have its home merely in the mental activities of the individual subject. For Hegel, however, this presumption is misleading, because one of the consequences of his 'Introduction' was that the only conceptions of freedom in modernity that have any philosophical relevance are those that have taken on an objective shape. Hence we could say that he simply takes for granted that the moral form of the freedom of the will is more than a merely subjective stance, because in the present it has already become a real motive for action (*Handlungsmacht*), even an entire culture of convictions. Furthermore, he solves this problem by assuming that moral reflection in fact forms an individual factical right, in the face of which the institutional order of society must repeatedly prove itself. In the second sphere of freedom, individuals must be able to feel they have been put in a social world that stands up to the rational test demanded by the categorical imperative (§ 138).[18]

Hegel then demonstrates the insufficiency of this moral form of freedom, its deficits with regard to a 'realm of actualized freedom', in two different ways, both of which we have already seen in the context of his critique of 'abstract right'. On the one hand, he pointedly outlines the social pathologies that would arise if subjects only understood themselves as 'free' in a moral sense (§§ 140, 141).[19] On the other hand, he offers reasons that make such a standpoint seem deficient on its own, requiring further development. The arguments found in the second line of argumentation (§§ 134–7, 141) contain his famous critique of 'abstract ought' (*abstraktes Sollen*) which even today stands at the centre of the debate over the value of Kant's conception of morality: if subjects only make their will dependent on the idea of the good that is, in principle, capable of universal acceptance, then Hegel objects that subjects lack a sufficiently concrete conception of the goals that could guide their actions. After all, this formal rule remains 'empty' and in a certain sense even circular, as long as it is not substantiated with references to the social institutions and roles in which a thinking subject finds itself at any given moment.

Just as in the transition from personal to moral freedom, Hegel develops the central determinations of the next, third and last sphere of freedom, which compensate for the flaws that characterize the previous stage. When it comes to 'social'[20] or 'ethical freedom', with which he concludes his investigation by presenting another three-stage account (§§ 142–360), he claims that it must be capable of giving content to individual conceptions of the good, filling them with concrete goals and responsibilities. Therefore, this third sphere must contain all the institutional structures and practices that, in modernity, can be shown to serve subjects as stations in the actualization of their still unsatisfied striving for a common good. Whether Hegel was moved to discern three such institutions as embodiments of social freedom by the conceptual necessities of his dialectical method, or by distinct, social-theoretical reasons, cannot be answered in any definitive way. In any case, the fact that later social theory has repeatedly attempted to divide the institutional order of modern societies into various integrated and normatively independent subsystems shows that Hegel's tripartite distinction between 'family', 'civil society' and 'the state' has proven itself to the present day.[21]

But the greatest achievement of the concluding part of the *Philosophy of Right* probably consists in the fact that for all three institutional structures, Hegel manages to name the 'subjective' and 'objective' components[22] that give each of them a specific role in the actualization of social freedom. The claim that Hegel pursues with his account of the sphere of 'ethical life' (*Sittlichkeit*) is to point out, along with the social conditions of individual self-actualization, the social institutional structure whose existence and activity allow modern society to maintain itself. Therefore, the three sub-spheres of the family, civil society and the state must form stations of individual self-actualization as well as subsystems of societal reproduction. Hegel fulfils this exceedingly challenging task by indicating, for each of these three institutional complexes, how they: (a) contribute to the formation of the subjective capacities that subjects, as members of society, require for actualizing all of their various freedoms; (b) are capable of providing the social roles and responsibilities that can serve subjects as rational goals for their self-actualization; and finally (c) provide a necessary and, taken altogether, sufficient contribution to preserving the 'material' conditions upon which the reproduction of modern societies depends. In conclusion, we should mention the still controversial question as to whether Hegel was only capable of arriving at such an impressive, even groundbreaking, synthesis of a theory of liberty and an analysis of society because he consistently and vigorously grasped the three institutional structures of his last, ethical sphere as embodiments of different forms of reciprocal recognition.

III   The impact of the work

Hegel's *Philosophy of Right* suffered the misfortune of a highly one-sided and prejudiced reception, and even today, any attempt to make use of his work must struggle with this unfortunate fact. Wherever Right Hegelianism did not succeed in anchoring an image of the text as a highly conservative work aimed at preserving the status quo, Left Hegelianism – from a Marxist standpoint – completed the process of insulating the text from the mainstream of modern political thought. Only British Hegelianism, with its idiosyncratic mixture of idealism and social reformism, was capable of leaving behind an adequate interpretation that does justice to Hegel's own intentions. Therefore, it is the anonymous influence of this one intellectual current to which we owe the fact that today there are an increasing number of efforts to pick up on the social or institutional-theoretical core of Hegel's doctrine of freedom and make it fruitful for the political philosophy of the present.

Notes

1   G.W.F. Hegel, *Political Writings*, ed. Laurence Dickey (Cambridge: Cambridge University Press, 1999).
2   Immanuel Kant, *Anthropology, History and Education*, eds Günther Zöller and Robert B. Louden (Cambridge: Cambridge University Press, 2007); Johann Gottlieb Fichte, *Schriften zur Revolution*, ed.

Bernard Willms (Cologne and Opladen: Westdeutscher Verlag, 1967).

3   G.W.F. Hegel, *Elements of the Philosophy of Right*, trans. H.B. Nisbet (Cambridge: Cambridge University Press, 1991). All sections mentioned in the text refer to this edition.

4   Terry Pinkard, *Hegel: A Biography* (Cambridge: Cambridge University Press, 2000), ch. 10. See also Franz Rosenzweig, *Hegel und der Staat* (Frankfurt/Main: Suhrkamp, 2010).

5   Allen W. Wood, *Hegel's Ethical Thought* (Cambridge: Cambridge University Press, 1990), pp. 71ff.; Ludwig Siep, 'Vernunftrecht und Rechtsgeschichte: Kontext und Konzept der Grundlinie im Blick auf die Vorrede', in *Grundlinien der Philosophie des Rechts* (Berlin: Akademie, 1997), pp. 5–30.

6   See Frederick Neuhouser, *Foundations of Hegel's Social Theory: Actualizing Freedom* (Cambridge, MA: Harvard University Press, 2000); John Rawls, *Lectures on the History of Moral Philosophy* (Cambridge, MA: Harvard University Press, 2000), pp. 349ff.

7   See Axel Honneth, *Suffering from Indeterminacy: An Attempt at a Reactualization of Hegel's Philosophy of Right*, trans. Jack Ben-Levi (Amsterdam: Van Gorcum Ltd, 2000).

8   Wood, *Hegel's Ethical Thought*, pp. 45–51.; Neuhouser, *Foundations of Hegel's Social Theory*, pp. 19–21.

9   See Rawls, *Lectures on the History of Moral Philosophy*, pp. 349ff.

10 Harry G. Frankfurt, 'Freedom of the Will and the Concept of a Person', in *The Importance of What We Care About* (Cambridge: Cambridge University Press, 1988), pp. 11–25.

11 See Rawls, *Lectures on the History of Moral Philosophy*, pp. 329ff.

12 Neuhouser, *Foundations of Hegel's Social Theory*, ch. 1.

13 Honneth, *Suffering from Indeterminacy*, ch. 3.

14 See Axel Honneth, 'Pathologies of the Social: The Past and Present of Social Philosophy', in *Disrespect: The Normative Foundations of Critical Theory* (Cambridge: Polity, 2007), pp. 3–48.

15 Neuhouser, *Foundations of Hegel's Social Theory*.

16 See Honneth, *Suffering from Indeterminacy*.

17 See Neuhouser, *Foundations of Hegel's Social Theory*, pp. 27ff.

18 Ibid., p. 26.

19 See Honneth, *Suffering from Indeterminacy*.

20 Neuhouser, *Foundations of Hegel's Social Theory*.

21 See Axel Honneth, *The Struggle for Recognition: The Moral Grammar of Social Conflicts*, trans. Joel Anderson (Cambridge: Polity, 1995), pp. 94f.

22 See Neuhouser, *Foundations of Hegel's Social Theory*, pp. 32f.

Part II

Systematic Consequences

3

The Fabric of Justice: On the Limits of Contemporary Proceduralism

Now that the debate over the relationship between liberalism and communitarianism has abated just as suddenly as it emerged two decades ago, the gap between philosophical theory and political praxis appears to be growing again. Back when the writings of Michael Walzer, John Rawls or Charles Taylor were broadly discussed among intellectuals, political philosophy seemed to have the power to inform political praxis with theoretical ideas and clues.[1] For a brief moment, it seemed that philosophical efforts to properly define the concept of social justice had an influence on the development of political aims and programmes.[2] Yet today, after the challenge of communitarianism has subsided, we are faced once again with the same malaise about a disconnect between political philosophy and political action, between theory and praxis. There appears to be a general consensus about the fact that liberal-democratic societies are based on normative foundations, which requires legal guarantees for the individual autonomy of all citizens. Furthermore, most would agree that these principles of legal and political equality require economic redistribution, allowing the disadvantaged to make effective use of their legally guaranteed rights. However, these general principles of social justice are without any informational value for the praxis of political representatives and social movements. When it comes to complex social problems such as welfare state reform, these widely accepted principles quickly lose their explanatory and advisory effect. This gap does not consist in a mere temporal delay between philosophical explanation and practical application, for more is needed than time, effort and persistence to transform theoretically developed principles of justice into guidelines for political action.

Instead, these normative principles seem to be formulated in a manner that prevents us from deriving guidelines for political action. It appears that we are constantly forced to draw on other norms that lack philosophical grounding, just to have a prospect of arriving at a 'just' solution.[3]

In the face of this widening gap between philosophical theories of justice and political praxis, perhaps we should take a step back and get a clear view of the first side of this split. After all, it is certainly possible that conceptual faults in the theory are responsible for its growing detachment from political action. In what follows I will attempt to gradually distance myself from the premises of the dominant liberal theory of justice in order to take up an external perspective, which will allow me to subject this theory to critical examination. I will proceed by first developing three elements of what seems to be the broad consensus among nearly all theories of justice. Without taking account of the many differences between various individual approaches, I claim that a basic proceduralist schema, the notion of just distribution and a certain fixation on the state combine to make up the theoretical foundation of our current theory of justice (I). Second, I will examine and question each of these three theoretical building blocks, beginning with the paradigm of distribution, which I regard as the key to criticizing the other key elements of the theory (II). Third, after I have demonstrated the dubious nature of all three theoretical elements, I can begin to draft a normative counter-proposal. I will start with the question of how we should conceive of the material of social justice if the distribution of goods does not constitute a sufficient solution. I will then go on to outline a response to the other two questions that arise from the deficits of both the basic proceduralist schema and the fixation upon the state (III). Finally, I will make some indications about the consequences of reconceiving the theory of justice in this fashion. Here I will come back to my starting point: the relationship between a philosophical theory of justice and political praxis. Obviously, the guideline for my approach will be the question of how we are to conceive of the fabric or material of social justice.

I

Today there seems to be a broad consensus within philosophical circles about the premises of a theory of social justice. Although we might find scattered resistance to individual elements, most agree on the procedure of justification and its main area of application. Both are seen to derive from the idea that principles of justice are the expression of a common desire to grant each other equal freedom of action. Although this abstract principle appears coherent, it brings together two different theoretical complexes, each of which derives from a different definition of liberty. On the one hand, what we call social justice has its measure in the guarantee of our personal, purely individual autonomy. On the other hand, principles of justice must be conceived of as the result of a shared process of will formation that depends on intersubjective cooperation.[4] I will refer to the former element of this construction, which concerns the reciprocal granting of individual autonomy, as its 'material' component. I will call the second component, which deals with the generation of principles of justice, its formal principle.

The material component embodies the fact that a striving for the liberation of the individual from external impositions and personal dependencies is considered an essential achievement of free societies. The modern form of individual liberty should, in principle, have its measure in the unhindered pursuit of individually chosen aims. This new conception of liberty alters significantly the substantive task of justice: whereas it once primarily consisted in assigning each person his or her place in the social hierarchy and ensuring a corresponding livelihood, it now consists in granting all subjects equal space to pursue their individual preferences. Though this formulation might sound inconspicuous, it would soon give birth to a crucial notion in our current conception of justice: the fewer limits others impose on us – that is, the more independent we are of our partners in interaction – the greater our individual freedom. Although this liberal emphasis on individuality does not automatically imply the isolation of the subject, the images used to lend rhetorical support to this conception, as well as the examples used to convey it to a broader audience, suggest that social bonds can generally be regarded as limitations on individual freedom. It is through these channels that the individualistic notion of personal autonomy has seeped into modern theories of justice. This has given rise to the influential idea that creating a just society means conceding all subjects a form of self-determination that allows them to be as independent as possible of their partners in interaction.[5] The most important consequence of this one-sided notion is a theoretical schema that we might term the 'paradigm of distribution'. Because our dependency on others is viewed as a threat to our individual freedom, the latter can only be secured if every individual possesses sufficient means to achieve his or her life plans. Accordingly, the substantive task of justice consists in distributing those 'goods' that enable all members of society to pursue their individual preferences. At the end of this developmental process, therefore, justice is equated with 'just distribution', without any thought as to whether we are justified in viewing individual freedom essentially as the use or enjoyment of goods.[6]

But before I go into the deficits of the distributional paradigm, I first want to present the other components of the contemporary concept of justice. I have already indicated that a certain tension can be found in the most general definition of social justice, because alongside the individualistic notion of liberty it also entails an element of willing intersubjective cooperation. The procedure by which we arrive at justified principles of distribution often involves a shared process of will formation that leads to the determination of normative principles. This form principle of recent theories of justice – constitutive proceduralism – results from considerations on the autonomy of individuals. Because the members of society are to be viewed as free and self-determined, a conception of justice must not seek to go over their heads in defining what counts as a just distribution of goods. Instead, these authors construct an 'original position', a social contract or similar situation of deliberation, in which hypothetical conditions of impartiality allow us to arrive at justified conclusions about distributional preferences.[7] Distributional principles are therefore determined not by means of a theory, but by a fair and just process of deliberation in which those affected arrive at a consensus. We can refer to this self-restriction as 'proceduralist', because the concrete distributional schema derives from a procedure that guarantees the consent of all involved. However, proceduralism is necessarily marked by a certain tension, because we must project specific conditions of justice onto the definition of the 'original position', conditions to which all involved must consent. After all, the parties in this original position are to deliberate as free and equal individuals – if indeed they are to arrive at decisions to which all can truly consent. This means that the specific preconditions of liberty to be decided upon must be settled *before* the participants begin to deliberate. In a certain sense, therefore, the theory must unintentionally anticipate the normative results of the procedure by positing specific conditions of autonomy.[8] And the more we view this procedure not as a mere thought experiment, but as a real process in the social world, the more this tension turns to conflict.[9]

But here as well, I would like to put aside these concerns until I have outlined the third element of currently prevalent theories of justice: the agency or authority entrusted with implementing principles of distribution in social reality. This can entail, at one end of the spectrum, shifting all responsibility to state institutions, or, at the other end, demanding that each individual be willing to apply these principles. Although it is not always clear whether more recent theories of justice include non-state authorities or individual behaviour in their considerations, their basic line of argumentation suggests that the only appropriate agency for realizing justice is the democratic state. This tendency to concentrate all formative power within the state results from a combination of two considerations, both of which sound plausible on their own. On the one hand, the members of society are not to be made responsible for realizing justice, because this would entail the danger of a dictatorship of virtues, an unreasonable demand on morally exemplary behaviour. On the other hand, only the constitutional state is to possess the legitimate means for effectively implementing distributional measures. Current theories of justice therefore envision a moral division of labour, according to which citizens are to fashion principles of justice, while the democratically controlled state retains the sole authority to implement them.[10] The obvious danger of focusing so strongly on the state is that everything outside the latter's legal jurisdiction would remain immune to demands for justice. Social spheres such as the family or private companies, which for good reason are only partially penetrated by the law, cannot be drawn upon or made responsible for the implementation of justice. I will return to this point later in a more detailed analysis of these three components of contemporary theories of justice.

II

Until now I have only outlined some of the theoretical premises that I regard as common to all currently dominant conceptions of justice. Although there are certainly differences in detail, these theories agree that the epitome of justice in modernity consists in ensuring individual autonomy. This type of autonomy is to be secured and guaranteed by providing all citizens with the basic goods required for realizing individual life plans. The principles according to which these goods are to be justly distributed, however, are to be determined not by the theory itself, but by those affected. To do so, the theory formulates a procedure – either a thought experiment or a real act – that informs us about the principles of distribution that participants would arrive at under free and fair conditions. The agency entrusted with the practical implementation of these principles is the constitutional state, which ensures their proper realisation via a legitimate system of laws. Of course, much depends on the concrete determinations made at each individual stage of the process. The normative shape of these theories of justice varies greatly depending on whether the basic goods are made up exclusively of material resources or include certain capacities; it depends on how the conditions of impartiality are determined and the pattern of state activity. But again, I am interested not in particular versions of these theories, but rather in the general image they project. The first thing that catches the eye is that the material of justice nearly always consists in generally valued goods to be distributed according to principles still to be determined. This presupposes a common interest in these means, which are required for forming and pursuing autonomous, freely chosen life plans.[11] For these theories, what makes up a just social order is merely a question of what counts as a just distribution of basic goods.

At first sight, this might seem self-evident, since we do seem to owe part of our individual liberty to our having opportunities and means for attaining freely chosen aims. Financial resources provide us with multiple options in life, and a broad palette of career offers allows us the purposeful realization of our capacities. But these formulations contain a subtle presupposition that cannot be so easily assimilated to the schema of distributive goods. In order to perceive the possession of money as a chance for liberty, subjects must have already formed a conception of which aims they deem worthy of pursuing. In order to regard career offers as paths for realizing their capacities, subjects must already grasp some of their dispositions and talents as valuable and worthy of realization. None of these preconditions has the character of a determinate good, for unlike 'things', they cannot be 'possessed', but must be acquired with great effort within, and through, interpersonal relationships. However, these random examples are not yet objections, but are only intended as a key for developing a critique of the entire schema of distribution.

The connection between these last two brief considerations lies in the fact that goods can only be grasped as useful means for realizing individual liberty if we presuppose that people are 'autonomous'. We cannot determine what it means to grasp financial resources or career opportunities as chances for freedom by considering the meaning of these goods themselves, but only by defining our respective relation to them. Therefore, even the most comprehensive and well-considered list of basic goods cannot tell us what it would mean to ensure conditions of personal autonomy. The real issue would always be found below the threshold of what could be formulated in such a list. As far back as Kant, and probably ever since Rousseau, we have defined 'autonomy' as a certain type of individual relation-to-self that allows us to be confident of our needs and beliefs, and to value our own capacities. These forms of self-respect may be articulated and represented with the aid of goods, but they cannot be acquired and maintained through them.[12] Instead we achieve autonomy along intersubjective paths by learning to understand ourselves, via others' recognition, as beings whose needs, beliefs and abilities are worth being realized. However, this will only be possible if, at the same time, we recognize those who recognize us, because in their behaviour towards us we should be able to see our own value as in a mirror. Therefore, if individual autonomy is to emerge and flourish, reciprocal intersubjective recognition is required. We do not acquire autonomy on our own, but only in relation to other people who are willing to appreciate (*wertschätzen*) us, just as we must be able to appreciate them.[13]

But if relations of reciprocity, and not goods, represent the conditions of autonomy, then current theories of justice completely fail to grasp the structure of justice. According to the paradigm of distribution, that which ensures equal autonomy can somehow be distributed. This is to assume that the 'material' of justice always exists in a pre-formed, thing-like state – something that subjects can accumulate individually. But neither can be true if we only arrive at autonomy through reciprocal recognition. These relations can never be self-contained and static like concrete goods, nor can we consume or enjoy them individually, because they always require the cooperation of other subjects. Autonomy is a relational, intersubjective entity, not a monological achievement. What helps us to acquire autonomy is not cut out of the same cloth as a good that can be distributed; it is fashioned out of living relations of reciprocal recognition that are just to the degree that they allow us to reciprocally value our needs, beliefs and abilities. Of course, we can also refer to such practical intersubjectivities as 'goods' in an

Aristotelian sense, but then we must not infuse them with the economic meaning implied by the distributional schema.[14]

These objections undermine only the first cornerstone of today's dominant theories of justice. The paradigm of distribution has proven unsuitable for properly determining the material of justice in modernity. Instead of 'goods', we should speak of relations of recognition; instead of 'distribution', we should think of other patterns for granting justice. Before I go into more detail, I must first clarify whether this inversion has any implications for the other building blocks of modern theories of justice. Can proceduralism maintain its state-centricity if the fabric of justice is no longer seen to consist in distributable goods but in intersubjective relations of reciprocity?

As we have seen, proceduralism is based on the idea that theory cannot determine just principles (of distribution). Because subjects must be presupposed as partially autonomous, they, or their representatives, are to be the hypothetical originators of principles formulated under fair and impartial conditions. But however we view the matter, deliberating actors must be assumed to freely control the material of their decisions. The material and subject-matter of their impartial decisions must be viewed as a freely formable mass, for otherwise the room for decision would be limited by external and alien conditions. Here we see the immanent link between proceduralism and the paradigm of distribution. We can only view principles of justice as the result of a fair procedure if we also presuppose that subjects can determine the material of their decisions as freely and arbitrarily as they do movable goods. In order to maintain the fictional notion that principles of justice can be created autonomously, proceduralism must define the material of justice as a disposable good; that about which we make normatively justified decisions is to be conceived of as a kind of evenly divisible mass that can be supplied to entitled subjects and groups. The idea of the distribution of goods is thus an entirely appropriate presupposition for this form of proceduralism. But if we remove this premise – that is, if we can conceive of the material of justice no longer in terms of exchangeable goods, but instead as reciprocal social relations – then this also affects the basic conditions of proceduralism. We can no longer picture deliberating agents dealing with something that they can control freely in accordance with their own conceptions of justice. Relations of recognition, which have proven to be the decisive conditions of personal autonomy, do not consist of material that could be allocated at will. We cannot place ourselves in a position vis-à-vis these 'goods' in which we are the decision-makers and preside over their just organization or equal distribution.[15] These relations of recognition instead represent historically contingent forces that influence us behind our backs. To want to detach ourselves from them in order to get sight of them is to entertain an illusion that is just as empty and idle as the desire to shape them as we please.

It appears to me that this undermines the second cornerstone of currently prevalent theories of justice. As soon as distributable goods are no longer regarded as the material of justice, we can no longer conceive of the process of generating principles of justice as a fictitious procedure within an original position. However fair, impartial and free this procedure might be, by eliminating the distributional schema, we deprive those involved of the capacity to even conceive of a just social order as being a matter of the resources or means at their disposal. I will deal later with an alternative conception, which views this deliberative procedure as a palpable occurrence within the democratic public sphere, but first I will discuss how this theoretical dismantling has affected the last remaining component of current theories of justice.

This last cornerstone consists in the assumption that the state alone possesses the appropriate and universally accepted means for implementing principles of justice, imposing a distribution of basic goods – agreed upon by social agents in fictitious deliberations – in the form of enforceable laws. The connection between such a division of labour and the paradigm of distribution is so obvious that it hardly needs mentioning. The task of realizing justice must be left to the state, because it is the only authority that possesses the power to distribute the goods needed to enable individual autonomy. But what becomes of this state-centrism once we abandon the notion of distributional justice and replace it with the idea that relations of recognition are what primarily constitute the breeding ground and enabling condition for individual autonomy? The first problem derives from the circumstance that we owe our autonomy to our involvement in various different social relations, each of which can be thought of as irreplaceable. Alongside the democratic legal community, in which we are obligated to respect each other as free and equal citizens, we are involved in multiple forms of familial and work relations – which are becoming ever more precarious – in which we apparently acquire other facets of our self-respect.[16] But what is important at this point is the fact that only one of these forms of practical intersubjectivity can be directly and immediately influenced by the state. It is only with regard to legal relations that the state can be conceived of as intervening in relations of recognition by altering the range of subjective rights and entitlements, including new social groups, or declaring modified situations legally relevant. Therefore, within this legal sphere, in which we recognize each other as free and equal citizens and thereby become aware of our political autonomy, it still makes sense for us to conceive of the realization of justice as a directive activity of the state. The other spheres of reciprocal recognition, however, are accessible to state influence only within very strict bounds. Neither in the family nor in the workplace can the state simply intervene to improve conditions of recognition, without running the risk of impinging on these spheres' autonomous conditions of existence. Conversely, these are the two spheres of action that appear especially significant in terms of promoting individual self-respect in a general and commonly understandable manner. After all, the family is the place where the emotional groundwork is laid for our self-confidence and our capacity to articulate needs.[17] And in the social exchange of services, we acquire the no less important capacity to view our works and our skills as valuable and socially needed[18] – both of which make up core components of our capacity to live without 'shame and anxiety' (Adam Smith) and thus autonomously. But what if the democratic state only possesses highly limited means for intervening in the relations of recognition inherent in these spheres? Would we have to give up the aim of ensuring just conditions that promote autonomy simply because there appear to be no other agencies of justice available?

In order to solve this difficult issue, we should borrow from the theories that have developed in the wake of Michel Foucault's decentring of the concept of power, applying the latter to theories of justice. Whereas until recently most political scientists and sociologists were convinced that political directives could only run from top to bottom via the activity of the state, we now know this is not true, because political power is largely exercised through a broad and decentred network of semi-governmental, civilian organizations. If we try to make this conception fruitful for the theory of justice, we will quickly see that traditional approaches focus excessively on the state. Because political rule is reproduced through different, loosely connected points, social justice is fought for and secured by many agents connected through network-like structures, all of which are found on the terrain of civil society. The institutions we find as soon as we look beyond the state's own measures consist of 'pre-state' organizations, associations and collectives that work to improve conditions of recognition in the name of justice. We need only think of family-like self-help groups, trade unions, church communities or other civilian groups in order to get a picture of just how many social agents are involved in realizing justice. The structural model for such pre-state agencies can be found in Hegel's 'Corporations',[19] whose function primarily consisted in establishing the moral principle of a certain social sphere – 'civil society' – and reinforcing it in practice.[20]

Although these organizations admittedly lack the binding power that gives state measures such strong potential for influencing conditions of recognition, this does not mean that pre-state networks must remain without any influence on how individual autonomy is secured and expanded. I claim that our image of justice is strongly restricted by this current fixation on the state. That we cannot perceive of the activities of such civil organizations as moral interventions, or as instances of the social promotion of justice, is the consequence of a restricted view inherent in currently prevalent theories of justice.

III

Until now, I have mostly employed what might best be termed a 'therapeutic' approach. I have intended to show, purely negatively, that the currently dominant image of justice blinds us to the latter's true structure and to the way it works. We misunderstand the place that justice has in our everyday praxis if we attempt to grasp it according to models of distribution and theories of original positions. In this third and last part, I will take up the alternative conceptions I have only hinted at until now and sketch the outlines of a different, more appropriate, conception. If I were to outline this conception with a few key points, I would say that, first of all, the distributional schema would have to be replaced by the involvement of all subjects in a given relationship of recognition. Second, a normative reconstruction uncovering the basic moral norms that underlie that relationship of recognition would have to replace the use of a fictitious procedure. Third, the exclusive focus on the regulative activity of the state would be supplemented by a decentralized consideration of non-state actors and organizations. Now, to briefly explain these three steps.

Clearly, even the alternative model of justice I have in mind must start by acknowledging the normative idea that all members of modern societies must possess the same capacities and conditions for individual autonomy. What distinguishes this alternative conception is thus not its moral core, but its material implications. Everything turns upon how we understand the social promotion of autonomy, upon whose crucial role both sides agree. As long as we view liberty as something that all individuals can achieve on their own, it suffices to assume individually disposable goods to be the material of justice. With the help of these goods, individuals are capable of creating a space for the pursuit of their freely chosen life plans. On this account, the task of social justice in modernity consists in ensuring that each individual has an equal and sufficient share of such goods. By contrast, my alternative conception understands individual autonomy not as a monological but as an intersubjective matter. Individuals achieve self-determination by learning, within relations of reciprocal recognition, to view their needs, beliefs and abilities as worthy of articulation and pursuit in the public sphere. This does not obviate distributional justice, but it does demote it from *the* decisive principle of justice to a dependent variable in relations of recognition.[21] The alternative, intersubjective conception of autonomy fundamentally transforms the architecture of the theory of justice. This is not only true of its material, but also of its form principle and agent-relation (*Akteursbezug*), all of which take on a new definition as soon as we grasp individual liberty as a result of relations of recognition.

The material of justice must now be regarded as a special class of intersubjective relations in which citizens accord to each other normative worth. This type of reciprocally granted entitlement to a certain level of consideration provides the background against which subjects learn to experience themselves as deserving respect, thereby attaining autonomy. But unlike material goods, these relations of recognition can be neither generated socially nor distributed according to a given set of rules. Instead they are historically contingent structures, which have assumed the shape of institutional practices in which subjects are involved or from which they are excluded. Such historically given relations of recognition are what make up the material of justice. We cannot take up the stance of an individual or discursive legislator towards these relations; rather we must first content ourselves with observing and accepting them. However, even within this highly restricted role, we know that if the relations of recognition emerging before us are to fulfil their constitutive function, they must presuppose a moral principle. Subjects can only ascribe to each other normative worth, in the light of which they are capable of valuing themselves, if both sides agree on a moral principle that can serve as a source of their reciprocal ascriptions and statements. No relation of recognition, not even those past relations in which subjects respected each other as *un*-equals, can do without a mutually agreed upon norm. These shared principles work to ensure that a praxis of reciprocal recognition can be developed and preserved at all. With these normative foundations of all recognition, however, our alternative theory of justice does possess some initial criteria for judging existing institutions and policies. After all, the demands made by these moral principles coincide with the conditions under which subjects ideally attain a measure of self-respect; therefore, we could say tentatively that it would be 'just' to install and socially equip an existent social sphere as is demanded by the underlying norm of recognition.[22]

Before I can make this thesis more plausible and substantial, I must first discuss which principle of justification we should apply in this context. We saw that the theories I dealt with in the first part of this essay hypothetically construct an impartial procedure of deliberation in which citizens agree upon certain norms. But this kind of proceduralism is unacceptable for the position I will sketch here, because it must presuppose that the material of justice is given historically. But if we are not capable of arbitrarily moving and distributing the material of our moral intentions, it is useless to search for hypothetical principles to which we could then commit. The result of already existing relations of recognition demands instead that principles of justice be justified by the historical material. This means that we may justify principles not through the use of a constructed procedure, but only by locating them in the relations of communication themselves, in their conditions of validity. This alternative procedure could thus be termed 'reconstructive', because it does not 'construct' an impartial standpoint from which to justify principles of justice, but 'reconstructs' them out of the historical process of relations of recognition in which they are always already at work.[23] Compared to proceduralist approaches, this type of reconstructive theory of justice is both more trustful and more sceptical of historical reality. It is more trustful because it sees within already established relations of communication the normative principles that underlie demands for social justice. It can therefore restrict itself to explicating the principles that socialized subjects are already guided by in their relationships of recognition. However, if these preconditions are absent – that is, if we are dealing with ethically damaged and demoralized social relationships – this theory of justice will be relatively powerless. It, too, will have to resort to an impartial standpoint in order to not wholly lose sight of the principles of social justice.[24] This extreme case also demonstrates why a reconstructive theory of justice is generally more sceptical than its proceduralist alternatives, because it does not trust a fictitious procedure of agreement to inform us realistically about principles of justice. It will always be doubtful whether these principles overtax existing social relations.

But the scepticism reaches even further. There might be hopes that in the course of this normative reconstruction, we will come across an historically existent discursive method – the very same method appealed to fictitiously by proceduralists. If that were the case, we could discern a special relation of recognition in modern social reality, one in which citizens achieve autonomy by participating in democratic processes of will formation, thereby defining together the principles of social justice.[25] Under these circumstances, the theory could pull out of the business of determining principles of social justice, for it need only distil the normative preconditions under which the discursive results of the already existing procedure can count as justified. The reason why I distrust such an historically situated form of proceduralism[26] is that individual autonomy demands more and other forms of social recognition than are guaranteed by participation in public processes of will formation. Subjects need intersubjective esteem and consideration even in the social roles they play apart from being legal subjects, where their own commonly practised self-legislation enjoys insufficient legal protection. With that, we pick up where we left off before turning to the proceduralist theory of justice.

I have mentioned several times that subjects depend on the recognition of their needs, beliefs and abilities in order to take part in social life. It does not suffice to conceive of autonomy as arising solely from intersubjective respect for subjects' decision-making competence; rather, subjects need to be appreciated for their particular needs and individual deeds. Only when citizens see all these elements of their personality respected and recognized will they be capable of acting with self-respect and committing themselves to their own respective life paths. For this reason, the reconstructive procedure cannot restrict itself to uncovering the principle of recognition within already established legal relations. While subjects thereby respect each other's capacity to form reflexive judgements, there are still other, equally significant relations of recognition that provide individuals with the experience of being appreciated for their needs and abilities. Normative reconstruction must be directed towards the entire spectrum of reciprocal social relationships if we are to truly disclose all the conditions under which subjects achieve autonomy. Alongside legal relationships, we must also include familial relationships and societal relations of work within our theory of justice. Even if citizens can only intervene in these spheres through the restricted mechanisms of democratic law-making, these conditions of recognition also prove significant for justice because they have a strong influence on the flourishing and failing of individual autonomy.

Just as in the egalitarian legal relations under the democratic rule of law, individuals are also obligated within the family and the exchange of services to recognize each other as free and equal. Unlike in traditional societies, both of these weakly regulated spheres must satisfy the demand for symmetrical and egalitarian recognition.[27] However, in the course of normative reconstruction we find out quickly that very different moral aspects serve here as sources of reciprocal esteem. In democratic legal relations the deliberative equality of all subjects forms the normative basis of the respect that subjects grant each other, whereas within the family the particular needs of the members are what constitute the normative points of orientation for recognition; and within the social exchange of services, the work or achievement (*Leistung*) of those involved constitutes the relevant criterion. A reconstructive theory of justice therefore faces the challenge of defending not only one normative principle in the name of individual autonomy, but three. Depending on the respective social sphere, the moral aspect of either deliberative equality, justice of needs (*Bedürfnisgerechtigkeit*) or justice of achievement (*Leistungsgerechtigkeit*) must be emphasized and reinforced.[28] This kind of pluralism, as unwieldy as it may seem, accommodates the distinctions that subjects actually make in individual issues of justice. As many empirical investigations have now shown, subjects constantly distinguish between the same three spheres mentioned above in their everyday praxis, in order to apply the respectively appropriate principles of justice.[29]

The fact that this alternative theory of justice corresponds to empirical reality means that it might reduce philosophy's distance from political praxis after all. The task would be to demonstrate the institutional, material and legal conditions that would have to be fulfilled in order for different social spheres to take account of the norms of recognition upon which they are based. With the aim of promoting individual autonomy, they would have to defend deliberative equality within democratic legal relations, equity of needs within familial relationships, and justice of achievement in relations of work. Not only that, they would also have to demand that all subjects be involved in these relationships of recognition. Such a theory of justice would also find itself in agreement with the moral convictions entertained by subjects in their everyday praxis. Conversely, however, the theory cannot make the application of its own principles – not even its differentiations – dependent on the outcome of democratic will formation. After all, the theory knows too well that such decisions are only provisional, partial and distorted as long as citizens cannot raise their voices free of all anxiety and shame. For the sake of this element of individual autonomy and elementary freedom of public expression, this theory of justice must demand advocative relations in which subjects attain self-respect not only in the democratic public sphere, but also in their familial relationships and in their working life. Nevertheless, they cannot rely solely on the state to realize their intentions; rather, they must count on the cooperation of non-state organizations. Their activities merely require rejuvenation by means of both more powerful and more realistic conceptions of justice in order to employ the right moral vocabulary in the right place. And at least this prospect might nurture the hope that a reconstructive, pluralistic theory of justice can close the gap between philosophical theory and political praxis.

Notes

This chapter is based on a lecture for the Siemens Foundation (Munich) in December 2008. I wish to thank Heinrich Meier for the friendly invitation, as well as Jürgen Habermas for his extremely kind introduction and moderation.

1 Axel Honneth, ed., *Kommunitarismus: Eine Debatte über die moralischen Grundlagen moderner Gesellschaften* (Frankfurt/Main: Campus, 1992).
2 The former political relevance of political philosophy has been made most apparent by the discussions over the writings of Amitai Etzioni, for instance in *The Spirit of Community: Rights, Responsibilities and the Communitarian Agenda* (New York: Crown,

1993). For an account of the political discussion in Germany, see Christel Zahlmann, ed., *Kommunitarismus in der Diskussion: Eine streitbare Einführung* (Berlin: Rotbuch Verlag, 1992).

3 David Miller, *Principles of Social Justice* (Cambridge, MA: Harvard University Press, 2003), ch. 1.

4 For a good overview of this tension at the heart of modern theories of justice, see Bernd Ladwig, 'Freiheit', in Gerhard Göhler, Matthias Iser and Ina Kerner, eds, *Politische Theorie: 22 umkämpfte Begriffe zur Einführung* (Wiesbaden: VS Verlag für Sozialwissenschaften, 2004), pp. 83–100; Albrecht Wellmer, 'Models of Freedom in the Modern World', in *Endgames: The Irreconcilable Nature of Modernity: Essays and Lectures* (Cambridge, MA: MIT Press, 1998), pp. 3–68.

5 For a critique of this individualistic or privatistic conception of individual freedom, see Charles Taylor, *The Ethics of Authenticity* (Cambridge, MA: Harvard University Press, 1991); Joseph Raz, *The Morality of Freedom* (Oxford: Clarendon Press, 1986); and Michael Sandel, *Liberalism and the Limits of Justice* (Cambridge: Cambridge University Press, 1982).

6 As far as I know, we have yet to see a systematic critique of the distributional schema. However, see the remarks made by Iris Marion Young, *Justice and the Politics of Difference* (Princeton: Princeton University Press, 1990); and Jürgen Habermas, 'Reconciliation through the Public Use of Reason', in *The Inclusion of the Other: Studies in Political Theory*, eds Ciaran P. Cronin and Pablo De Greiff (Cambridge, MA: MIT Press, 1998).

7 For what has now become the classic formulation, see John Rawls, *A Theory of Justice* (Cambridge, MA: Harvard University Press, 1971).

8 Habermas, 'Reconciliation through the Public Use of Reason', pp. 49ff.

9 This is how I understand the basic intention of the theory of justice that Jürgen Habermas develops in *Between Facts and Norms: Contributions to a Discourse Theory of Law and Democracy*, trans. William Rehg (Cambridge, MA: MIT Press, 1996). Here he understands the principles of the modern constitutional state as institutionalized conditions enabling a democratic procedure of public self-government. I will later refer to this intention as 'historically situated proceduralism'.

10 With the very different intention of criticizing exaggerated conceptions of global justice, Thomas Nagel has described how liberal theories of justice concentrate all the power of ensuring justice in

the democratic constitutional state. See 'The Problem of Global Justice', *Philosophy and Public Affairs*, vol. 33 (2005), pp. 113–47.

11 Rawls, *Theory of Justice*, pp. 78ff; John Rawls, *Political Liberalism* (New York: Columbia University Press, 1993), 187ff.

12 The difference between the approaches of Rousseau and Kant obviously lies in the fact that only Rousseau makes the attitude of self-respect contingent on reciprocal recognition, or on being respected by others. See Frederick Neuhouser's groundbreaking work on this issue: *Rousseau's Theodicy of Self-Love: Evil, Rationality, and the Drive for Recognition* (Oxford: Oxford University Press, 2008). Kant, on the other hand, maintains that this attitude is the result of individual subordination to ethical laws. See Henning Hahn, *Moralische Selbstachtung* (Berlin and New York: Walter de Gruyter, 2008), pp. 52ff. Here I cannot go further into the subsequent theoretical development that began with Fichte.

13 See Axel Honneth, *The Struggle for Recognition: The Moral Grammar of Social Conflicts*, trans. Joel Anderson (Cambridge: Polity, 1995); Catriona Mackenzie and Natalie Stoljar, eds, *Relational Autonomy: Feminist Perspectives on Autonomy, Agency and the Social Self* (New York: Oxford University Press, 2000); Diana Myers, *Self, Society, and Personal Choice* (New York: Columbia University Press, 1989); and Paul Benson, 'Taking Ownership: Authority and Voice in Autonomous Agency', in John Christman and Joel Anderson, eds, *Autonomy and the Challenges to Liberalism: New Essays* (Cambridge: Cambridge University Press, 2005), pp. 101–26. Of course, we should mention that from the very start, Rawls introduces 'social bases of self-respect' as a primary good, even 'perhaps the most important primary good' (Rawls, *Theory of Justice*, p. 386). Most likely owing to the difficulties inherent in regarding conditions of self-respect as 'goods' to be distributed (see Gerald Doppelt, 'Rawls's System of Justice: A Critique from the Left', *Noûs*, vol. 15 [1981], pp. 259–307), Rawls states later, in *Political Liberalism*, that certain other primary goods such as 'equal basic rights and liberties' and 'fair equality of opportunity' count among social bases of self-respect (Rawls, *Political Liberalism*, p. 82), but can no longer be viewed as primary goods. In my view, these conceptual shifts only reveal the distributional paradigm's irresolvable difficulties in making intersubjective relationships and relations of recognition into the objects of a liberal theory of justice. Nevertheless, the intellectual honesty displayed by Rawls, here and elsewhere, in dealing with a problem that he clearly was aware of is certainly admirable.

14 Aristotle's 'ethical' goods lack the physical extension that gave rise to the notion of 'dividing up' these goods according to certain principles in order that more people, or everybody, might enjoy them. The subtle accommodation of ethical goods to material objects, thus allowing their distribution, merits its own investigation. See Max Scheler, *Formalism in Ethics and Non-Formal Ethics of Values*, trans. Manfred S. Frings and Robert L. Funk (Evanston, IL: Northwestern University Press, 1973), pp. 110ff.; Charles Taylor, 'The Diversity of Goods', in: *Philosophy and the Human Sciences: Philosophical Papers 2* (Cambridge: Cambridge University Press, 1988), pp. 230–47.

15 Anthony Laden has claimed that Rawls' distinction between 'allocative' and 'distributive' justice (Rawls, *Theory of Justice*, pp. 76ff.) allows us to avoid these difficulties. While allocative justice only ensures a certain distribution of a given amount of goods among people with 'known desires and needs', distributive justice indicates a normative principle that determines the rules under which people engage in fair cooperation and organize the fair distribution of the goods they produce. I do not, however, see how this distinction allows us to avoid the difficulty I (and others) have raised. Although Rawls states that the 'correctness of the distribution is founded on the justice of the scheme of cooperation', he thereby refers to principles that determine 'what is produced, how much is produced, and by what means' as well as who has what 'legitimate claims' (ibid.) to the product. The material meaning of justice continues to consist in the distribution of something grasped as being fundamentally 'producible'.

16 See Axel Honneth, 'Redistribution as Recognition: A Response to Nancy Fraser', in Nancy Fraser and Axel Honneth, *Redistribution or Recognition? A Political–Philosophical Exchange* (London and New York: Verso, 2003), pp. 110–97.

17 See Axel Honneth, 'Between Justice and Affection: The Family as a Field of Moral Disputes', trans. John Farrell, in *Disrespect: The Normative Foundations of Critical Theory* (Cambridge: Polity Press, 2007), pp. 144–62.

18 See Chapter 4 in the current volume; Diana Myers, 'Work and Self-Respect', in Gertrude Ezorsky, ed., *Moral Rights in the Workplace* (Albany: SUNY Press, 1987), pp. 18–27.

19 G.W.F. Hegel, *Elements of the Philosophy of Right*, trans. H.B. Nisbet (Cambridge: Cambridge University Press, 1991), §§ 250–6.

20 On the issue of 'Corporations' in Hegel, see Hans-Christoph Schmidt am Busch, *Hegels Begriff der Arbeit* (Berlin: Akademie

Verlag, 2002), pp. 129ff. (See also Chapter 4 in the current volume.)
A further model for such a decentred notion of institutions of
justice can be found in Durkheim's idea that morality of modern
societies can only be maintained through an entire network of
relatively independent, institutionalized bodies with the function
of constructing justice (Émile Durkheim, *Leçons de sociologie: Phy-
sique des moeurs et du droit*, 2nd edn [Paris: Presses Universitaires
de France, 1969]).

21 This essentially means that the criteria of just distribution of goods
(in the sense of distributable resources) arise from the normative
principles that determine the type of reciprocal recognition that
prevails in a certain social sphere. According to Anthony Laden
(see note 15), Rawls' conception of 'distributive justice' would
also have to be understood in this way. But instead of distinguishing between different types of recognitional relations, he regards
the relationship of equality between citizens as the only primary
relationship of recognition.

22 For a more fundamental treatment of the issue, see Honneth,
'Redistribution as Recognition'.

23 Habermas presents a similar justification for his 'reconstructive'
approach in *Between Facts and Norms* (pp. 82ff.). The difference
between our endeavours consists in the fact that he only treats
the historical development of the modern constitutional state as
an object of normative reconstruction, whereas I propose that,
given the demands on a theory of justice, we undertake such a
reconstruction with regard to the entire spectrum of the historical
development of all the spheres of recognition that are both central
and institutionalized in modern societies. Of course, this means I
am faced with the problem of having to claim that all three different spheres of recognition are embodiments of principles of recognition whose practical realization in our interactions demands
individual autonomy.

24 This formulation parallels Hegel's idea that the merely 'moral
point of view' – i.e. the internal nature of moral conscience
– always has an important role when 'the world of actuality is
hollow, spiritless, and unstable' (*Elements of the Philosophy of Right*,
§ 138, Addition).

25 Habermas, *Between Facts and Norms*, chs 3 and 4.

26 I regard the theory of justice that Habermas outlines in *Between
Facts and Norms* to be an instance of this form of proceduralism.

27 See Honneth, 'Redistribution as Recognition'.

28 Ultimately, my conception of social justice coincides with the proposal David Miller makes in his plural theory of justice. He suggests a three-part distinction between the principles of need, desert and equality (Miller, *Principles of Social Justice*) on the basis of everyday beliefs in justice. On the various disputes that arise from the fact that I regard such a distinction between different 'spheres of justice' as being in need of 'reconstructive' justification, see Chapter 7 in the current volume.

29 See Miller, *Principles of Social Justice*, ch. 4.

4

Labour and Recognition: A Redefinition

Never in the last two hundred years have there been so few efforts to defend an emancipatory and humane notion of labour as today. Developments in the organization of labour in industry and the service sector appear to have pulled the rug out from under any attempts to improve the quality of labour. A growing portion of the population is struggling just to gain access to job opportunities that can secure a livelihood; others work under radically deregulated conditions that hardly enjoy any legal protection anymore; still others are forced to watch their previously secure careers become deprofessionalized and outsourced. So hardly anybody will dispute Robert Castel's diagnosis that we are now faced with the end of that brief historical phase in which the welfare state made wage-labour a secure livelihood.[1] This development in the organization of labour, this tendency of a return to unprotected temporary, part-time and home work, is strangely mirrored in a shift that has occurred in the intellectual focus and interests of social science. Disappointed intellectuals, who forty years ago still placed their hopes in the humanization or emancipation of labour, have turned their backs on the world of work in order to focus on other topics far from the realm of production. In the face of these new circumstances, the critical theory of society appears to have occupied itself with issues of political integration and citizens' rights, without dwelling even for a moment on the threats to past achievements in the sphere of production. Even sociology, the scientific stepchild of capitalist industrialization, has largely abandoned its erstwhile bailiwick and is focusing increasingly on processes of cultural transformation.

However, these tendencies of intellectual retreat from the world of work in no way correspond to the sentiments of the population. Despite the many prognoses of an 'end of the work society', labour has not lost its relevance in the social lifeworld. The majority of the population continue to attach their own social identity primarily to their role in the organized labour process – and this majority has in all likelihood even greatly increased since the labour market has been opened to women as never before. Not only has labour not lost its significance in the lifeworld, but it continues to retain its normative significance as well. Unemployment remains a social stigma and is still regarded as a personal fault; precarious employment is still felt to be burdensome; and the growing flexibility of the labour market has met with reservations and general unease in broad circles of the population.[2] The longing for a job that provides not only a livelihood, but also personal satisfaction, has in no way disappeared; it is just that this longing no longer dictates public discourse or the arena of political debate. However, it would be empirically false and almost cynical to take this oppressive silence as a sign that demands for a reorganization of labour are a thing of the past. The gap between the experiences of the social lifeworld and the topics of social-scientific study has probably never been as wide as it is today. Whereas societal labour has almost entirely lost its significance in the social sciences, the hardships, fears and hopes of those immediately affected by societal working conditions revolve around this notion more than ever.

The reasons why social theory has turned its back on the issue of labour, however, are not merely opportunistic. It would be exceedingly short-sighted to suspect the silence of intellectuals and sociologists to be an expression of a lack of desire to deal any further with the real hardships of the population. Rather, the disappearance of the realm of labour from the focus of social theory conveys the realization that the currently existing relations of production make any proposals for a thoroughgoing improvement of the organization of labour appear mere wishful thinking (*Sollensforderungen*). The gulf between social reality and utopian expectations has become so deep, the distance between real conditions of labour and efforts at emancipation so large, that social theory has been forced to concede the current futility of all its theoretical endeavours.[3] It is not in the spirit of opportunism or triumphalism that the intellectual representatives of social movements have turned their backs on the sphere of societal labour; but they do so only grudgingly and with bitterness. Because the idea of emancipating labour from heteronomy and alienation has proven to be unrealistic, the organization of labour is now to be left to the globalizing forces of the capitalist labour market. The path thus demarcated, and most clearly so in Habermas's notion of a 'norm-free' self-regulation of the economic system,[4] has paved the way for the sobering situation with which we are now confronted: the hardships of all those who not only fear losing their jobs, but are also concerned about the quality of their jobs, no longer resonate in the vocabulary of a critical theory of society.

In what follows, I want to determine whether this development can still be reversed theoretically. How must we incorporate the category of societal labour into the framework of social theory so that we can make the prospects for qualitative improvement more than merely utopian? In order to get at this complex problem, I first want to propose that we distinguish between external and immanent criticism, and then apply that distinction to a critique of currently existing relations of labour. We can only speak of immanent criticism, in which normative demands no longer have the character of mere wishes, if the idea of meaningful and secure work already constitutes a rational claim embedded in the structures of social reproduction themselves (I). Second, I aim to show that societal labour can only become an immanent norm if it is linked to the conditions of recognition prevailing in the modern exchange of services (*Leistungsaustausch*). Every instance of labour that transcends the threshold of merely private, autonomous activity must be organized and structured in a certain specific way if it is to be worthy of societal recognition (II). Finally, I would like to develop the immanent demands connected to this structural linkage between labour and recognition with reference to the organization of the modern world of work. This should make clear that the idea – ultimately going back to Durkheim – of a just organization of the division of labour has more normative impact than might appear at first sight (III).

I

Since the beginning of the industrial revolution, there has been no shortage of utopian visions for reorganizing societal labour. The form of what would become capitalistically exploited labour, organized in factories and shops, exerted such a formative power – one which penetrated all spheres of life – that the normative expectations of the time were initially and primarily attached to the sphere of production. These emancipatory ideas initially received their impetus from the perception of the still visible types of labour embodied by the craftsman. Whereas the craftsman performed all the labour himself, creatively organizing the entire working process, and found the objectification of his own skills mirrored in the finished product, workers in the factory were utterly excluded from such a holistic experience of labour, because their activity was determined by others, fragmented and divorced from their own initiative. Depending on our perspective, the craftsman's activity was taken as a model of free and self-determined cooperation or of individual self-objectification. In the first case the new, capitalist form of gainful employment was condemned because it abrogated the interaction of working subjects; in the second case it was damned for dismantling the organic process in which workers' skills are objectified in a finished product, and for dividing up this process into individual segments having no meaning in themselves. This critique of the capitalist organization of work was additionally fuelled by incorporating aesthetic models of production into the vision of a non-alienated, self-initiated activity. Particularly among the socialist heirs of early German Romanticism, the idea spread that all human labour should possess the self-purposeful creativity exemplified by the production of works of art.[5]

As vivid and enthralling as all these ideas about the emancipation of labour were, they ultimately failed to have any effect on the organization of societal labour. Although the romanticized model of the craftsman and the aesthetic ideal of artistic production had sufficient impact to alter permanently our conception of a good and well-lived life, they exerted no real influence on the struggles of workers' movements, or on socialist efforts to improve working conditions and give workers control over their working conditions. The ambivalent effect emanating from these nineteenth-century workers' utopias is due to the fact that they were too weakly linked to the demands of economically organized labour. The modes of activity they honoured and elevated to paradigmatic models were too extravagant, so to speak, to serve as a model for organizing all the activities required for the reproduction of society. This drastic downside of the classic workers' utopias, however, was compensated by the fact that they evoked a mode of activity whose transparency as a process of objectification soon made them into a core element of the vision of the good life. Because we as human beings require the experience of trying out our acquired skills in the use of

materials and 'objectifying' them in a product, this activity continues to be recognized as an element of a well-lived life.[6] Yet, the fact
that the labour of the craftsman or the artist has become an integral
part of the good life still does not tell us which normative standards
socially organized labour must be able to fulfil. After all, in the
economic sphere, individually performed activities are subject to
demands that arise from the necessity of their being involved in the
societal exchange of services. For this reason, I would like to label
as forms of external criticism all attempts to criticize the given, capitalist work relations in the light of models of organic, solely self-
determined production. By pointing to performance structures that
cannot be equally constitutive of all instances of labour required in
the economic sphere, they all make normative appeals to modes of
activity that remain external to the object they criticize. The work
experiences that might be necessary for the good life of the individual cannot simultaneously supply the standard for judging the
socially organized sphere of production. The constraints and conditions that prevail here require the performance of activities that
starkly diverge from craftsmanship or art.

Certainly, the nineteenth-century workers' utopias gave flight
to our social imagination and opened up whole new spaces of
thinking. It is to them that we owe our conception of individual
fulfilment and successful cooperation, without which the archive
of our dreams of a better life would be significantly poorer. These
utopias of craftsmanship or artistic work provided ethical thought
with an impetus for expanding the traditional notion of 'the good'
to include labour. Ever since, we can hardly imagine a well-lived
life without an element of objectifying activity. But none of these
accomplishments has changed the fact that a critique of the capitalist organization of labour in the name of the ideal of craftsmanship
has the fault of coming from a merely external standpoint.[7] Social
struggles to improve working conditions in the economic sphere
are forced to appeal to norms that greatly differ from the utopian
conception of holistic activity. We only cross the threshold to an
immanent critique of the existing organization of societal labour if
we draw upon moral norms that already constitute rational claims
within the social exchange of services. After all, the institutionalized notion of labour as a contribution to a social division of labour
is linked to normative claims that reach all the way to the organization of the workplace.[8] Before I go into the conditions of such a
critique, I want to examine briefly one attempt to foist an immanent
critical substance onto holistic, craftsmanlike activity.

We saw that the weakness of a critique inspired by the ideal of the craftsman is that it singles out a form of activity that in no way embodies a guaranteed claim within the structures of societal reproduction. Even if certain instances of labour approach this ideal, this would still not justify the claim that all required forms of labour have to have the same shape. Of course, things would be different if it could be shown that every performance of socially necessary labour had a certain tendency towards organic holism, autonomous self-control and thus quasi-craftsmanlike organization. Regardless of what kind of activity is at issue, its individual purposefulness alone would require that subjects retain as much control as possible. I myself once sought to develop such an argument on the basis of industrial-sociological investigations in order to demonstrate that workers' daily resistance revealed the desire for autonomous control over their activity. I was convinced that the mere fact that employees constantly undertook subversive efforts to gain control over their work provided enough evidence to justify demands for more worker control in the workplace.[9] My aim was to apply the ideal of the craftsman not as an external, but as an internal standard for judging the capitalist organization of labour. If, on the basis of the structure of their work, employees have the desire to control their own work, this moral demand is immanently contained in the historically given relations of work and does not necessarily have to be externally opposed to these relations.

Only a short time later, Jürgen Habermas pointed out that I was guilty of drawing a 'genetically false conclusion', because I had taken the mere existence of certain desires and demands as grounds for their moral justification. He countered that only practical discourses, and not presumed moral demands, could morally justify decisions about which norms should be valid in a given organization of labour.[10] It took many years for me to realize that this objection also held the key to a far better solution, if only it could be incorporated into an appropriate critique. There is no doubt that the purpose of immanent criticism cannot be merely to assert claims and demands raised by certain groups at a certain time in the light of their social situation or work situation. The fact that these complaints are advanced from within society against existing rules gives them a truly immanent character, but they still lack any element of provable reason that could make them into justified standards of immanent criticism. At the time, I had sought to amend my argument rationally by showing that employees' subversive demands correspond to the autonomous structures 'anthropologically' embedded in the performance of labour. But regardless of whether such practices of resistance can be verified, it now seems to me far-fetched to impute a craftsmanlike substance to purposive activity as such. When it comes to most work in the modern service sector, we would not even know what it would mean to say that labour must be autonomous, purely objective and objectifying. In this sector, no product is constructed that could reflect acquired skills; rather, workers merely react with as much initiative as possible to the personal or anonymous demands of the employer or customer. In other words, it is a fallacy to claim that all socially necessary activities are naturally constituted along the lines of an organic and holistic form of labour such as craftsmanship.

If we, like Habermas, put aside the structure of labour and examine the norms for organizing it, we will be faced with a different issue. It is not surprising, after all, that the author of *The Theory of Communicative Action* suddenly speaks here of 'norms' that should pervade the organization of societal labour, while otherwise only speaking of a 'norm-free system' for the economic sphere. What makes Habermas's formulation so significant is that this shift in perspective raises the question of whether the modern capitalist organization of labour is based on moral norms that are just as indispensable for its functioning as the norms of mutual understanding are for the modern lifeworld. This is not to say that this is the perspective from which Habermas brings such norms into play; he does not doubt for a moment that these norms are relatively arbitrary and subordinated to the outcome of the conflict between capital and labour. According to Habermas, the difference between 'system' and 'lifeworld' consists in the fact that the coordination of action in the former only occurs through the mediation of purposive strategic stances, while in the latter it presupposes moral attitudes. That is why Habermas cannot ascribe any moral infrastructure to the capitalist economic sphere, even if he occasionally concedes that the modern organization of labour does contain certain norms.[11] These relations would be much different, however, if it could be shown that the functioning of the capitalist labour market also presupposed the existence of a whole series of moral norms. In this case, not only would the categorial opposition between 'system' and 'lifeworld' collapse, but it would also become possible to criticize relations of work from an immanent perspective.

Unlike external criticism, immanent criticism presupposes that we can find a standard that constitutes a justified, rational claim within the criticized relations themselves. The alternatives I have examined with the hope of finding such a criterion for the current state of the world of work have all proven to be insufficient. The silent protests of employees who oppose the fact that others control their work lack that element of demonstrable universalization required to make them into justified standards of immanent criticism. And given the multiplicity of socially necessary labour activities, it seems impossible and absurd to claim that their autochthonic, internal structures demand that they be organized in a unified, single manner. If we exclude these theoretical paths because of their inability to justify simultaneously necessary and rational claims, then in my view the alternative is to search for the roots of rational claims within the existing organization of labour. This line of argumentation, however, requires that we examine the capitalist labour market not solely from the functionalist perspective of economic efficiency. If we were to restrict ourselves to this perspective, the structures of the modern organization of labour would only display the thin layer of strategic rules that Habermas addressed in his system-theoretical constructions. If, by contrast, we view the capitalist labour market as also having the function of social integration, then the picture changes completely. We are then faced with a series of moral norms that underlie the modern world of work, just as the norms of action oriented towards achieving mutual understanding underlie the social lifeworld. In what follows, I want to dig up a mostly forgotten tradition in order to uncover the normative basis of the modern organization of labour. In this way I hope to revive the possibility of immanently criticizing the currently prevailing relations of labour.

II

In the *Philosophy of Right*, Hegel sought to uncover the elements of a new form of societal integration in the structures of the capitalist economy developing before his eyes. He was certain from the very beginning that the achievements of the new market-mediated system of satisfying needs could not be measured merely in terms of economic efficiency. Although he was also aware that this new market institution significantly increased the productivity of economic activity, he insisted that its function must not be restricted to this one physical achievement. Otherwise, this institution would lack any ethical anchoring in society and would thus remain without the necessary moral legitimacy. Therefore, Hegel sought to demonstrate that the entire system of the market-mediated exchange of labour, the purpose of which is to satisfy needs, could only find approval if it fulfilled certain normative conditions. For Hegel, the primary integrative function of this new economic form consisted in transforming *'subjective selfishness'* into a willingness to work for *'the satisfaction of the needs of everyone else'*.[12] Once the population's economic needs are to be fulfilled through transactions in an anonymous market, every (male) member of society must be willing to abandon his personal affinity for idleness and contribute to the common good with his own labour. For Hegel, this universal obligation to work requires that each individual must develop his skills and talents in such a way as to increase the 'universal resources'.[13] However, the willingness to contribute to the common good in this way now presupposed a corresponding service in return. Every participant in the market-mediated exchange of services has 'a right to earn his living':[14] that is, to nourish himself and his family at a given standard of living. In Hegel's eyes, therefore, the second normative achievement of the emerging economic system consists in the fact that it creates a system of mutual dependence that secures the economic subsistence of all its members. As we might say today, the expectation that each person must work is linked to the condition that each receive a living wage.[15] In order to emphasize the moral significance of these internal preconditions, Hegel coined the term 'recognition': in the system of market-mediated exchange, subjects mutually recognize each other as private autonomous beings who act for each other and thereby sustain their livelihood through the contribution their labour makes to society.[16]

Of course, Hegel was clear-sighted enough to see that the development of the capitalist market economy was in danger of coming into conflict with its own normative recognitional conditions. As long as the profit-oriented production of goods 'is in a state of unimpeded activity', 'profits' will be concentrated in the hands of the few, while 'the subdivision and restriction of particular jobs' will intensify for 'a large mass of people', which will in turn lead to 'dependence and distress'.[17] 'The rabble', a not insignificant portion of the population, will have no chance to gain market-mediated recognition for their labour, and will thus suffer from a lack of 'self-respect'. Owing to his understanding of the normative conditions of this new economic system, Hegel did not subscribe to the idea of maintaining the impoverished classes 'at their ordinary standard of living' through charitable contributions by the rich. He was convinced that as a result of such redistribution, 'the needy would receive subsistence directly, not by means of their labour, and this would violate the principle of civil society and the feeling of individual independence and self-respect'.[18] Instead, Hegel proposed supplementing the capitalist market economy with two organizations whose task it would be to ensure the normative conditions of existence for mutual recognition and 'self-respect'. While the 'Police' (*Polizey*) would have the function of intervening in the economic process in order to ensure a balanced relation of supply and demand, the 'Corporations' (*Korporationen*) – modelled after trade associations and unions – would help their members maintain their skills and abilities, and ensure their basic economic subsistence.

But these specific institutional solutions are not what is of particular interest in Hegel's description of the capitalist organization of labour. Both the so-called 'Police' and 'Corporations' constitute organizational structures whose formation and function are far too specific to the early phase of capitalist industrialization to be very relevant for us today. More significant for my purposes is the fact that Hegel derives the directions and design of these corrective institutions not from an external perspective, but from the normative principles of the very economic system he seeks to correct. Hegel was convinced that the moral presuppositions of the capitalist organization of labour required that the individual's labour not only be remunerated with a living wage, but also remain recognizable as a contribution to the common good on the basis of the skills needed to perform that work. The whole idea behind the reciprocal exchange of services demands that each individual activity embody a sufficiently complex and visible display of skills to prove worthy of the universal recognition linked to 'self-respect'. Therefore, Hegel insisted that where economic developments cause a given labour activity to sink below a certain required level of skills and independence, the 'Corporations' are charged with a task that the capitalist market economy should in fact perform on its own. These trade associations are to ensure that the skills of their members receive enough care and public attention to enjoy universal esteem in the future. Thus Hegel has the corporations fulfil a task that constitutes a normative claim anchored within the conditions of existence of this new organizational form of societal labour.

With such a normative conception of the capitalist organization of labour, however, Hegel stands in opposition to a conception that sees the opposite process at work in this new economic system. According to this alternative interpretation, the development of the capitalist economy leads not to a transformation of moral relations, but to the dissolution of social ethics (*lebensweltliche Sittlichkeit*). Even in Hegel's time, there were many theorists who advocated such a position, but it would be over a hundred years before Karl Polanyi would pinpoint this notion by grasping the capitalist market economy as a process in which the sphere of economic activity is 'disembedded' by having been divorced from all traditional customs and moral regulations.[19] Contrary to Hegel, Polanyi believed that the establishment of an all-encompassing market for labour and goods is accompanied by the creation of a 'self-regulating mechanism' that tolerates no form of moral restriction. In his view, it is only the law of supply and demand that holds sway, such that societal labour is organized solely for the purpose of the profitable sale of goods, and is only remunerated to the degree required for just this purpose. We need not think too long or hard to realize that if this thesis is indeed correct, then the strategy I have pursued thus far falls apart. If it is true, as Polanyi claims, that the formation of the capitalist economy completely subordinates the organization of labour to the laws of the market, then we can no longer speak of any kind of normativity in this new socially integrative mode of labour at all. This would of course also rob us of the chance to anchor a criticism of existing relations of work in the moral principles residing in the capitalist organization of labour.

Polanyi's thesis, however, which was initially accepted as being self-evident, has once again come in for criticism – one that is based on the observation that the market's coordination of societal action is faced with a series of problems that, ultimately, can only be solved through institutional and normative rules. If market actors did not make certain concessions with regard to the value of certain goods, the rules of fair exchange and the reliability of expectations, they would not have any clue as to the parameters they are to respect in their supposedly purely purposive considerations.[20] The 'social order' of the market, as it is termed today, thus encompasses not only positive legal regulations and principles that set the conditions for the freedom to contract and engage in economic exchange, but also a series of unwritten, inexplicit norms and rules that implicitly determine – before any market-mediated transaction takes place – how the value of certain goods is to be estimated and what should be legitimately respected in the act of exchange. It is probably best to grasp these reciprocal imputations as normative certainties of action that move agents to engage in such transactions in the first place. These expectations need not always be actually fulfilled, nor will they prove impervious to disappointment; nevertheless, they constitute the cultural and normative interpretive framework in which the market is necessarily embedded. In light of this thesis, which is all but diametrically opposed to that of Polanyi,[21] Hegel's definition of the capitalist organization of labour can be reformulated in a more precise, sociological form. The structures of a capitalist labour market could only develop under the highly demanding ethical precondition that all classes can expect to receive a wage that secures their livelihood and perform tasks worthy of recognition. Hegel therefore sought to prove that the new market system can only lay claim to normative approval on two conditions: first, it must provide a minimum wage; second, it must be apparent that all instances of labour represent a contribution to the common good.

The greatest difficulty in understanding the status of these normative presuppositions consists in the fact that they exert but minimal influence on actual economic developments, while aspiring to universal validity. What does it mean to say that the capitalist organization of labour is embedded in a horizon of moral norms that ensure legitimacy, if Hegel regards these norms as incapable of preventing the autonomization of purely profit-oriented production? The only way to solve this contradiction is to understand these norms as a counterfactual basis for the validity of the capitalist organization of labour. Social actors can only grasp the meaning of this new economic system and view it as being in the 'common interest' if they presuppose the norms Hegel uncovers – this claim implies that the market-mediated organization of labour rests on normative conditions that remain valid even if they are invalidated in practice. To speak of 'embedding' in this context means making the functioning of the capitalist labour market dependent on normative conditions that it itself cannot necessarily fulfil. Events in the mostly opaque labour market are founded on moral norms that remain valid even if they are violated by actual developments. At the same time, these normative certainties form the moral resource that social actors can draw upon when questioning the existing rules of the capitalist organization of labour. What is needed is not an appeal to a realm of higher values or universal principles, but the mobilization of those implicit norms that constitute conditions of understanding and acceptance entrenched in the modern labour market. Social movements that have fought against unreasonable wages or the de-qualification of their professions would in principle only need to make use of the moral vocabulary already found in

Hegel's analysis. This would encompass aims such as the defence of labour that is sufficiently complex and not wholly externally controlled, or the fight for a living wage, both of which constitute thoroughly normative claims summarized by Hegel in the term 'self-respect'. His determinations, however, are certainly insufficient for the purpose of normatively explaining all the deficiencies of the capitalist labour market that have ever been challenged by workers. Although he focuses his attention on the new forms of recognition that the capitalist market offers all male adults, the resort to the compensatory device of the 'Corporation' causes him to lose sight of the central experience of the majority of workers: the emptying of their labour of all qualitative content.

It would be eighty years before Émile Durkheim made the first earnest effort to interpret demands for qualitatively meaningful labour as claims that are immanent to the new economic system.[22] Like Hegel, Durkheim also investigates the structures of the capitalist organization of labour primarily with a view to the contribution they can make to the social integration of modern societies. And just like his predecessor, he runs into a series of normative conditions that underlie market-mediated conditions of exchange, which exist in the peculiar form of counterfactual presuppositions and ideals.[23] In *On the Division of Social Labour*, Durkheim asks whether modern societies, with their constantly expanding and increasingly market-mediated division of labour, are at all capable of creating a feeling of solidarity and community among their members. Just like the author of *Philosophy of Right*, he is convinced that the mere prospect of economic growth and efficiency is not enough to inject the new economic system with the type of moral legitimacy required for successful social integration. This is not to say that Durkheim searches for sources of solidarity that lie outside of this socioeconomic system and could constitute the point of reference for his analysis. The last thing he wants to do is sketch a more modern civil religion or collective ethos in order to eliminate the threat of weak social bonds. Instead, he sets out to identify the conditions that could alter our sense of social belonging within the structures of the new, capitalist organization of labour. The solidarity needed to integrate even modern societies should flow not from sources of moral or religious tradition, but from economic reality.

This undertaking requires the same methodological operation that Hegel employed in his analysis of 'civil society'. The capitalist organization of labour must be presented not in its accidental, empirically given form, but through the normative traits that make it justifiable. If we were to give an empirical description of this new economic system, we would gain no insight into why it should be a source of ethical integration or solidarity. Over long stretches of Durkheim's stylized analysis, we find precisely the same line of argumentation as in Hegel's dialectical depiction of the liberal economic relations characterized by the emerging capitalist economy.[24] Both demonstrate that under the new economic conditions, every adult member of society is entitled to make a contribution to the common good and to receive an appropriate living wage in return. Although Durkheim does not use the term 'recognition', the core of his argument can easily be rendered with its help: market-mediated relations give rise to social relations in which the members of society are able to form a particular, 'organic' form of solidarity, because the reciprocal recognition of their respective contributions to the common good gives them a sense of being connected to each other. Whereas Hegel focused primarily on market participants' economic independence, which was to be preserved through a living wage, Durkheim attaches special value to the fairness and transparency of the social division of labour. Durkheim felt that the new economic system could only take on the function of social integration if it fulfilled two moral conditions, both of which consisted in counterfactual presuppositions in all exchange relations in the labour market. For employees to be able to consent freely to a labour contract, there must be a level playing field for acquiring the necessary qualifications, and all social contributions must be remunerated in accordance with their real value for the community.[25] For Durkheim, therefore, justice and fairness are not normative ideals externally imposed on the capitalist organization of labour, but constitute functionally necessary presuppositions within this economic framework. Without their existence, a sense of social belonging could not arise. The same is true of the second normative determination that Durkheim brings into play in his attempt to give an overview of the moral necessities of this new economic system: if market-mediated relations of labour are to ensure social integration, they must not only be organized in a fair and just manner, but also satisfy the demand that individual activities be related to each other in a way that is as transparent and clearly arranged as possible.

At this point Durkheim takes a decisive step beyond Hegel by proposing a criterion for organizing individual labour activities. His argument begins with his insight that capitalistic relations of work can only generate 'organic' forms of solidarity if all workers can experience them as a common, cooperative effort in the common interest. This requires that the cooperative connection between subjects' own activity and that of their fellow workers must be made clearly visible from the perspective of each individual task. However, Durkheim maintains that this will only be possible if the various labour activities are sufficiently complex and demanding, such that each individual can feel a halfway meaningful connection to all other socially necessary labour activities. He does not hesitate to interpret the demand for meaningful work as an entitlement anchored within the normative conditions of the capitalist economic system:

> The division of labour presumes that the worker, far from being hemmed in by his task, does not lose sight of his collaborators, that he acts upon them and reacts to them. He is, then, not a machine who repeats his movements without knowing their meaning, but he knows that they tend, in some way, towards an end that he conceives of more or less distinctly. He feels that he is serving something.[26]

It may be true that Hegel also entertained such ideas in speaking of 'self-respect' as a form of recognition to which every member of the market-mediated society is entitled, but Durkheim was the first to go a step further and detail the normative implications of the new social system, including the entitlement to a kind of labour that is felt to be meaningful.[27]

III

The currently existing and thoroughly deregulated relations of work seem to scorn the views of Hegel and Durkheim on the moral conditions inherent in the capitalist economic system. The actual circumstances of societal labour, be it in the post-Fordist regime in industrial democracies, or in the low-wage countries of the second and third world, are marked by such unreasonable and oppressive conditions that any demand for sustained improvement must sound like mere wishful thinking. Just as I mentioned at the beginning of this chapter, we are further away than ever from an effective critique of working conditions that could have any practical consequences. Nevertheless, the analyses offered by Hegel and Durkheim have not totally lost their significance. If we take a look at recent developments in economic sociology or in economic institutionalism, we gain ever more theoretical insights into the fact that the capitalist labour market is dependent on normative conditions concealed beneath the praise for the 'self-regulating powers of the market'. However, not all of the market's pre-economic presuppositions that appear in the altered perspective of these rather new disciplines are also moral in nature. The majority of the rules analysed instead resemble institutional conventions and social networks.[28] We do not encounter moral norms in the strict sense until we come to share Hegel's and Durkheim's conviction that the capitalist labour market must not merely be a means for increasing economic efficiency, but also a medium of social integration. Only under this premise, which is in no way self-evident, does it become apparent that the functioning of the market depends on the fulfilment of moral promises that are to be described with terms such as 'self-respect', 'a fair day's pay for a fair day's work' and 'meaningful work'. In responding to the question of whether we have immanent criteria for criticizing the existing relations of work, therefore, everything depends on whether we decide to analyse the capitalist market from the perspective of system integration or social integration. If we restrict ourselves to the former perspective, then we will find pre-economic conditions and rules in the market, but no moral principles. If instead we take up the latter perspective, we will get sight of all the moral implications, which, according to Hegel and Durkheim, guarantee the market's normative embedding in the social lifeworld.

Faced with a choice between these two different perspectives, the voices of those affected by the capitalist labour market can perhaps be legitimately raised after all. It may have become apparent in the course of this chapter that we cannot justify our criticism of given relations of work on the basis of employees' own judgements. If we did, we would have no argument for why such public complaints and lamentations should enjoy any kind of moral validity at all. Perhaps, however, we can bring this malaise into play at a higher level, where it functions not as a normative source of criticism, but as a device for facilitating our choice between the two perspectives mentioned here. The choice between taking up the perspective of system integration or social integration cannot be merely left up to the arbitrary will of the individual theorist. Rather, the latter must justify his or her choice according to which of the two perspectives is more appropriate in each individual case. But as long as employees struggle against unreasonable labour conditions, and as long as the majority of the population suffers under capitalistic working conditions, there is little reason to analyse the capitalist labour market from the perspective of capitalist efficiency.[29] At least the sons and daughters of civil society – to paraphrase Hegel – seem to be convinced that the market has as many claims upon them as they have rights in relation to it.[30] In any case, the reactions of those who populate the labour markets of modern capitalism can only be appropriately explained if we take up the perspective of social integration instead of system integration. We can only grasp the fact that people suffer under the currently prevailing working conditions, and are not merely indifferent to them, if the market continues to be analysed as part of the social lifeworld. If, however, we adopt this perspective, we will get sight of all those moral conditions on the capitalist labour market that I have reconstructed here with the help of Hegel and Durkheim. And despite the overwhelming pressure of the current reality, there is little reason to abandon this reservoir of moral principles.

Notes

1   See Robert Castel, *From Manual Workers to Wage Laborers: Transformation of the Social Question*, trans. and ed. Richard Boyd (New Brunswick, NJ: Transaction Publishers, 2003). I have reviewed the German edition of this book in *Literaturen*, vol. 2 (2001), pp. 58–9. See also Eva Senghaas-Knobloch, *Wohin driftet die Arbeitswelt?* (Wiesbaden: VS Verlag, 2008), part I.

2   See, for example, Christoph Morgenroth, 'Arbeitsidentität und Arbeitslosigkeit – ein depressiver Zirkel', *Das Parlament – Aus Politik und Zeitgeschichte*, vols 6–7 (2003), pp. 17–24; William Julius Wilson, *When Work Disappears: The World of the New Urban Poor* (New York: Vintage Books, 1996).

3   Jürgen Habermas, 'The New Obscurity: The Crisis of the Welfare State and the Exhaustion of Utopian Energies', in *The New Conservatism: Cultural Criticism and the Historian's Debate*, ed. and trans. Shierry Weber Nicholsen (Cambridge, MA: MIT Press, 1989), pp. 48–70.

4   Jürgen Habermas, *Theory of Communicative Action*, vols 1–2, trans. Thomas McCarthy (Boston: Beacon Press, 1981–7). I have expressed doubts about this de-normativation of the economic sphere in *Critique of Power*, trans. Kenneth Baynes (Cambridge, MA: MIT Press, 1991), ch. 9.

5   A good overview of these craftsmanship or aesthetic workers' utopias is given in Ernst Bloch, *The Principle of Hope*, trans. Neville Plaice, Stephan Plaice and Paul Knight (Cambridge, MA: MIT

Press, 1986), ch. 36. For a review of the romanticist undercurrents of socialism, see George Lichtheim, *Origins of Socialism* (Durrington: Littlehampton Book Services Ltd, 1969).

6   See Martin Seel, *Versuch über die Form des Glücks* (Frankfurt/Main: Suhrkamp, 1995), pp. 142–50.

7   This is of course even more true for attempts to revive the ideal of craftsmanship and holistic activity. See Richard Sennett, *The Craftsman* (New Haven and London: Yale University Press, 2008).

8   I drew my first impulse for discussing the normative dimension of the societal exchange of services instead of labour from an essay by Friedrich Kambartel: 'Arbeit und Praxis', *Deutsche Zeitschrift für Philosophie*, vol. 41, no. 2 (1993), pp. 239ff; see also his *Philosophie und politische Ökonomie* (Göttingen: Wallstein, 1998).

9   Axel Honneth, 'Arbeit und instrumentales Handeln', in Axel Honneth and Urs Jaeggi, eds, *Arbeit, Handlung Normativität* (Frankfurt/Main: Suhrkamp, 1980), pp. 185–233.

10 Jürgen Habermas, 'A Reply to My Critics', in John Thompson and David Held, eds, *Habermas: Critical Debates* (Cambridge, MA: MIT Press, 1982), pp. 219–83; n. 11, p. 312.

11 See Richard Münch, 'Zahlung und Achtung: Die Interpenetration von Ökonomie und Moral', *Zeitschrift für Soziologie*, vol. 23, no. 5 (1994), pp. 388–411.

12 G.W.F. Hegel, *Elements of the Philosophy of Right*, trans. H.B. Nisbet (Cambridge: Oxford University Press, 1991), § 199.

13 Ibid.

14 Ibid., § 236, Addition.

15 Hans Christoph Schmidt am Busch, *Hegels Begriff der Arbeit* (Berlin: Akademie Verlag, 2002). I owe several impulses in the following line of argumentation to this excellent monograph.

16 Ibid., pp. 59–65.

17 The formulations cited here all stem from *Philosophy of Right*, §§ 243–4.

18 Ibid., § 245; see also Schmidt am Busch, *Hegels Begriff der Arbeit*, p. 146.

19 Karl Polanyi, *The Great Transformation: The Political and Economic Origins of Our Time* (Boston: Beacon Press, 2001), part II, ch. 5.

20 See Jens Beckert, 'Die soziale Ordnung von Märkten', in Jens Beckert, Rainer Diaz-Bone and Heiner Ganssmann, eds, *Märkte als soziale Strukturen* (Frankfurt/Main: Campus, 2007), pp. 43–62.

21 For a good overview of the debate, see Christoph Deutschmann, 'Unsicherheit und soziale Einbettung: konzeptuelle Probleme der Wirtschaftssoziologie', in Beckert et al., *Märkte als soziale*

Strukturen, pp. 79–93. Talcott Parsons naturally plays an important role in this debate as well, as he also assumes a series of normative preconditions for market activity: 'The Motivation of Economic Activities', in *Essays in Sociological Theory* (New York: Free Press, 1954), pp. 50–68. Furthermore, Parsons uses the term 'recognition' at a key point in his argumentation, because in his view normative conditions must ensure that workers recognize each other's fulfilment of their roles in the labour process and thereby attain 'self-respect' (p. 58).

22 Émile Durkheim, *The Division of Labor in Society*, trans. George Simpson (New York: Free Press, 1964).

23 I cannot discuss the various difficulties involved in Durkheim's analysis here. For a useful overview, see Steven Lukes, *Émile Durkheim: His Life and Work, A Historical and Critical Study* (London: Penguin, 1973), ch. 7; Hans-Peter Müller, 'Die Moralökonomie moderner Gesellschaften', afterword in Émile Durkheim, *Physik der Sitten und des Rechts*, ed. Hans-Peter Müller (Frankfurt/Main: Suhrkamp, 1999), pp. 307–41.

24 Steven Lukes refers indirectly to the affinity with Hegel by drawing parallels between Durkheim's analysis and that of the British Neo-Hegelian T.H. Green. See *Émile Durkheim: His Life and Work*, pp. 265, 271, 300.

25 Durkheim, *The Division of Labor in Society*, pp. 389–95.

26 Ibid., p. 372.

27 A short text from 1898 makes clear that Durkheim was indeed aware of all these normative implications of his sociological analysis: Émile Durkheim, 'L'individualisme et les intellectuels'; English translation, 'Individualism and the Intellectuals', in Robert Bellah, ed., *Émile Durkheim on Morality and Society: Selected Writings*, trans. Mark Traugott (Chicago: University of Chicago Press, 1973), pp. 43–57.

28 Mark Granovetter, 'Economic Action and Social Structure: The Problem of Embeddedness', *American Journal of Sociology*, vol. 91, no. 3 (1985), pp. 481–510.

29 Pierre Bourdieu et al., *The Weight of the World: Social Suffering in Contemporary Society* (Cambridge: Polity, 1999).

30 *Philosophy of Right*, § 238.

5

Recognition as Ideology: The Connection between Morality and Power

In the same measure that the concept of recognition has become the normative core of several different emancipation movements over the last several years, there have also been increasing doubts as to its critical potential. This theoretical scepticism has doubtlessly been fostered by the experience that we live in a culture of affirmation in which publicly displayed recognition often bears the marks of mere rhetoric and has the character of being just a substitute for material remuneration. Praising certain characteristics or abilities seems to have become a political instrument whose unspoken function consists in inserting individuals or social groups into existing structures of domination by encouraging a positive self-image. Far from making a lasting contribution to the autonomy of the members of our society, social recognition appears merely to serve the creation of attitudes that conform to the dominant system. The reservations about this new critical approach thus amount to the thesis that practices of recognition do not empower persons, but subject them to domination. Processes of reciprocal recognition, in short, encourage subjects to adopt a particular self-conception that motivates them to voluntarily take on tasks or duties that serve society.[1]

These fundamental reservations recall the considerations that moved the Marxist theoretician Louis Althusser over thirty years ago to view the practice of public recognition as the common mechanism of all forms of ideology.[2] His roughly outlined arguments, which dealt exclusively with state policies, were later taken up by Judith Butler, who, by drawing on Jacques Lacan's work in psychoanalysis, fashioned these arguments into a tenable concept.[3]

As is well known, Althusser made use of the double meaning of the French concept of *'subjectivation'* in order to elucidate what he understood by ideology: individuals become 'subjects', i.e. persons who are aware of their responsibilities and rights, only to the extent to which they are subjected to a system of practical rules and role-ascriptions that lends them a social identity. Once we understand the act of subjection according to the model of public affirmation, 'recognition' suddenly loses all of its positive connotations and becomes the central mechanism of ideology. On this account, to recognize someone is to encourage them, by means of repeated and ritual invitations and demands (*Aufforderungen*), to adopt precisely that self-conception that conforms to the established system of behavioural expectations.

However, Althusser himself never employed this concept of ideology in a critical sense, restricting himself instead to a purely descriptive use of it.[4] Without making any normative judgements, he described the institutional act of recognition as a mechanism for creating subjects who behave in conformity with a given social system. For a critical theory of society that seeks to locate its normative foundation in the act of reciprocal recognition, however, Althusser's conceptual determinations pose a difficult challenge; a theory of recognition is forced to ask whether social recognition might also occasionally take on the function of securing social domination. In this new context, the concept of ideology loses its merely descriptive significance and becomes a pejorative category, indicating forms of recognition that must be regarded as false or unjustified, because they fail to promote personal autonomy, instead engendering attitudes that conform to practices of domination.[5]

Of course, it would be wrong to accuse the theory of recognition of having ignored negative phenomena of subjection and domination from the very beginning. After all, this approach owes its entire critical impulse to social phenomena of lacking or insufficient recognition. It seeks to draw attention to practices of humiliation or degradation that deprive subjects of a justified form of social recognition and therefore of a decisive condition for the formation of their autonomy.[6] Conversely, this way of formulating the issue makes clear that 'recognition' has always been treated as representing the opposite of practices of domination or subjection. Such forms of exercising power were to be regarded as phenomena of withheld recognition, intentional disrespect or humiliation, such that recognition itself could never come under suspicion of functioning as a means of domination. This presumption of innocence, however, is no longer self-evident in view of the considerations to which Althusser's concept of ideology gives rise. The latter draws attention to forms of recognition that, by employing methods of ritual affirmation in order to create a self-image that conforms to social expectations, can be effective as a means of social domination. They thus contribute to the reproduction of the existing relations of domination. We could easily cite past examples that demonstrate just how often public displays of recognition merely serve to create and maintain an individual relation-to-self that is seamlessly integrated into a system based on the prevailing division of labour. For example, the pride that 'Uncle Tom' feels as a reaction to the constant praises of his submissive virtues makes him into a compliant servant in a slave-owning society.[7] The emotional appeals to the 'good' mother and housewife made by churches, parliaments or the mass media over the centuries caused women to remain trapped within a self-image that most effectively accommodated the gender-specific division of labour.[8] The public esteem enjoyed by heroic soldiers continuously engendered a sufficiently large class of men who willingly went to war in pursuit of glory and adventure.[9] As trivial as these examples may be, they do make strikingly clear that social recognition can always also operate as a conformist ideology, for the continuous repetition of identical forms of recognition can create a feeling of self-worth that provides the motivational resources for forms of voluntary subordination, without employing methods of repression.

However, these cases all owe their suggestive power entirely to the certainty afforded by hindsight. The choice of examples itself, indeed the very way they are described, is the result of a moral judgement that can be made only from the perspective of our morally advanced present. Because we live in an epoch that regards itself as being morally superior to past ages, we are certain that the esteem enjoyed by the virtuous slave, the good housewife and the heroic soldier was purely ideological. Yet if we put ourselves in the past, it becomes much more difficult to distinguish between a false, 'ideological' form of recognition and one that is correct and morally imperative, because the criteria of which we were so convinced suddenly become uncertain. Why should the slave's experience of being esteemed for his submissiveness by his white masters not allow him to attain a feeling of self-worth that provides him with a certain degree of inner autonomy? And does the public recognition of women as caring mothers not give them a measure of compensation for the disrespect they have endured as a result of their exclusion from roles outside the home? And finally, the set of values characteristic of male heroism may have provided men who suffer from social insignificance, owing to unemployment or lack of qualifications, an opportunity to become part of an independent, male subculture in which they could gain compensatory prestige and reputation. In each case, these possibilities of interpretation reveal that upon closer inspection of the historical circumstances, a particular *dispositif* of esteem that in retrospect seems to be pure ideology can in fact prove to be a condition for a group-specific attainment of increased self-worth. Once we examine particular forms of recognition in terms of the sociocultural conditions prevailing at the time, determining their ideological contents seems all the more difficult. Only in cases of revolt against dominant practices of recognition do we have any grounds for speaking of mere ideology. In general, however, this difficulty diminishes over time; the greater the historical distance, the more likely we are to possess generally accepted criteria that allow us to distinguish retrospectively between ideological and morally imperative forms of recognition.

With regard to the present, however, this theoretical problem retains its intricacies. As long as we have no empirical evidence that people experience particular practices of recognition as repressive, constricting or fostering stereotypes, it is extremely difficult to distinguish between ideological and justified forms of recognition in any reasonable way. This difficulty is a result of the fact that when we speak of acts of recognition, we always refer to the public display of a value or achievement that is to be attributed to a person or social group. To speak in this connection of an 'ideology' is therefore to claim that intrinsically positive and affirmative practices in fact bear the negative features of an act of willing subjection, even though these practices appear *prima facie* to lack all such discriminatory features. This raises the question of how public displays of social worth, i.e. recognition, can nevertheless bear features of domination. This problem constitutes the topic of this chapter. As an introduction, I summarize what we, after a number of recent attempts to clarify this issue, can understand today by a practice of recognition. Here we will see that the concept of recognition is normative inasmuch as it indicates the rational behaviour with which we can respond to the evaluative qualities (*Werteigenschaften*) of a person or group (I). These conceptual considerations, however, only appear to offer a solution to the problem of how to distinguish between ideological and morally justified forms of social recognition. We will see that ideologies of recognition are only rarely entirely irrational; rather, they mobilize evaluative reasons contained within our horizon of values (II). A solution to our problem can only be found in the attempt to dissect and spell out the conditions of various forms of recognition, thereby revealing the 'irrational core' of all merely 'ideological' forms of recognition. I suspect that this irrationality does not lie on the semantic surface of our evaluative vocabulary, but is to be found instead in the discrepancy between evaluative promises and material fulfilment (III).

I

In a certain sense, the problem I wish to focus on here cannot even exist for Althusser. His concept of recognition is one-dimensional, permitting no distinctions between 'correct' and 'incorrect', 'right' and 'wrong', 'justified' and 'ideological' practices of recognition. Instead, every form of recognition is necessarily ideological; merely by making a demand upon or 'calling upon' addressees imposes upon them an imaginary unity that they in no way possess as individuals. By contrast, an attempt to distinguish between 'ideological' and appropriate forms of recognition must begin by giving a positive definition of 'recognition'.[10] Although recently there has been strong growth in the research on 'recognition', there remains a great deal of dispute over its conceptual core. Indirectly drawing on Hegel, the concept is used generally to depict vague attitudes or practices through which individual subjects or social groups receive affirmation for certain specific qualities. Not only does the relation of recognition to the Kantian concept of 'respect' remain unclear, but it has also become more apparent than ever that the concept of recognition encompasses semantic components that differ in English, French and German usage, and that the relation between these various components is not especially transparent. In German, the concept essentially indicates only the normative act of according positive social worth, while the English and French usage also encompasses the epistemic senses of identifying or recalling something. An additional difficulty consists in the fact that in all three languages, the concept can be used to indicate speech acts in which one admits or acknowledges a point, in which case 'recognition' has a primarily self-referential sense.[11] Finally, a Wittgensteinian interpretation has come to rival the Hegelian usage of the term; 'recognition' here functions as a performative response to the actions (*Lebensäußerungen*) of other people. Owing to the writings of Stanley Cavell in particular, who makes do without any recourse to Hegel, the category of 'acknowledgement' has penetrated the inner circle of analytic philosophy.[12]

In this thicket of conceptual confusion and unanswered questions, it is only by giving categorial definitions that do not shy away from simplifying the issue or excluding certain elements that we can gain some clarity. Here we must take account of the fact that recognition represents a moral act anchored in the social world as an everyday occurrence. I assume four premises upon which there seems to me to be sufficient consensus. First, it can be claimed that the original mode of recognition consists in the meaning emphasized in the German usage of the term: the affirmation of positive qualities of human subjects or groups. However, this is not to say that we cannot establish any systematic connections between this and other definitions of the term. Second, there is now general agreement that recognition is an act that cannot consist in mere words or symbolic expressions, because only the corresponding modes of comportment can produce the credibility so normatively significant for the recognized subject. Insofar as we limit ourselves to intersubjective relationships, we should speak of recognition as a 'stance' (*Haltung*), i.e. as an attitude realized in concrete action.[13] Third, we can assume that such acts of recognition represent a distinct phenomenon in the social world, which cannot, therefore, be understood as a mere side-effect of a separate action, but must instead be explicitly intended. Whether they be gestures, speech acts or institutional policies, such expressions or measures always represent acts of recognition inasmuch as their primary purpose is to affirm the existence of another person or group. This basic conceptual determination rules out, for example, defining positive attitudes that are inevitably accompanied by other interests in interaction as being a form of recognition. If I have a strong desire to play chess with another person on a regular basis, I may express a certain amount of esteem for the other person's intellectual abilities, but my primary purpose is to play chess together. A fourth, broadly agreed-upon premise can be summarized by the claim that recognition represents a conceptual species comprising a number of various sub-species. 'Stances' of love, legal respect and esteem thus accentuate and display various aspects of the basic attitude we understand generically as recognition.

These four premises only summarize what we assume is meant by recognition in a halfway clear use of the term. Recognition should be understood as a genus comprising various forms of practical attitudes whose primary intention consists in a particular act of affirming another person or group. Unlike what Althusser had in mind, such recognitional stances are unambiguously positive, because they permit the addressee to identify with his or her own qualities and thus to achieve a greater degree of autonomy. Far from being a mere ideology, recognition constitutes an intersubjective prerequisite for the ability to fulfil one's life goals autonomously.[14] Yet the real challenge in clarifying the use of this concept begins once we turn to the epistemic character of such affirmative behaviour; the decisive question here is whether we should understand recognition as an attributive or receptive act. When it comes to finding an appropriate characterization for a generic case of recognition, we appear to be faced with two alternatives for our cognitive relation to our partners in interaction. We can understand the affirmation contained in such an act either as an ascription of a new, positive quality, or as a perception of qualities that a person already possesses, thus reinforcing or manifesting them secondarily. In the first case, recognition would represent the ascription or addition of a status that the concerned subject could not have previously possessed; in the second case, recognition would be a particular act of perception by which we become aware of an already present status that a subject has independent of our perceiving it. Another way of defining this is by saying that recognition is productive in the first case and merely reproductive in the second; the status or positive qualities possessed by a person or a social group are either produced in the act of recognition or simply reproduced in a particular meaningful way.

It is not easy to choose between these two conceptual models, because each seems to possess certain distinct advantages. I believe that the perception or reception model permits us to account better for our intuition that recognition must be an act motivated by practical reasons: we thereby react in a correct or appropriate way to the reasons contained in the evaluative qualities that human beings possess in different respects.[15] By contrast, the attribution model is free of any admixture of this kind of value realism. Here we account for our intuition that recognition is a constitutive act in which we ascribe particular qualities to a person or group. The disadvantage of this latter model represents the advantage of the reception model: if recognition merely attributes determinate qualities to another person, then we possess no internal criteria for judging the correctness or appropriateness of such acts of ascription. There would be no limits to the permutations that recognition could take, because we would have to regard everything as an ability or status just because it has come about by an attributive act. The only way out of this problem consists in claiming that the legitimacy of a given act of recognition is measured according to the normative quality of the way recognition comes about. However, the concept of recognition would then lose all the moral implications that are supposed to distinguish it from a sociological 'labelling approach'.

Now, at first sight, matters look no better for the other approach – the reception or response model. In order to be able to claim that an act of recognition constitutes a 'correct' response to the evaluative qualities of a person or group of persons, we must presuppose the objective existence of values in a way that is no longer reconcilable with our knowledge of how they are constituted. It may seem right for us to continue to place recognition in the 'space of reasons' so that it is not deprived of its character as a moral action. Only if recognition is motivated by reasons we can articulate can it be understood as an intentional act and thus belong in a broad sense to the domain of morality. The proposal that we identify this type of reason as 'evaluative' is convincing in that, by recognizing others, we appear to attest to the value of a person or group. The moral constraints we respect in the act of recognition result from the valuable qualities to which our recognitional behaviour gives public expression. The problem starts only when we begin to give a more precise definition of the status of such evaluative reasons. Here it seems that we have no choice but to fall back upon a kind of value realism that is no longer reconcilable with our other basic ontological convictions. However, once we concede the possibility that these kinds of values represent the certainties of our lifeworld, whose character can be subject to historical modifications, the situation changes. The qualities we would have to perceive in persons or groups in order to respond to them 'correctly' in our recognitional behaviour would thus be no longer unchangeable and objective, but historically variable. In order to arrive at a halfway plausible theory, however, we would have to add some further elements to the notion of recognition outlined here. We would have to conceive of the lifeworld as a kind of 'second nature' into which subjects are socialized by their learning successively to appreciate the valuable qualities of other persons. This learning process would have to be conceived of as a complex one in which we acquire modes of behaviour corresponding to the perception of evaluative qualities, whose particularity would obviously compel us to restrain our natural egocentrism. As a result, we could then understand human recognitional behaviour as a bundle of habits linked to the revisable reasons for the value of other persons in the process of socialization.[16]

However, this line of argumentation has not yet solved the real difficulty posed by this type of moderate value realism. We have already said that the valuable qualities we can appropriately recognize in other persons can only be real within the experiential horizon of a particular lifeworld. Those who have been socialized successfully into the culture of that lifeworld take these values to be objective givens of their social environment, just as they initially take other cultural particularities for granted. This entails the threat of a kind of relativism that is fundamentally irreconcilable with the normative aims of the concept of recognition, because the values according to which we measure the appropriateness of our recognitional behaviour would only be valid within one single culture. As a consequence, the relativism associated with the response or reception model would no longer differ from that of the attribution model. In both cases the validity of recognitional stances – be they acts of ascription or appropriate responses – would be contingent upon the normative facts of a given form of life. In my opinion, we can only avoid this difficulty by equipping this moderate value realism with a robust concept of progress. This would involve assuming there to be a definite direction to the cultural transformations of valuable human qualities, which would allow us to make justified judgements about the trans-historical validity of a particular culture of recognition.[17] Without going into the details of such a concept of progress, which I believe must be defined as a form of reflection on the knowledge that guides us in the lifeworld,[18] the main idea behind it is that with the differentiation of the evaluative qualities we observe and notice on the basis of our socialization, the normative level of our relations of recognition rises as well. With every value that we can affirm by an act of recognition, our opportunities for identifying with our abilities and attaining greater autonomy grow. This should suffice to justify the idea that our concept of recognition is anchored in a moderate form of value realism.

But before I return to the question of how we can distinguish between ideological and justified forms of recognition, I still need to deal with at least one other problem; it arises from the fact that we speak of ideologies mostly as transformations of consciousness or evaluative systems of statements whose source lies not in inter-subjective behaviour, but in institutionalized rules and arrangements. Like Marx, who held the civil form of the contract to be an institution that produces ideologies,[19] we assume that the specific constitution of certain institutions is what originally leads to the emergence of illusory or fictionalizing beliefs. If patterns of recognition are now also thought to be capable of engendering such ideologies, we will have to clarify the fact that not only persons can grant recognition, but social institutions as well. We must therefore shift from the level of intersubjective recognition to the level of institutionally guaranteed recognition.[20]

We can make this transition by recognizing that institutional rules and practices can contain certain particular conceptions about which human evaluative qualities should receive recognition in which specific way. For instance, the value that a person, as an individual with needs, should be recognized as possessing is expressed in the institution of the modern nuclear family, while the normative fact that members of modern societies are to be respected as free and equal subjects is expressed in the principle of equality, institutionalized in modern legal systems. In both cases, institutions can be understood as embodiments of the specific form of recognition that subjects accord each other on the basis of specific evaluative qualities. However, we have to distinguish between those institutions that 'express' patterns of recognition and those institutional rules and practices that articulate particular forms of recognition in a merely indirect way or only as a side-effect. The routines typical of all institutions convey particular conceptions of human subjects; though they do not intentionally accord recognition, they can be understood as crystallizations of patterns of recognition. For example, the rules that regulate the remuneration of labour, safety precautions, health care and vacation time for workers in certain specific industries reflect forms of recognition that result from social struggles, e.g. in the organizational practices and routines concerning the treatment of hospital patients. The schemata of perception and behaviour, which are the prerequisite for the particular treatment of individuals in these organizations as members or clients, can be understood as sediments of practices of recognition in the lifeworld. Of course, the direction of these sediments can be inverted: for instance, if a certain organization takes on a leading role in the creation or discovery of new evaluative qualities. In this case, modified patterns of recognition are established in the rules and practices of an institution before they find expression in the narrative praxis of a given lifeworld. This second case of institutional recognition is surely crucial when it comes to the question of how, and in what sense, certain specific patterns of recognition possess an ideological character, owing to the fact that they encourage subjects to freely subordinate themselves to the prevailing system of rules and expectations.

II

So far my main concern has been to find an appropriate understanding of the concept of recognition. Faced with an alternative between an attribution model and a reception model, I have chosen a moderate value realism. We should understand recognition as a way of rationally responding to evaluative qualities we have learned to perceive in others to the degree that we have been integrated into the second nature of our lifeworld. This suffices to give us a sense of the difference between this conceptual definition and Althusser's suggestion that every form of recognition represents an instance of ideology. He holds that regardless of how subjects are addressed, the mere ascription of social worth represents an ideological practice, because it creates both the illusion of unity and identity as well as the willingness to accept corresponding behavioural expectations. By contrast, the thesis developed in this essay assumes the possibility of an appropriate and rational form of recognition, which would consist in giving performative expression to existing evaluative qualities. However, this does not yet give us a clear enough sense of why this conception of recognition should indicate a moral act at all. Although we are dealing with an act that is mediated by evaluative reasons, this by itself in no way indicates that this act is necessarily moral. Its character as a moral act does not become apparent until we take a closer look at what I have already described as a 'restriction of egocentrism'. In a certain sense this idea builds on Kant, who, when introducing his concept of respect, wrote that every conception of worth compels us to impose a restriction on our actions which 'thwarts' our 'self-love'.[21] We could continue this line of thought by saying that to recognize others is to perceive an evaluative quality in them that motivates us intrinsically to behave no longer egocentrically, but rather in accordance with the intentions, desires and needs of others. This makes clear that recognitional behaviour must represent a moral act, because it lets itself be determined by the value of other persons. When we take up the stance of recognition, what guides our behaviour are not our own intentions, but the evaluative qualities of the other. If that is the case, we must be able to distinguish between as many forms of moral action as there are values worthy of recognition. This is why I have come to the conclusion that we have to distinguish between three sources of morality corresponding to the various forms of recognition in our lifeworld. As I have claimed in agreement with several other authors, the value horizon of modern societies is characterized by the idea that humans, as beings who have needs, who are equally entitled to autonomy and equally capable of achievement, should possess a value to which diverse forms of recognitional behaviour correspond (love, legal respect, social esteem).[22]

Before I pursue this thought any further, I want to address the question that should in fact stand at the centre of this essay. I had said that we cannot exclude the possibility that forms of social recognition possess a purely ideological function if they encourage an individual relation-to-self that suits the existing dominant order. Instead of truly giving expression to a particular value, such ideological forms of recognition would ensure the motivational willingness to fulfil certain tasks and duties without resistance. At this point it probably makes sense to further narrow the set of public value statements and conceptions of the human subject that could play any role at all in such ideological forms of recognition, for the majority of the evaluative classifications we might currently encounter in our current lifeworld do not even meet the prerequisites for being credible as ideological forms of recognition.

First of all, the systems of belief that might be at issue in the case of such ideologies have to give positive expression to the value of a subject or group of subjects. These ideologies are only capable of fulfilling the function ascribed to them if they give individuals the opportunity to relate to themselves affirmatively, such that they see themselves encouraged to adopt certain specific tasks willingly. Thus we must exclude classifications of an obviously discriminatory character; systems of belief in which specific groups of persons are denied worth – racism, misogyny or xenophobia – cannot represent ideological forms of recognition, because they usually injure the self-image of their addressees. Ideologies that are to be effective in terms of social recognition cannot exclude their addressees, but must instead contribute to their integration.

Second, in order to achieve the desired effect, these systems of beliefs must be 'credible' in the eyes of the addressees themselves. If the latter have no good reason to identify with the value statements addressed to them, then these statements will fail to fulfil their performative function. This limiting condition is in no way trivial. It is obvious that if positive value statements are to strengthen the self-image of a person or group of persons, they have to be realistic – that is, they have to apply to abilities or virtues that the addressees really do possess. It makes just as little sense to praise police officers for their mathematical skills as it does to praise outstanding mathematicians for their physical strength, unless both are being honoured for achievements unrelated to their respective careers. But there is a second, more important element to the criterion of 'credibility', one that is related to the expansion of the realm of evaluative reasons: people will only accept value statements that go beyond the value they have already achieved in the process of overcoming one-sided or inappropriate interpretations. In other words, ideological forms of recognition can only employ value statements that live up to the evaluative vocabulary of the present. Praise for already discredited evaluative qualities will not be credible in the eyes of the addressees. Therefore, the criterion of credibility also contains a component of rationality with a clear historical or temporal index. Today, a woman who is praised for her virtues as a good housewife will have little reason to identify with this value statement to such a degree that she could regard her own feeling of self-worth as having been thereby reinforced.

Correspondingly, 'normalizing' patterns of recognition cannot be viewed as 'ideological' forms of recognition.[23] After all, the term 'normalization' in this context means that a person or group has been recognized for having certain qualities or an identity that they view as a restriction on their sphere of autonomy.[24] Therefore, a normalizing form of recognition cannot move us to develop an affirmative self-conception that would lead us to willingly accept tasks and sacrifices imposed upon us by others. The matter is a bit more complicated when we only suspect the effect of an act of normalization, without having any empirical evidence that the addressees are displeased with or object to such an act. In these situations, the negative judgement assumes that its addressees would actually reject the qualities ascribed to them if they indeed knew all the details, for they would then have a sense that their autonomy has thereby been restricted. Therefore, this idea essentially amounts to the claim that a pattern of recognition is 'normalizing' if it serves to maintain a restrictive, evaluatively anachronistic ascription of identity in an unjustified manner, while ideological forms of recognition can only maintain their repression-free effect with the aid of contemporary, evaluatively rational value statements.

Perhaps we can name a third condition that has to be fulfilled in order for forms of social recognition to take on an ideological function: such value statements have to be not only positive and credible, but also contrastive, in the sense of giving expression to a particular new value or special achievement. This restriction follows from the fact that individuals can identify with the definitions ascribed to them only if they have the sense of being distinguished in a certain way. A value statement, which the addressees have to be able to apply to themselves in comparison with the past or with the surrounding social order, will have to evince a contrast that guarantees that they will feel distinguished in some special way. If an existing form of social recognition is only expanded to include a previously excluded social circle, it will lack this aspect of definitive accentuation eliciting the motivational willingness to subject oneself voluntarily.

With these three restrictions, not all of which are equally important, I have begun to outline only the conditions for partially successful ideological forms of recognition. They can evoke an individual self-conception that motivates a subject to accept tasks and obligations freely and willingly only if the value statements employed are simultaneously positive, credible and contrastive. But taken together, these conditions for success make clear that such ideological forms of recognition cannot simply represent irrational systems of beliefs; rather, they must mobilize evaluative reasons with the power to rationally motivate their addressees to apply these reasons to themselves. In contrast to ideologies that have an exclusionary character and virtually shatter the evaluative perceptual horizon of the present by blinding individuals or groups to the evaluative qualities of others, ideological forms of recognition operate within an historical 'space of reasons': they only expand, so to speak, the evaluative qualities we have learned to perceive in other humans by adding a new meaning – one which, when taken up successfully, creates a self-conception that conforms to a person's function in society. As with every new accentuation inherent in social recognition, these kinds of rational ideologies are also located within the horizon of value that encompasses the normative culture of recognition in modern societies. They also cannot avoid making semantic use of the principles of love, legal equality or achievement which shape the given conditions of reciprocal recognition all the way down to our evaluative awareness. The question we must therefore pose is how we can draw a distinction between justified and unjustified forms of social recognition. At what point does a new accentuation become an ideology with the function of merely evoking a relation-to-self that conforms to a given social role?

We do not get a clear sense of the full extent of the difficulties we face here until we recall that the historical development of recognition generally occurs as the disclosure of new points of view within the horizon of general principles. By invoking an overarching principle of recognition, one brings a new, previously neglected value into play whose consideration compels us to broaden our evaluative horizon and thereby intensify or expand recognition. In my view, during the last two centuries, new needs have constantly been asserted by invoking the normative meaning of 'love' – the well-being of the child, the wife's need for autonomy, and so on. These needs have gradually led to a deepening of reciprocal care and affection; the same dynamic can be observed in the relations of recognition obtaining in modern law, where legal proceedings pertaining to previously neglected life-situations have brought about an unambiguous increase in legal equality. I would also speak of a dialectic between the general and the particular even with regard to the achievement principle, since here an unbroken symbolic struggle over the meaning of 'work' and 'pay' has brought us to the threshold of a broader conception of social contributions and achievements. But the more we become aware of the fact that relations of recognition have been transformed, expanded and improved historically by means of new accentuations of general principles, the more difficult it becomes to identify merely ideological forms of recognition. Who can tell us for sure that an apparently functional, ideological evaluation is not just one of those shifts in accentuation by means of which the struggle for recognition unfolds historically? The issue is simple only in cases where the concerned parties actually resist new forms of evaluative distinction. Here we have at least an initial reason to question changed forms of recognition and to suspect that a mere ideology could be at work. But in the absence of such protest, where individuals seem to attain a stronger sense of self-respect through a new form of recognition, we initially lack all criteria for distinguishing between ideological and justified shifts in accentuation. In the final part of this essay, I would like to present a recent example in order to at least sketch the first outlines of an answer to the question.

III

Ideological forms of recognition have to represent positive classifications whose evaluative contents are sufficiently credible for their addressees to have good reason to accept them. Any new form of distinction must be able to alter their relation-to-self so as to promise a psychic premium of heightened self-respect, provided that they do in fact regard the abilities, needs and virtues associated with this distinction as being their own. Today, the primary examples of such ideologies appear to be advertisements that set up a schema of recognition in which a certain specific group of persons feels the urge to conform to a set of given standards. If the corresponding practice can be carried out with the help of an item advertised in a more or less concealed way, advertising has attained its goal. However, the example of consumer advertising is only partially sufficient to illustrate ideological forms of recognition. In general, the content of these advertisements is received with the mental reservation that the commodity on offer cannot really alter our life practices in any substantial way. But if certain specific advertisements cross this threshold and have an actual effect on our behaviour, then we could say that they wield the same power as ideological forms of recognition: they would then possess the 'regulative' ability to engender modes of behaviour by promising the advantage of an increase in self-esteem and public affirmation. Using Foucault's terminology, the power exercised by ideological forms of recognition is productive and not repressive. By promising social recognition for the subjective demonstration of certain abilities, needs or desires, they engender a willingness to adopt practices and modes of comportment that suit the reproduction of social domination.[25] But even by having clarified the type of power represented by ideological forms of recognition, we have not yet determined how they could be identified within the unbroken flow of a many-layered struggle for recognition. Although the comparison with modern methods of advertisement gives us a clear sense of the fact that such ideologies must speak to their addressees in a way that reinforces the former's evaluative credibility, justified demands for new accentuations of social recognition can no longer be made without taking on elements of a symbolic political aim that draws public attention to them. Instead of continuing to address this question on a merely conceptual plane, I will now take a look at an empirical example in the hope that it might further clarify matters. From the multiplicity of new patterns of recognition currently found in our society's culture – the increased value accorded to female housework in connection with the achievement principle, an appreciation of belonging to social minorities in connection with legal equality, the idea of giving recognition to 'public service' (*Bürgerarbeit*) – I would like to pick out one instance that shows all signs of being a purely 'ideological' form of recognition. This should reveal whether there are any criteria for determining the ideological content of forms of recognition with any real certainty.

Recently, the sphere of work in developed capitalist economies has undergone a far-reaching structural transformation, with the result that employees have come to be addressed in a new way. Current management literature speaks no longer of 'wage-workers' or the 'labour force', but instead of creative 'entrepreneurs' of their own labour, or 'entreployees' (*Arbeitskraftunternehmer*).[26] The shift in accentuation accompanying this change in nomenclature takes up the discourse of individual self-fulfilment in order to apply it to the organization of labour in the sphere of production and the provision of services. Growing needs for self-fulfilment in the sphere of labour should be accommodated by levelling hierarchies, raising the autonomy of teamwork and providing a higher degree of self-management, thus increasing the chance of conceiving of one's own activity as an autonomous expression of acquired skills. Furthermore, this new nomenclature seems to be accompanied by a whole new way of conceiving of one's own profession, since subjects should regard their work no longer as the fulfilment of a necessity, but as the realization of a 'vocation' or 'calling'. The idea of labelling labourers as employers of their own labour-power urges us to regard every job change or every new change in working conditions as a result of these subjects' own decisions, made solely in accordance with the intrinsic value of their respective job. Therefore, this modified nomenclature also seems to be accompanied by a new accentuation of the achievement principle, since wage-labourers are required to perform all the autonomous, creative and flexible activities previously reserved for the classical entrepreneur. This new form of recognition asserts that every qualified member of the labour force is capable of planning his or her career path as a risk-filled enterprise, requiring the autonomous application of all of his or her skills and abilities.

In this case it certainly seems reasonable for us to discern the outlines of 'ideological' recognition with regulative power. The suspicion is that the shift in accentuation of recognition primarily has the function of evoking a new relation-to-self, which encourages willing acceptance of a considerably modified workload. The increased demands for flexibility and the deregulation of labour that have accompanied capitalism's neoliberal structural transformation require the ability to productively market oneself, an ability engendered by referring to workers as 'entreployees'.[27] Yet, there is a gap between this initial suspicion and a justified claim; overcoming this gap requires a set of criteria that can be developed only with difficulty. If this new way of addressing employees really is to be considered a case of recognition, we can say that it fulfils the conditions of an ideological form of recognition: subjects have good evaluative reasons to apply the altered distinction to themselves and thereby attain a higher degree of self-esteem or self-respect. Therefore, we cannot follow the standard path taken by every critique of ideology, which consists in demonstrating the irrationality of a system of beliefs that is viewed as ideological, for in an evaluative sense at least, the new form of recognition must be sufficiently rational to be 'credible' in the eyes of employees, enabling the latter to apply it to themselves. Therefore, I believe we must spell out in even greater detail the conditions for conferring social recognition, so that we might be able to reveal the characteristic deficiencies of ideological forms of recognition. To do so, I pick up my argumentation where I last left off: the discussion of recognition as a suitably rational, moral response to the evaluative qualities of human beings.

At the very beginning of this essay, I pointed out that recognition may not consist in mere words or symbolic expressions, but must be accompanied by actions that confirm these promises. An act of recognition is incomplete, so to speak, as long as it does not lead to modes of behaviour that give real expression to the actual value articulated in the original act. However, recognition can reasonably be said to be 'fulfilled' only in cases of simple interaction between two people. As soon as we turn to instances of generalized recognition provided by social institutions, we can no longer suppose recognition to be consummated in the corresponding modes of conduct or forms of institutional activity. Although institutionally generalized forms of recognition also ultimately find expression in transformed habits, they are primarily fulfilled in the realm of institutional policies and practices. In order to establish new modes of generalized forms of recognition, legal definitions would have to be changed and material redistribution would have to take place.

Hence, alongside the evaluative dimension of the credibility of social recognition, we must also consider the material element, which, according to the degree of complexity of a given social interaction, consists in either appropriate individual conduct or suitable institutional procedures. An altered form of social recognition will

only be 'credible' if, in addition to being rational from an evaluative point of view, it does justice to a new value quality in material
terms. Something in the physical world – be it modes of conduct
or institutional circumstances – must change if the addressees are
to be convinced that they have been recognized in a new manner.[28]

It is this second, material dimension that provides a key to the
difficult task of distinguishing between justified and ideological
forms of recognition. As we have seen, the latter are able to develop
their regulative power only if their evaluative vocabulary is sufficiently rational to reveal credible modes of fashioning a new and
affirmative self-conception. Generally speaking, such ideological
forms will be more successful, the more fully they account for the
evaluative expectations that point the way towards progress in the
culture of reciprocal recognition. But the deficiency by which we
might recognize such ideologies could consist in their structural
inability to ensure the material prerequisites for realizing new evaluative qualities. Between the evaluative promise and its material
fulfilment, there would be a chasm; the provision of the institutional prerequisites would no longer be reconcilable with the dominant social order. If we apply this criterion to the example I have
illustrated above, then my belief will prove to be true. The new
manner of addressing employees and qualified workers as entrepreneurs of their own labour-power might contain an evaluative
promise of recognizing a higher degree of individuality and initiative, but it in no way ensures the institutional measures that would
allow a consistent realization of these new values. Instead, employees are compelled to feign initiative, flexibility and talents where
there is no material basis for doing so. This new form of recognition
is not deficient or irrational in an evaluative sense, but it does not
meet the material demands of credible, justified recognition, for the
institutional practices required for truly realizing the newly accen-
tuated value are not delivered in the act of recognition. But if we
add the components of material fulfilment that together constitute
the rationality of recognition, then we can claim that ideological
forms of recognition suffer a second-level rationality deficit. Even
if they are rational in the sense that they derive from the historically changing realm of evaluative reasons, they remain irrational
in the sense that they do not go beyond the merely symbolic plane
to the level of material fulfilment. A second instance of a novel
form of recognition that could prove ideological from this point of
view is the now fashionable notion of 'public service', whereby a
social group is granted a symbolic distinction that could encourage

willing subjection, without introducing corresponding measures at the institutional level.

Of course, even the criterion formulated here ought not to lead us astray into an overly self-confident hermeneutics of suspicion. We can never exclude the possibility that the gap between an evaluative promise and its material fulfilment is merely a temporal one, a mere a delay in the realisation of the institutional prerequisites. On the level of institutional recognition, just as is the case in simple interaction, we should expect lengthy learning processes before the evaluative substance of a new form of recognition can find expression in changed modes of conduct or institutional arrangements. But all in all, the criterion of material fulfilment does provide us with a useful means of testing in advance whether an alteration in a given form of recognition might in fact bring about an increase in regulative power. Institutional patterns of evaluative distinction that lack any prospect of yielding material change can then in good conscience be labelled ideological forms of recognition.

Notes

I wish to thank the participants at the conference on 'Power and Recognition' at the University of Utrecht (13–15 March 2003), the colloquium on 'Philosophy and Social Sciences' in Prague (20–4 May 2004), and my own research colloquium on social philosophy for valuable suggestions and questions. Particularly helpful were the proposals offered to me by Bert van den Brink, Rahel Jaeggi and David Owen

1   Patchen Markell, *Bound by Recognition* (Princeton and Oxford: Princeton University Press, 2003); Kelly Olivier, *Witnessing: Beyond Recognition* (Minneapolis: University of Minnesota Press, 2001); Markus Verweyst, *Das Begehen der Anerkennung: Subjekttheoretische Positionen bei Heidegger, Sartre, Freud und Lacan* (Frankfurt/Main: Campus, 2000).

2   Louis Althusser, 'Ideology and Ideological State Apparatuses', in *Lenin and Philosophy and Other Essays*, trans. Ben Brewster (New York: Monthly Review Press, 2001), pp. 127–88.

3   Judith Butler, '"Conscience Doth Make Subjects of Us All": Althusser's Subjection', in *The Psychic Life of Power: Theories in Subjection* (Stanford: Stanford University Press, 1997), pp. 106–31.

4 Raymond Geuss, *The Idea of a Critical Theory: Habermas and the Frankfurt School* (Cambridge: Cambridge University Press, 1981), ch. 1.

5 Ibid., pp. 12ff.

6 Axel Honneth, 'The Social Dynamics of Disrespect: On the Location of Critical Theory Today', trans. John Farrell, in *Disrespect* (Cambridge: Polity, 2007), pp. 63–79.

7 Gert Raiethel, *Geschichte der nordamerikanischen Kultur*, vol. I: *Vom Puritanismus bis zum Bürgerkrieg 1600–1800* (Frankfurt/Main: Zweitausendeins, 1995), ch. XXXI.

8 Karin Hausen, 'Die Polarisierung der "Geschlechtsckaraktere" – Eine Spiegelung der Dissoziation von Erwerbs- und Familienleben', in Werner Conze, ed., *Sozialgeschichte der Familie in der Neuzeit Europas* (Stuttgart: Klett-Cotta, 1976), pp. 363–93; Bärbel Kühn, 'Vom Schalten und Walten der Hausfrau: Hausarbeit in Rat, Tat und Forschung im 19. und 20. Jahrhundert', in Birgit Bolognese-Leuchtenmüller and Michael Mitteerauer, eds, *Frauen-Arbeitswelten: Zur historischen Genese gegenwärtiger Probleme* (Vienna: Verlag für Gesellschaftskritik, 1993), pp. 43–66.

9 René Schilling, *Kriegshelden: Deutungsmuster heroischer Männlichkeit in Deutschland 1813–1945* (Paderborn: Ferdinand Schöningh, 2002).

10 Axel Honneth, 'Der Grund der Anerkennung: Eine Erwiderung auf kritische Rückfragen', in *Das Andere der Gerechtigkeit* (Frankfurt/Main: Suhrkamp, 2004), pp. 303–41.

11 Avishai Margalit, 'Recognition II: Recognizing the Brother and the Other', *Aristotelian Society Supplementary*, vol. 75 (Bristol: The Aristotelian Society Publications, 2001), pp. 127–39.

12 Stanley Cavell, 'Knowing and Acknowledging', in *Must We Mean What We Say?* (Cambridge: Cambridge University Press, 2002), pp. 238–65.

13 Heikki Ikäheimo, 'On the Genus and Species of Recognition', *INQUIRY*, vol. 45, no. 4 (2002), pp. 447–62; Arno Laitinen, 'Interpersonal Recognition: A Response to Value or a Precondition of Personhood?', *INQUIRY*, vol. 45, no. 4 (2002), pp. 463–78.

14 A difference becomes apparent from Althusser's theory at this point, one whose social-ontological nature lies so deep that we can hardly discuss it here. As a matter of principle, Althusser does not concede subjects the possibility of gaining a higher degree of autonomy in their actions and decisions, assuming instead that individuals can become socially identifiable subjects only by

being subjected through public recognition to a web of social rules with no room for variation in terms of individual autonomy. By contrast, I assume (as does Durkheim) that such social rules of recognition have to be able to be differentiated according to the room they allow for autonomy.

15 Laitinen, 'Interpersonal Recognition: A Response to Value or a Precondition of Personhood?'.

16 John McDowell, 'Two Sorts of Naturalism', in *Mind, Value and Reality* (Cambridge, MA: Harvard University Press, 2001), pp. 267–97; Eva Lovibond, *Ethical Formation* (Cambridge, MA: Harvard University Press, 2002), part II; Axel Honneth, 'Zwischen Hermeneutik und Hegelianismus', in *Unsichtbarkeit* (Frankfurt/Main: Suhrkamp, 2003), pp. 106–37.

17 Honneth, 'Zwischen Hermeneutik und Hegelianismus'.

18 Axel Honneth, 'The Irreducibility of Progress: Kant's Account of the Relationship between Morality and History', in *Pathologies of Reason: On the Legacy of Critical Theory*, trans. James Ingram (New York: Columbia University Press, 2009), pp. 1–18.

19 Karl Marx, *Capital: A Critique of Political Economy*, vol. I, trans. Ben Fowkes (London: Penguin, 1976), pp. 181–91.

20 Emmanuel Renault, 'Reconnaissance, Institutions, Injustice', *De la Connaissance: Revue de Mauss*, Semestrielle no. 23 (2004), pp. 180–95.

21 Immanuel Kant, *Groundwork of the Metaphysic of Morals*, trans. H.J. Paton (New York: Harper and Row, 1964).

22 Axel Honneth, 'Redistribution as Recognition: A Response to Nancy Fraser', in Nancy Fraser and Axel Honneth, *Redistribution or Recognition? A Political–Philosophical Exchange* (London and New York: Verso, 2003), pp. 110–97.

23 Carolin Emcke, *Kollektive Identitäten: Sozialphilosophische Grundlagen* (Frankfurt/Main: Campus, 2000); Hans-Uwe Rösner, *Jenseits normalisierender Anerkennung: Reflexionen zum Verhältnis von Macht und Behindertsein* (Frankfurt/Main: Campus, 2002).

24 Emcke, *Kollektive Identitäten*, pp. 237ff.

25 Wolfgang Detel, *Macht, Moral, Wissen: Foucault und die klassische Antike* (Frankfurt/Main: Suhrkamp, 1998), pp. 55ff.

26 Sven Opitz, *Gouvernementabilität im Postfordismus: Macht, Wissen und Techniken des Selbst im Feld unternehmerischer Rationalität* (Hamburg: Argument, 2004), ch. 8; Günter Voss and Hans J. Pongratz, 'Der Arbeitskraftunternehmer: Eine neue Grundform der Ware Arbeitskraft?', *Kölner Zeitschrift für Soziologie und Sozialpsychologie*, vol. 50, no.1 (1989), pp. 131–58. See also Chapter 10 in the

current volume. [Tr.: The authors suggest the term 'entreployee' in a short English summary of their argument: 'From Employee to "Entreployee": Towards a "Self-Entrepreneurial" Workforce?', *Concepts and Transformation*, vol. 8, no. 3 (2003), pp. 239–54.]

27 Opitz, *Gouvernementabilität im Postfordismus*, ch. 8.

28 This is what John L. Austin means when he states that specific performative statements count as being successful or completed if something or other happens as a result (*How to do Things with Words* [Cambridge, MA: Harvard University Press, 1975]). With my notion of 'material fulfilment', I am applying his analysis of performative statements to the specific case of 'recognition'.

6

Dissolutions of the Social: The Social Theory of Luc Boltanski and Laurent Thévenot

Moral categories have all but disappeared from the theoretical vocabulary of sociology. When it comes to explaining social orders, neither beliefs about legitimacy nor feelings of injustice, neither moral disputes nor normative consensus plays a significant role anymore. Instead, sociology views the object of its study either as anonymous processes of self-organization or as the result of cooperation between strategic actors. The disciplines that serve as a model for these studies are biology or economics, whose conceptual models are considered adequate for explaining a process as complex as the reproduction of societies. In light of these theoretical reorientations, one cannot avoid the impression that contemporary sociology is striving to finally leave behind its founding fathers. After all, for Max Weber and Émile Durkheim, as well as Talcott Parsons, it was obvious that a basic conception of the social world could only be gained by making use of the concepts, models and hypotheses of a theory of morality. Practical philosophy was the breeding ground, so to speak, and the discipline that guided classical sociology. But ever since Habermas's *Theory of Communicative Action*, the last grand attempt at a theory of society on the basis of practical philosophy, that has all been forgotten. Until recently, it seemed that Habermas's book represented the end of the tradition of normative sociology. That this is not the case, that there is still a current within social theory that draws on moral-philosophical sources, is largely due to the efforts of a small group of researchers in France centred on Luc Boltanski and Laurent Thévenot. The work of this extraordinarily productive circle originated in a critique of the sociology of Pierre Bourdieu, and is constantly opening up new paths of inquiry in its efforts to explain the integration of modern societies as a conflict-filled interaction between differing moral beliefs.[1] The founding text of this socio-logical school is *De la justification*[2] by Boltanski and Thévenot, pub-lished in 1991. The book, which has now been translated into English,[3] deserves careful analysis for the simple reason that it is by far the most interesting contemporary attempt to give sociology a new basis in moral philosophy.

I

Even in the way they formulate the starting point of their study, Boltanski and Thévenot adopt the perspective taken up by the clas-sical sociologists in their efforts to found a theory of society. Like Weber, Durkheim and Parsons, these two authors locate the key problem of sociology in understanding what it means that indi-vidual actors normally coordinate their aims and thereby contrib-ute to the production of social orders. But in explaining the consensus required to bring about such coordination, Boltanski and Thévenot do not employ the two strategies that once domi-nated the field. Neither do they follow Durkheim by locating the necessary consensus in an antecedent collective consciousness, nor do they follow modern economists by viewing this coordination as the fortunate result of the coincidence of individual strategies (26ff.).[4] By rejecting both these conceptual models, the authors must seek out a third type of explanation, one which – unlike Durkheim – takes account of the interpretive authority of the indi-vidual actor, without – unlike modern economists – denying the influence of comprehensive social systems of interpretation. Boltan-ski and Thévenot present their answer to this problem in three steps which, taken together, form the first element in their theory of society.

The first step of their argument consists in assuming that actors generally coordinate their aims by resorting to previously learned models of moral order that justify legitimate modes of social coex-istence. Unlike Bourdieu once claimed, the members of society are not to be conceived of as individuals who are unaware of their own motivations, and whose patterns of social behaviour are largely determined by unconscious interpretive powers. Instead, they are to be grasped as beings who possess cognitive abilities of self-determination, inasmuch as they can, on their own initiative, resort to wholly different conceptions of order in the coordination of their individual aims. In this first step, therefore, the assumption of a plurality of models of social coexistence is not a merely arbitrary addition, but a necessary component of their entire theory: because subjects can be viewed as competent and cognitively autonomous actors, they have to be capable of resorting to more than one model of social order if they are to be able to choose among these orders according to their own criteria.

In the next step of their argument, the two authors introduce a distinction borrowed from American pragmatism, one which greatly modifies this claim: although subjects can coordinate their actions almost unconsciously and automatically, provided that no interruptions occur in their interaction, once that interruption occurs, they must direct their attention to their previous, routine cognitive and moral assumptions. Therefore, individuals can only become conscious of the models of order they use to coordinate their aims in so-called 'unnatural' situations that interrupt the flow of their lifeworld practices. Once that happens, they are faced with what John Dewey and George H. Mead would have termed the 'functional requirement' of examining what they previously assumed valid in order to adapt to changed conditions. Like other theorists with such a pragmatic bent, Boltanski and Thévenot also believe that scientific observation must make use of these moments of disruption, of 'breakdown' and 'crisis' (36), in order to study the true structures of social integration. We gain insight into the background normative beliefs that enable the coordination of individual actions through the perspective of participants who must deal with a disruption of their interaction by reflecting on their conflicting conceptions of order.

The third step consists in proposing that we grasp such 'unnatural' moments, in which we discursively examine our previously accepted conceptions of order, as the hinges of social reproduction: social life is characterized by an 'imperative to justify', which in the face of regularly occurring crises compels the members of society to reciprocally uncover their latent conceptions of order and justify them to each other. These stations of discursive justification represent the conscious, reflexive side of social reproduction, which makes explicit what was once implicit in the flow of routine lifeworld interactions: partners in communication are forced to offer arguments and justifications for why a problematic segment of their lifeworld should be solved within the horizon of one model of order rather than another. They must justify why a task of coordination which has become questionable can only be dealt with in the way they prefer.

Of course, the authors are aware that in these moments, in which the social order is broken through consciously, there is always the alternative of a violent solution. The party with the most power can interrupt the discursive argument and impose its own conception of order on the other party (38). However, Boltanski and Thévenot intentionally limit their scope to 'peaceful' forms of coping with such argumentative confrontations: 'Civil war . . . along with tyranny (which bases the order of the polity on force and fear)' (38) is excluded from their study. The authors do not make clear whether they intend to restrict their study to democratic societies; and they are very reluctant to define in more detail the type of society to which their study is meant to apply. We only find out that the study focuses on 'differentiated', 'complex' societies characterized by the fact that a number of competing conceptions of order can fulfil the task of coordination in a given sphere of action (173). And we might add that the focus is on societies in which such interpretive conflicts are solved in an argumentative and peaceful manner. There is no reason not to presume that the object of inquiry in *On Justification* is essentially the Western democratic state.

These three premises delineate the theoretical framework of the book. Its primary achievement – the power of its theoretical penetration and the wealth of impulses it offers – only truly comes to the forefront once the authors begin to gradually fill in this hollow normative theory of society. They are not content to give a merely formal analysis of the discursive interruptions of social life; they are less concerned with the rational conditions underlying argumentative conflicts than they are with the moral topics and conflict scenarios typical of everyday life in Western society. In that sense, the study is intended to be no less than a comprehensive, empirically oriented analysis of all the moral disputes and conflicts that could arise in the social lifeworld of a society such as that of France. To that end the authors are faced with two tasks, both of which pose a significant challenge: first, they must attempt to reconstruct all the moral models of order that serve contemporary societies as normative sources for coordinating social action; second, they must get an overview of the types of social conflicts in which discrepancies over the legitimacy of practised models of order begin to appear. The grandeur of their study consists in the wealth of empirical observations, hermeneutic speculations and textual analyses that Boltanski and Thévenot employ in carrying out these two tasks. At the same time, the study demonstrates the limits of developing a sociological theory without the use of any structural determinations.

II

According to the general thesis of our two authors, coordinating individual aims always requires mutual agreement on the moral norms that determine which future expectations are considered legitimate. As we saw above, these intersubjectively presupposed conceptions of order generally remain in the pre-reflective background of the uninterrupted course of events in the lifeworld. Individual actors only become aware of them when interaction breaks down; this breakdown forces us to reflect on what were previously implicit beliefs. For Boltanski and Thévenot, the first task is to gain insight into the basic principles that normative models of order must obey by attempting to comprehend such breakdowns. Furthermore, they intend to hermeneutically reconstruct the models of order that are most significant when it comes to maintaining our social order.

What remains unclear throughout the entire study are the details of the method used to define the formal properties of the models of order currently in practice. Although they do not say it explicitly, they apparently believe that modernity is characterized by a number of normative principles that legitimate social order must obey (74ff.). This implicit premise becomes especially clear when they introduce the first basic principle of orders of justification or 'polities' (*Rechtfertigungsordnung*) currently in effect. According to Boltanski and Thévenot, all familiar models of a legitimate social order must be committed to the 'principle according to which the members of a *polity* share a *common humanity*', and therefore must forbid extreme forms of discrimination or exclusion (74). This prerequisite of moral universalism is not argued for in the book, but is merely claimed to be an empirical given in 'our' societies. Certainly it would have been necessary to go into more detail about the structural-historical or social-historical reasons for why such a universalistic idea of human beings should be a normative condition of modern societies at all. This is all the more true of the second basic principle that, in the eyes of Boltanski and Thévenot, determines all currently valid conceptions of order. They claim that all customary, contemporary models of justification are guided by the notion that social superiority is justified by a special contribution to the 'common good' (76f.). Even though the authors use confusing formulations ('investment formula'), they probably mean that each model of a justifiable social order must be founded on the principle of achievement, which normatively determines which rung 'originally' equal members of society should occupy in the social hierarchy. The more 'sacrifices' or contributions a certain person or group of persons makes to the common good, the higher the status they should occupy within society. When the authors argue that this second principle should be valid in all present normative models of order, they not only mean that there must be different, competing conceptions about such contributions or sacrifices, but above all that the idea of individual achievement must dominate the entire spectrum of justifications for contemporary social orders. In 'modern' society, all conceptions of a legitimate social order are, without exception, determined by the following principle: achievements considered to be especially valuable are to be honoured by being accorded a higher status or 'worth'.

That is how the achievement principle becomes the decisive norm for justifying modern social orders, without being explicitly declared as such. Almost inconspicuously, the two authors smuggle a premise into their investigation that is in no way self-evident and needs much stronger justification. Even a glance at the empirical research generally shows that the members of Western society tend to assert wholly different principles when it comes to judging problems of social justice. Depending on the type of social relationship assumed to obtain for a certain problem of distribution, they employ normative criteria such as social equality, individual needs or personal achievement. Observations such as these are what motivated David Miller to undertake a pluralistic attempt at a theory of justice.[5] When it comes to defining the moral norms that, in modern societies, determine what counts as a just distribution of goods and burdens, we must assume a plurality of principles whose validity depends on the nature of the social relationship in question. Of course, Boltanski and Thévenot aren't interested in advancing a normative theory of justice; as sociologists, they seek insight into the background normative beliefs that members of contemporary societies use to generate a world of practical commonality. Nevertheless, Miller's approach cannot be considered entirely irrelevant for this inquiry, for even he bases his theory on sociological investigations and comes to the conclusion that, alongside the achievement principle, there are other, entirely different, basic criteria for judging the moral legitimacy of social orders, all of which have significance in the lifeworld. If we relate this consideration back to the work of Boltanski and Thévenot, there is a question as to whether we should in fact regard all currently widespread conceptions of justified social orders as adhering to the achievement principle. It does not seem accurate to claim that people, always and everywhere, coordinate their aims by implicitly presupposing a normative order that rewards special achievement with superior social status. There are just as many spheres or forms of relationship in which people advance conceptions of legitimacy that obey criteria such as individual need or legal equality. Here as well, only structural considerations are likely to enable the authors to gain a greater awareness of their own premises. Instead of directly and immediately offering a definition of the formal properties of contemporary beliefs about justice, it would have been advisable to first ask whether certain types of social practices or institutions of modernity demand entirely different normative principles than that of individual achievement. The fact that Boltanski and Thévenot ignore such considerations is a considerable deficit, one which the reader encounters in many places in the book. The connection between institutional structures and spheres of value, between social sub-systems and the corresponding norms, remains entirely unclear; the impression arises that individual actors' interpretive achievements are not bound to any socio-structural guidelines at all.

After they have defined the formal properties of modern conceptions of order with the help of this form of universalism and the achievement principle, the authors proceed to survey their concrete embodiments. One might expect a methodological procedure along the lines of Charles Taylor's grand investigation in a different field, *Sources of the Self*.[6] This would involve a kind of historical-hermeneutic reconstruction of ideas of just social orders that obtain in modernity. One might also expect that the authors would undertake an empirical investigation of the currently widespread forms of just coexistence, be it through group discussions, interviews or questionnaires. But Boltanski and Thévenot employ neither of these two methodological strategies. They attempt neither historical hermeneutics nor empirical illustration, but instead base their investigation on the history of political philosophy, because they presume that the roots and models of all currently valid conceptions of social justice are to be found in the paradigmatic works in this field. The authors do not really explicitly justify this unusual procedure anywhere in the text; rather, a justification only appears implicitly in very few places. For instance, in one aside, the authors write that modern political philosophy has given many contemporary societies their definitive character (71f.). If we summarize the various remarks on this issue in the text, their justification for resorting to the canon of political thought ultimately amounts to the claim that, even today, all our conceptions of justice and social coexistence have been decisively influenced by the great philosophical classics. We would have to add that it is via the formation of cultural traditions that certain ideas in the philosophical tradition have managed to influence our everyday notions so strongly that even contemporary social cultures of justification largely feed on past models of political thought.

This notion is not unattractive, even if it is highly speculative and no great effort is made to justify it. The authors certainly do not want to claim that the classical works of political philosophy themselves are the source of the conceptions of order that we use to coordinate and justify our everyday actions. This assumption would take us across the threshold of cultural idealism, in which our everyday social consciousness is nothing but an archive of past theoretical history. Their claim is most likely that the power of certain philosophical works to influence our consciousness has been great enough to produce, through the obscure pathways of cultural inheritance, the paradigms or archetypes we currently use to reach agreement on potential forms of social justice. In these situations of justification, we do not make reference to the writings of Aristotle or Rousseau, but employ patterns of argumentation that were explicitly formulated for the first time in these works, and which have become a part of our collective intellectual property through repetition and propagation. Nevertheless, Boltanski and Thévenot appear to waver occasionally with regard to how their claim is to be interpreted. Sometimes it seems that the works they cite only illustrate certain narratives of justification (73), and other times they have a tendency to treat these same texts as sources of our current conceptions of justice (74). However, only the first, weaker interpretation is adequate for understanding the rest of the text, which avoids any hint of cultural idealism.

When it comes to selecting the texts used to illustrate their claims, the authors apply the same criteria that they discerned when it came to explaining the formal properties of contemporary conceptions of order. Therefore, the only works of classical tradition that can be viewed as paradigmatic are those in which a particular achievement principle is developed on the basis of moral universalism – a principle that is capable of justifying a social hierarchy. Boltanski and Thévenot claim to be able to distinguish between as many such foundational texts as there are distinct criteria of achievement in our beliefs about justice. The authors do not exclude the possibility that other classical points of reference could be used to illustrate these ideas of 'social worth', nor do they claim that these paradigms of justice could not be supplemented with other models in the future (71).[7] On the basis of these restrictions, the authors draw on six texts in the history of ideas in order to elucidate the competing conceptions of justice at work in our culture of justification: Augustine's *The City of God* founds the paradigm of charismatic individual achievement; Bossuet's *Politics Drawn from the Very Words of Holy Scripture* develops the idea of a domestic hierarchy (*häusliche Rangordnung*) in which the head of the household is charged with the protection of the family; Hobbes' *The Elements of Law, Natural and Politic* presents a status hierarchy based purely on the esteem a person enjoys in the eyes of the public; Rousseau's *Social Contract* lays the basis for a civil order in which social worth is based on the degree to which a person represents the common good; Saint-Simon's *Du système industriel* outlines the contours of a system of industrial strata based entirely on a person's usefulness for the satisfaction of the overall needs of society; and, finally, Adam Smith's *Theory of Moral Sentiments* develops the market economy principle of a scale of value centring upon the socially useful achievement of wealth (78–123). Again, none of these works are to be viewed as sources of our contemporary conceptions of justice in the sense that we all have their title or their wording explicitly in mind. Wherever the name of an author appears in this list, another name could just as easily be inserted, provided that the author founded a similar achievement principle. What is decisive is solely the fact that these are philosophical works that have contributed in some way to the emergence and development of ideas of social hierarchy that continue to be relevant today.

For that reason, it would be otiose to criticize individual decisions in the composition of the list. Certainly, the selection of names and works blatantly reflects the preferences of these two authors raised in the tradition of French philosophy. In terms of which texts have had the most historical influence, it is rather odd that they should choose Bossuet as the founder of the notion of a domestic hierarchy, given the fact that German authors have produced far more influential justifications of patriarchal values. Not a line in the entire book illuminates the partly convoluted and partly obvious channels through which these writings have exercised their paradigmatic influence. Not a word is said about the history of the reception of these works, nor do the authors take a look at the political circumstances surrounding their publication, as if the ambitious plan to offer a genealogy of our current conceptions of justice could be achieved by merely presenting the central ideas of a few classic texts. But the real deficit of this list is not that it ignores the history of the reception of these works or that it has a culturally limited perspective, but that it omits an entire class of works in political philosophy that continue to be influential today. No mention is made of Kant's political republicanism, nor of John Locke's classical liberalism, even though their fundamental egalitarianism is at least as significant for our contemporary conceptions of justice. This gap in particular reveals just how problematic it is to anchor every form of polity in the achievement principle. Alongside widespread conceptions of justice in which our social order is normatively founded on some kind of achievement and should thus be hierarchically organized, there are broad currents of civil egalitarianism, such as in the writings of Locke or Kant. The exclusion of these works is neither inadvertent nor due to carelessness, but instead the result of a kind of reductionism with regard to basic normative concepts; and this has its roots in a much earlier stage of the investigation.

But these six conceptions of justice are supposed to contain not only the principles of the formation of various hierarchies, but also the corresponding normative core of an entire image of society, even an entire lifeworld. It is no accident that the authors term these polities '*cités*' or 'communities', which is meant to express the fact that these are conceptions of an entire way of life, a comprehensive system of norms and practices. Boltanski and Thévenot make the bold claim that the horizon of our everyday acts and experiences is always determined by the categories of the model of order according to which we interpret a given situation. My surroundings appear to me in the light of the normative agreement that regulates the relationship to my partners in interaction within a certain segment of the social world. Just how far-reaching the consequences of this idea are for the authors only becomes clear once we realize that they even include material artefacts within this morally constituted horizon: 'In order for persons to reach agreement, . . . the quality of things must have been determined in a way that is consistent with the principles of worth invoked' (130). Depending on the type of hierarchy previously accepted for a given situation, the objects upon which people act take on different meanings for them: in the world of the family, to paraphrase an example used by the authors, a table acquires the meaning of an invitation to a common meal; in the industrial world it is a worktable; and in the market world, it is a place of assembly. As members of societies, our normative relations-to-world are as numerous as the principles of moral agreement we have already accepted in our interaction. Therefore, actors familiar with all of modernity's constitutive value orders are constantly compelled to move back and forth competently between six different lifeworlds.

It is never clear why the authors expand their considerations on the socially constitutive role of polities into an analysis of the lifeworld. The text occasionally makes reference to the works of Bruno Latour in order to make plausible why material objects have to be included in sociological analysis.[8] But these remarks certainly do not justify why we should understand particular lifeworlds according to the criterion of underlying beliefs about justice. After all, this thesis is linked to the strong premise that the customary categories of practical philosophy explain the entirety of our relations to the world. Whatever we experience, and however we perceive persons, circumstances and things, we do so with the help of categorial schemas that derive from a certain presupposed conception of a legitimate social order (133ff.). It is not too problematic that this assumption conceives of our social environment as something that is always already disclosed in terms of certain interests and projects; these are ideas that Boltanski and Thévenot could easily have picked up from the works of Merleau-Ponty or early Heidegger. What is confusing about this premise is instead the fact that the 'ready-to-hand' character (*Zuhandenheit*) of our world results entirely from moral guidelines that stem from our mutually accepted conceptions of order. The pragmatic quality of our social life is thereby reduced to a single way of normatively justifying social orders. Our world discloses itself as meaningful to us not through the horizon of our instrumental interests, or through needs to control our environment or manage our survival, but solely through the deep-seated desire for evidence of the legitimacy of our social institutions.

This phenomenological or perhaps even 'transcendental' turn takes Boltanski and Thévenot far beyond what the classical authors of their discipline would have accepted when it comes to sociology's dependence on moral philosophy. The founders of the discipline regarded the philosophical categories used to grasp moral beliefs or value orientations as a challenge to search for corresponding phenomena in the structures of social reproduction. This gave birth to sociological concepts such as value spheres, collective consciousness and systems of action. By contrast, in *On Justification*, the categories of political philosophy are taken as direct expressions of the content of our everyday social consciousness, without transferring them into socially congealed structures. This moral content, the so-called 'polities', are viewed as a 'transcendental' framework within which different lifeworlds are constituted. Ultimately, the various spheres of the social world are, for Boltanski and Thévenot, nothing but the product of practices of moral justification. The difficulties that result from privileging moral philosophy in such a one-sided manner become constantly apparent in the neglect of structural sociological categories and alternative, non-moral guidelines for action. There is no effort to pursue the question of how moral beliefs are embodied in institutions and stable systems of action; nor is there an examination of whether there are other, non-moral interests that motivate social reproduction. If these deficits still only appear indirectly at this point, they become all the more apparent once the authors turn to the treatment of crises or breakdowns in the process of justified interactions.

III

The image we receive from the study is one in which reality is differentiated into several partial sub-worlds, whose inner connection results from the specific achievement principle embodied in each respective conception of order. Members of society are forced to coordinate their actions with the aid of models of justified sociality; they do so by resorting to an arsenal of inherited 'polities' and understand their correspondingly legitimated interaction within the horizon of their shared moral beliefs. Yet this image, as Boltanski and Thévenot make clear from the beginning (36f.), addresses the rather improbable – that is, harmonious – side of social life; but in reality, there is dispute and conflict over the appropriate justification for their relations of interaction. Only by taking up these everyday disputes do the authors enter the arena in which the empirical research of their theoretical circle moves.[9] Here we also find the plan of a 'sociology of critique', which, unlike critical sociology, abstains from any normative judgements and strictly focuses on observing the critical activity of competent actors.[10] The entirety of the work of this intellectual circle centred on Boltanski and Thévenot is founded on the idea that we constantly argue about the meaning and appropriateness of our models of justification.

The two authors take a first step towards defining the meaning of such disputes by distinguishing between two distinct forms of breakdown in our daily routine activities. The possibility that the agreement underlying our interactions will be disturbed can arise when either the conditions of application or the appropriateness of the corresponding normative structure comes into question. In the first case, which is termed 'contention' (187), actors must interrupt their routine actions because one of the participants questions whether the commonly presupposed polity or order of justification is applied in a fair and appropriate fashion. In the second case, which is termed a 'clash' (187), their interaction comes to a halt because they disagree about which potential order of justification should be applied. Clearly the authors intend to take the philosophically familiar distinction between internal and external critique, pull it down from the level of theoretical language and apply it to everyday action: in 'contention', actors mobilize internal criteria of problematization by inquiring about the appropriate conditions for applying an already accepted conception of justice, while when they 'clash', they assert external criteria by doubting the appropriateness of a previously practised model of order. With this extremely skilful theoretical manoeuvre, the authors suggest that even everyday actors in everyday situations perform intellectual acts that, normally, are only asked of philosophers or critical theorists. Boltanski and Thévenot argue that in our everyday actions, each of us is always already involved in the business of normative critique, even before the academic intellectual pulls out the big guns.

In order to demonstrate that 'theoretical' critique stands on the same level as the kind of critique that each of us practises in our everyday lives, the two authors must, in principle, show that their own knowledge is in no way superior to that of normal actors. After all, the intention of replacing what was previously regarded as critical sociology with a 'sociology of critique' demands removing the gap between these two levels of knowledge.[11] The case of 'contention', the first arena of conflict, does not seem to present any difficulties for Boltanski and Thévenot; they merely 'observe' what involved actors do when, within the framework of a basically accepted polity, doubts are raised about the status hierarchy derived from that order (133ff.). According to the authors, the means generally used for settling these arguments represent discursive events they term 'tests'. This refers not to the official procedures that regulate the granting of educational titles, but instead to the nearly inconspicuous and daily occurring situations in which we commonly test, without the pressure of acting, whether the previously practised distribution of status positions really does conform to the underlying polity. As the examples presented in the study illustrate nicely (136ff.), each of these normatively regulated worlds is accorded a specific, characteristic test procedure. For example, within a civil order, a parliamentary investigation serves to clarify whether a certain representative, in light of rumours about inappropriate behaviour, truly possesses the competence and 'stature' that has been accorded to him or her. Within the 'world of fame', an intersubjectively examinable, experimental phase ensures that researchers must prove that their project deserves the recognition they claim it does. What is particular about these test procedures, as Boltanski and Thévenot repeat tirelessly, is that the distinction between criteria of correctness and justice has been eliminated entirely. Because the material objects, in the meaning accorded to them by the commonly presupposed polity, are included in the corresponding test procedure, the 'just' placement of a person in a status hierarchy must be proven with reference to how 'properly' he or she copes with 'ready-to-hand' objects (33, 41, 130).

But even at this point, we could point out that it would be careless to exclude social developments in which participants begin to apply, either intentionally or unintentionally, 'inappropriate' or normatively misplaced criteria for examining social 'worth'. Our socialization might certainly equip us with a 'sense of the common' for what is the appropriate respective procedure in a given context for determining actual ability and achievement (201ff.). Normally we tend to judge politicians according to their moral integrity and expertise, artists according to their inspirational power and the strength of their aesthetic expression, and craftsmen according to their technical skills and their familiarity with materials. But even in this relatively familiar social sphere, often enough there are tendencies to measure social worth and achievement according to criteria that do not correspond to the seemingly appropriate and socially trained criteria. We all are familiar with studies that currently show an increasing tendency to evaluate artistic creativity according to success in the market, and it is not rare for citizens to vote on the basis of the image a politician projects in the media, rather than on his or her moral reliability. And we constantly encounter the claim that measuring students' performance always involves an underlying assessment of their sociocultural *habitus*. Even Boltanski and Thévenot would not reject the possibility of such developments, in which alien and inappropriate criteria of excellence overarch social spheres of values. It is no accident that they occasionally refer to Michael Walzer, who has made the agreement between social tasks and the corresponding internal principles of distribution the guideline of his theory of justice.[12] All the more crucial is the way the authors account for such shifts or phenomena of 'overarching' within their theory. The study itself offers no clear answer to this question, but even makes the problem vanish by relegating it to the sphere of external critique. Yet these do not represent conscious demands for a new principle of justification in a sphere that was previously regulated in a different manner; instead, these are mostly unintentional developments in which an inappropriate principle of social worth has asserted itself 'behind the backs' of those involved. An analysis of society cannot remain neutral in the face of such occurrences by merely describing them as given facts. After all, one of its basic theoretical assumptions is that each polity and each socially differentiated sphere of value is characterized exclusively by its own procedure for examining abilities and achievements. Yet, somehow, Boltanski and Thévenot ignore the inner normativity of their own conceptual toolkit. Although they seem to assume a necessary connection between a polity and corresponding criteria of distribution, they deny it in the very next step. As if driven by a guilty conscience for possessing more knowledge than the actors they investigate, the two authors deny what they have indirectly claimed: each socially established, intersubjective system of moral norms of action has a specific criterion of excellence; if it is overarched by alien, inappropriate criteria, then this represents a theoretical misdevelopment or social pathology.

Another way of describing the problem in the moral-sociological approach employed by Boltanski and Thévenot is that they have a tendency to quickly and repeatedly rein in the same structural assumptions upon which their argument relies and towards which it aims. In this connection, such assumptions merely refer to claims about the ability of intersubjectively shared norms and practices to engender social institutions. In sociological analysis we have to count on such 'systems' of normatively regulated action if we are to be capable of recognizing what is fixed and temporarily stable in the flow of permanent change. But in *On Justification*, such long-lasting crystallizations of normatively coordinated action deriving from customs, habits or law seem to be entirely absent. Although the authors talk of 'orders' of justification or 'polities', they do not really take seriously what the sociological concept of 'order' entails. This problem – the simultaneous denial and usage of normative structures – becomes more intense once Boltanski and Thévenot go on to analyse 'clashes' as a second form of social dispute over the appropriate polity. It is uncertain from the very beginning whether such orders are meant to indicate mere conceptions and beliefs, or in fact real structures.

As we saw above, the two authors use the concept of conflict to indicate social discord and disputes that concern not the appropriate interpretation of a polity, but the possible application of different orders of justification or polities to one and the same situation. Actors' habitual intersubjective actions can be interrupted not only by one of the participants calling into question the previously practised application of an accepted normative structure, but also by interacting subjects casting doubt on the legitimacy of the polity, because they view it as inappropriate to the sphere of action in question. Judging by the number of pages they dedicate to this second type of moral disagreement (213–73), Boltanski and Thévenot seem to assume this is the most widespread form of social disagreement. According to this notion, the major point of disagreement in Western democracies refers to which of the culturally available models of achievement are to be applied to which sphere of social interaction. If we set aside the implausibility of reducing the spectrum of contemporary ideas of social justice to those based on the achievement principle, the image the authors develop of Western societies is certainly not wrong. Many diagnoses agree that the gradually occurring transformations of capitalist welfare states are largely marked by conflicts connected with changes in the normative grammar of certain spheres of action. However, even this attempt to give their notion some empirical plausibility contains more than we could reconcile with the descriptions offered by the authors, because they do not claim that the starting point of such conflicts lies in the normative constitution of social spheres, such that we could not regard them as changes or transformations. Instead the study seems to maintain that actors always engage in moral conflicts under conditions in which they are wholly free to decide which order of justification they will use to try and solve a certain problem of action. This peculiar voluntarism expresses more clearly than anywhere else in the book that Boltanski and Thévenot possess no concept of normatively regulated spheres of action.

The difficulties of this central part of the study begin with the fact that it is not entirely clear whether moral conflicts represent the collision of one normative image of society with another image, or with an institutionalized structure of norms. The text gives the impression that the first alternative is right, that the proposal of a changed polity only collides with the beliefs of those who cling to the previously proven regime. But that cannot be the case, because every polity is supposed to form an entire lifeworld, and thus lead to stable habits of action and perception. The demand to change the normative arrangement collides not with pure conceptions or beliefs, but with habitualized practices that have become second nature, and whose aggregate state is notably more solid than that of mental states. But that contrasts with the authors' presupposition that such conflicts could be mediated in the mode of 'compromise' or deliberation; they repeatedly argue that in the wake of moral 'denunciation', both parties see themselves challenged to examine their respective arguments in order to arrive at a compromise (277ff.). But how can a normative attitude that we can hardly control – because it has become second nature – be changed in a purely deliberative fashion? If the habitual and proven polity forms a self-evident element of our lifeworld, it will be more persistent than the conception of a mere negotiation of moral conflicts would allow. The reason the authors become entangled in all these contradictions is that they fail to sufficiently explain their own concept of the polity. If the latter is intended as a conception of order we can use to reliably coordinate our interaction, then it has the character of institutionalized systems of action, in which role expectations, moral obligations and social practices form a holistic whole. To claim that such structures, like beliefs, can be changed by arguments alone would be a grave category error.

But this inconsistency is not the only problem in the authors' treatment of moral conflicts. The above-mentioned tendency to deny theoretically immanent normativity returns here in a more intense form, leading to difficulties for which there is no solution in sight. The authors appear to presuppose that all six distinct polities can be employed anytime and anywhere as a normative pattern for proposing a change in our interaction. Regardless of whether we are dealing with industrial companies, domestic life, hospitals or political events, one of the participants must always be able to call the previously accepted social order into question by demanding a rearrangement according to one of the unused ideas of social justice. In order to explain what that would mean empirically, one only need imagine a father who one day recommends to his family that in the future, the entire household shall be reorganized according to the market order. Or imagine a natural scientist who attempts to overthrow the division of labour in the laboratory by proposing a familial arrangement of caring authority as a model for coordinating the laboratory's diverse activities. The point is not that such bizarre proposals and revolts do not occur in our social world; the issue is whether an analysis of society can relate to these proposals as neutrally as Boltanski and Thévenot do. The institutionalized normative structures dealt with above, or the correctly understood polities, have not developed by accident; they have emerged from practical experiences in which certain norms of recognition have proven over time to be sensible or appropriate when it comes to managing central problems of coordination. An analysis of society cannot simply abstract from the result of normative learning processes, but must instead take them up as theoretical elements in its own categorial apparatus. The central spheres of society would then represent spheres of action that are irreconcilable with any arbitrary set of norms, or, rather, only with those that have already proven superior and sensible. Of course, that does not mean that every social task can only be solved with the use of one particular regime of moral norms; different spheres of action between which we distinguish today have proven, in this normative sense, to be much more plastic than Parsonian functionalism would have us believe. The moral order of the family has undergone just as much change as the industrial working world or state welfare programmes.[13] But the process of iteratively examining alternatives has significantly reduced the assortment of models of order at our disposal. Within the family we can no longer – at least not without appearing obdurate, irrational or ridiculous – resort to the regime of patriarchal or charismatic leadership. For the same reason, it would be odd to demand a pure market order or an industrial system of organization in schools. Sociological observers cannot add such restrictions in our normative options as their own value judgement. As normative facts, they belong to empirical reality, just as do increasing divorce rates or more strongly individualized life-paths. For that reason, Boltanski and Thévenot cannot act as if all six models of justice are available for all areas of coordinating individual action. If they had taken more account of the implicit normativity of liberal-democratic societies, they would have realized that some of these models would be inappropriate for certain tasks; in fact, their application would even represent moral regress.

Occasionally the two authors appear to want to answer this objection. For instance, where they address the sense of the common or the sense of morality (*Gemein- oder Moralsinn*), they write that competent actors must be able to 'recognize the nature of the situation and be able to bring into play the corresponding principle of justice' (146). This is the same claim we saw above with relation to the implicit normativity of a society. Normally we learn in the course of our socialization which polities have proven appropriate to which class of tasks, such that we exclude alternative solutions from the very start. The sociologist who describes the choice of such alternatives as regressive or absurd makes use of a generalization of normative knowledge that he or she has acquired as a member of society. Therefore, the theorist's critique of misdevelopments does not go over the heads of the actors, but derives solely from an analysis of their implicit knowledge. Boltanski and Thévenot would have had to arrive at this conclusion if they had taken to heart the thought developed in this quote. But the citizens' 'sense of morality' is only rarely mentioned (216, 227), and instead we find talk of a normatively unstructured society. On almost every page, the study runs into the danger of dissolving, so to speak, the moral structure of the social. Only rarely do the orders of justification take on the solid form of institutionalized normative structures, and there are almost no historically excluded alternatives in the moral arrangement of social relations.

This lack of insight into the normative constitution of society, however, should not lead us to call for a return to Bourdieuian structuralism or Parsonian functionalism. The excessive structure and self-standing moral logic their approaches ascribe to society need to be pared down theoretically and opened up. It is the task of Boltanski and Thévenot's study to clear out and liberate these approaches while retaining the primacy of moral integration; that is how they have taught us to perceive the fragile and contested nature of normative orders. But perhaps they have gone too far. Whereas Bourdieu saw determinative forces at work in the formation of social *habitus* and Parsons only saw one-dimensional systems of action, Boltanski and Thévenot do not even leave the ruins of such normative guidelines. Their study portrays society merely as an arena of social action in which, anywhere and anytime, all arrangements allowed by culturally inherited polities are possible. Had the authors been aware of the pre-structured normative nature of society, they would have realized that they should not have contented themselves with a mere 'sociology of critique'. An analysis of society, compelled by the object of its investigation, forces us to criticize the respective form of the social.

Notes

1 For a good overview of the position and role of this approach within contemporary sociology, see Hans Joas and Wolfgang Knöbl, *Sozialtheorie: Zwanzig einführende Vorlesungen* (Frankfurt/Main: Suhrkamp, 2004), pp. 739–44. See also Peter Wagner, 'Soziologie der kritischen Urteilskraft und der Rechtfertigung', in Stephan Moebius and Lothar Peter, eds, *Französische Soziologie der Gegenwart* (Konstanz: UVK, 2004), pp. 417–48; Mohammed Nodi, *Introduction à la sociologie pragmatique* (Paris: Armand Colin, 2006).

2 Luc Boltanski and Laurent Thévenot, *De la justification: Les économies de la grandeur* (Paris: Gallimard, 1991).

3 Luc Boltanski and Laurent Thévenot, *On Justification: Economies of Worth*, trans. Catherine Porter (Princeton: Princeton University Press, 2010).

4 All page references refer to the 2010 English translation.

5 David Miller, *Principles of Social Justice* (Cambridge, MA: Harvard University Press, 2003); see also Chapter 7 in the current volume.

6 Charles Taylor, *Sources of the Self: The Making of Modern Identity* (Cambridge, MA: Harvard University Press, 1992).

7 In their pioneering study *The New Spirit of Capitalism* (trans. Gregory Elliott [London: Verso, 2007]), Boltanski and co-author Ève Chiapello attempt to demonstrate that since the 1980s, the 'spirit' of capitalism has begun to change, because a new model of order, the '*cité par projets*', is increasingly being used to justify and normatively secure capitalism. This means that a seventh conception of justification could be added to the six already outlined in *On Justification*; the normative core of this new conception consists in linking achievement to creativity, flexibility and innovation.

8 Bruno Latour, *The Pasteurization of France*, trans. Alan Sheridan and John Law (Cambridge, MA: Harvard University Press, 1993); Bruno Latour and Steve Woolgar, *Laboratory Life: The Construction of Scientific Facts* (Princeton: Princeton University Press, 1986).

9 See Luc Boltanski, Yann Darré and Marie-Ange Schiltz, 'La dénonciation', *Actes de la Recherche en Sciences Sociales*, vol. 51 (1984), pp. 3–40; Luc Boltanski and Laurent Thévenot, eds, *Justesse et justice dans le travail* (Paris: PUF, 1989).

10   See Luc Boltanski, 'Critique sociale et sens moral: Pour une soci-
     ologie du jugement', in Tetsuji Yamamoto, Edward G. Andrew,
     Roger Chartier and Paul Rabinow, eds, *Philosophical Designs for a
     Socio-Cultural Transformation: Beyond Violence and the Modern Era*
     (Lanham, MD: Rowman & Littlefield, 1999), pp. 248–73; Robin
     Celikates, 'From Critical Social Theory to a Social Theory of Cri-
     tique', *Constellations*, vol. 13 (2006), pp. 21–40; Wagner, 'Soziologie
     der kritischen Urteilskraft und der Rechtfertigung'.
11   See the detailed and informative account by Robin Celikates,
     *Kritik als soziale Praxis: Gesellschaftliche Selbstverständigung und kri-
     tische Theorie* (Frankfurt/Main: Campus, 2009).
12   Michael Walzer, *Spheres of Justice: A Defense of Pluralism and Equal-
     ity* (New York: Basic Books, 1983).
13   See Judith Stacey, *In the Name of the Family: Rethinking Family Values
     in the Postmodern Age* (Boston: Beacon Press,1996); Robert Castel,
     *From Manual Workers to Wage Laborers: Transformation of the Social
     Question* (Piscataway, NJ: Transaction, 2002); Stephan Lessenich,
     *Die Neuerfindung des Sozialen: Der Sozialstaat im flexiblen Kapitalis-
     mus* (Bielefeld: Transcript, 2008).

7

Philosophy as Social Research: David Miller's Theory of Justice

The gap between theory and practice within political philosophy seems to be greater today than ever before in its long history. On the one hand, its focus on justifying principles of justice, inspired by the pioneering work of John Rawls, has reached a previously unattained level of conceptual abstractness and ethical universality. But, on the other hand, it has lost the power to influence the self-understanding of political actors and advise them in the face of institutional barriers and cultural challenges.

In light of this growing chasm between philosophical theories of justice and political practice, the German translation of David Miller's *Principles of Social Justice* must feel liberating.[1] Although the original edition was published over ten years ago, when the brewings about communitarianism still ensured that theories of justice enjoyed a measure of resonance within political debate, the author's aim is perhaps more important today than at the time of publication. David Miller, Professor of Political Philosophy at Oxford, was convinced early on that there was something wrong about the entire construction of liberal theories of justice. It was not that Rawlsian theories were not argued for cogently or did not display an impressive measure of internal consistency; nor was he bothered by the priority given to the value of equality in the treatment of problems of justice in the political sphere. What upset Miller was instead the fact that this value was intentionally applied to all social spheres, and was even made into the point of reference for the perspective of justice. He felt that by hypostasizing equality as the sole principle of justice, these approaches divorced theory from praxis, conceptions of justice from the pre-theoretical world of beliefs. Empirical conceptions of justice no longer played a role in philosophical theory, because the latter already maintained an exclusive methodological commitment to the principle of equality. Miller therefore argued that the state of the theory of justice was, from the very beginning, a reflection of its own forgetfulness of empirical facts. Both the degree of its irrelevance in public discourse and its failure in the face of concrete challenges derive from these theories' concentration on one single principle, and thus from the fact that they ignore the differentiated nature of empirical beliefs about justice. The true intention of Miller's book was to counter this tendency and offer an opposing conception based on pre-theoretical beliefs, in order to make them the guideline for a theory of justice. He addresses the distinctions made today in our every-day societal life when it comes to finding just solutions to problems of distribution, and bases his theory on the thesis that people apply not only one, but three principles of justice. On his view, a theory of justice that lives up to its audience cannot be monistic and uphold one single principle, but must be pluralistic and embrace the three principles that people themselves assert.

I

Of course, Miller is not alone in his attempt to counter the monism of traditional liberal theories of justice with a pluralism of princi-ples of justice. As far back as 1983, Michael Walzer's *Spheres of Justice* advanced a 'complex' model of justice, whose essential idea consisted in ascribing one exclusive principle of legitimate distri-bution to different social privileges and burdens.[2] His major argu-ment was that each divisible task or benefit in a society possesses a general, intuitively determinable meaning, which in turn deter-mines a rational manner of distribution. In the field of sociology, we find a similar proposal in *On Justification* by Luc Boltanski and Laurent Thévenot, who develop the notion that each sphere of action in a society possesses distinct criteria for according or denying privileges.[3] What distinguishes these authors from Walzer is the mere fact that the specific principles of distribution are deter-mined not hermeneutically but empirically. While these two approaches largely agree that the diversity of social goods (or burdens) necessitates a plurality of principles of justice, Miller takes an entirely different approach, starting with the observation that subjects apply very different principles of distributive justice depending on the type of relationship at issue.

Miller arrives at this point of departure by reviewing empirical studies on the judgements and decisions of normal subjects facing problems of distribution. Mostly these are large-scale quantitative investigations in which randomly chosen subjects in different countries are asked to fill out questionnaires with questions on various kinds of conflicts surrounding the just distribution of goods. Yet Miller is cautious enough not to blindly trust the results of such empirical polls and unquestioningly make them the basis of his own theory. Just as he believes that a normative theory of justice depends on the determination of factical beliefs about justice, social-scientific research on justice requires the aid of philosophical theory. In the third chapter of his book, which precedes his evaluation of the empirical research, Miller attempts to clarify the reciprocal dependence between social science and political philosophy, between empirical research on justice and a normative theory of justice. In a time when these two disciplines are being increasingly torn apart by scientific specialization and professionalization, these pages take on a special significance. Miller is right to believe that empirical research remains 'blind' to everyday moral norms as long as its classifications have not been subjected to philosophical evaluation. Although such categorial pre-judgements will not always help to dispel all the difficulties of evaluating the material, they will ensure that there is a clear and consistent distinction between moral and non-moral patterns of justification with regard to certain forms of behaviour or judgement. One of the greatest problems involved in interpreting questionnaires on people's attitudes about social justice is the fact that the answers do not indicate whether they derive from proper moral or other social-technical considerations. For instance, a plea for egalitarian wage-forms is not necessarily an expression of a social ethos, but can just as easily be linked to the desire to live in a society that is as harmonious and stable as possible. In order to minimize such problems of interpretation, Miller suggests that empirical sociologists consult moral philosophy and normative theories of justice. After all, a significant part of the work in these fields consists in making rational and generally acceptable distinctions between different types of motivating moral behaviour and judgement.

Therefore, what is true for empirical research on justice is, according to Miller, also true for philosophical theories of justice. Just as sociology depends on the conceptual explanations of political philosophers, the latter is dependent on the former's investigations into everyday culture. Miller illustrates his claim that normative theories need to be supplemented with sociological research by turning to Rawls' theory of justice.[4] As much as the author of *A Theory of Justice* sought to reconcile his major principles with basic beliefs about justice held by normal citizens, he shows little interest in empirical studies that inquire into people's actual beliefs. For all of the scrupulous effort Rawls puts into moral psychology, economic theory and other individual disciplines within his procedures of justification, the complete absence of empirical moral psychology is all the more striking. Even though his theory is particularly dependent on consulting such investigations, they do not play any role in his argumentation. Miller does not concern himself with the reasons for this glaring omission, but concentrates entirely on the attendant theoretical consequences. Because Rawls pushes aside all research on everyday feelings about justice, not even taking critical notice of them, despite all appearances he ultimately ends up founding social justice as a whole on the single value of equality. Had he instead consulted the empirical research, Miller argues, Rawls would have quickly realized that the citizens he describes regard more than just one principle of justice as necessary and justified.

By taking this detour through a methodological discussion whose results have near political-scientific relevance, Miller arrives at the true object of his investigation. As mentioned above, he draws the empirical material for his argumentation from a series of sociological studies that use quantitative methods and often employ cultural comparisons to determine citizens' actual beliefs about justice. The results of this laborious procedure are to be used as a basis for a theory of justice that coincides more strongly with the substantive beliefs of normal subjects. In order to do so, however, Miller cannot content himself with reviewing the available material. Because this research mostly lacks what he regards as a necessary, preliminary philosophical clarification, he must subject the results of these studies to categorial examination. What Miller manages to achieve with this philosophical reconstruction (Chapter 4), and the way he internally combines the review of the material with a conceptual interpretation, can both be regarded justifiably as highlights of the fusion between social research and philosophy. At first sight, the results of the various empirical studies appear to be a chaotic conglomeration of various different attitudes about the legitimacy of various rules of distribution. The criteria employed in the responses appear to depend not only on the type of good to be distributed, the urgency of need and the proximity to the respective beneficiary, but also on the degree of one's involvement in the conflicts to be solved. In any case, a superficial look at the empirical material reveals hardly any systematic elements from which we could draw conclusions about whether the interviewees employ consistent rules in the solution of problems of distribution. Such an order begins to take shape once Miller begins to sort out the responses according to specified criteria, sorting them into larger clusters. Without ever giving the impression of doing injustice to the material, he thereby manages to take the manifold responses and gradually inject some regularity into the rules of distribution they apply.

Even the very first and central finding that Miller comes across in his reconstruction of the empirical material contrasts starkly with standard philosophical theories of justice. Contrary to the claim that principles of equality dominate our current moral culture, people appear to make use of very different rules of distribution in their everyday life. Depending on which social relationship is concerned in a given problem of distribution, they go beyond the principle of equality and bring to bear the normative considerations of need and desert. Miller also notes that within the pluralism of these various principles, even the idea of equal distribution plays a merely secondary role. It only comes into play where subjects feel that social relationships between citizens are at issue, whereas in all other contexts the principle of need or desert has priority. If we further analyse these fine, but nevertheless mostly implicit distinctions between different types of social relationships, we then find that the interviewees once again separate patterns of interaction lying outside of the domain of the constitutional state into two distinct spheres. With striking regularity, subjects set apart spheres characterized by commonly shared values and experiences of solidarity from the domain in which purposive-rational relationships dominate under the legitimate validity of economic aims. In light of these differentiations, it is not surprising that the interviewees generally tend to apply the principle of desert within the first of the two non-state relationships and the principle of need within the second. If we are dealing with problems of distribution within the sphere of economic activity, previously performed work generally represents the criterion for a just solution; if such problems arise in the context of networks of solidarity and intimate relationships, individual need is generally the applicable criterion of distribution.

Of course, in the framework of these differentiations, which amount to the according of three different, independent principles of distribution to three distinct relationship contexts, Miller has to recognize that there are also a number of overlaps and blurry lines. So, for instance, a large majority of the interviewees feel that the principle of desert should be applied in economic life only to the degree that it is capable of securing the basic livelihood of workers. Below this threshold, however, they favour the principle of need, which should be able to ensure – in the form of a minimum wage – that elementary needs are satisfied. Often the interviewees are uncertain about where exactly the borders lie between the various different zones of application for the different principles of distribution. In these cases, ethical collisions typically arise that are often solved by resorting to social-technical considerations. But for the most part, Miller finds that the image of a relatively stable tripartite division between independent principles of distribution remains. While the idea of equal distribution has priority when it comes to the civic (*staatsbürgerlich*) sphere, the principle of desert should dominate in the economic sphere and the principle of need should prevail in the sphere of smaller, integrated communities of values.

Now, to take this merely empirically reconstructed tripartite distinction as a sufficient basis for justifying a pluralistic theory of justice would amount to sheer positivism. That the population makes relatively differentiated judgements about justice with few deviations, and that citizens make use of different principles of distribution depending on the social context, cannot be the only reason to propose a tripartite theory of justice.[5] In order to move from empirical facts to normative principles, we need an additional step in the argumentation, one which explains why it is right to comply with the moral differentiations made by everyday citizens. We still need a sketch of the normative aspect that justifies fashioning the factical pluralism of everyday judgements about justice into a systematic theory of justice. Miller takes on this task, making no bones about its urgency, in the second chapter of his book – even before the presentation of the empirical material. Here he develops the outlines of a conception of justice whose only source of justification lies in our shared intuitive beliefs.

II

From a distance, the strategy that Miller chooses in order to avoid a mere positivist theory of justice recalls the notion of 'reflective equilibrium' developed by Rawls.[6] Just as Rawls justifies the validity of his theory by trying to find an equilibrium within a constant shifting between philosophically proven principles and 'considered judgements', Miller also seeks to justify his conception through a process of reflective balancing. The only difference is that the two variables in the procedure are not moral principles and considered everyday intuitions, but actual judgements about justice and our socially proven intuitions. Miller argues that a theory of justice can be justified adequately if empirical judgements and our intuitive, but theoretically cleansed, beliefs can be brought into harmony. Therefore, the general assumptions that he believes form the 'grammar' of our understanding of social justice must be characterized as the counterpart of empirical sociological findings.

In his reconstruction of the core of our intuitions, Miller keeps to the entirely classical idea according to which 'justice' means giving 'to each his or her own' (*suum cuique*). In line with this conception, every subject deserves to be treated in a way that is appropriate to his or her individual properties. Justice therefore demands that rather than indiscriminately treat people equally, we take their particularity into account and accordingly treat them equally or unequally. But if our intuitions about justice merely consisted in this one, principal idea, they would be unfounded. We would know that we are supposed to treat others according to their respective particularities, but we would not have any shared criterion for sorting and evaluating the complementary demands. In Miller's view, we compensate for this uncertainty in our intuitive conceptions of justice by taking the type of our relationship with other persons as the standard for judging which of their properties are relevant for determining what is just. According to the nature of the ties that bind us to our fellow citizens, the demands they are justified in making of us can change. 'To each his or her own' would consequently mean treating each person according to the normative duties that are characteristic for the type of social relationship that binds us together.

Again, these remarks are intended not as descriptions of our factical beliefs about justice, but as reconstructions of our intuitive beliefs about justice. With these indications about the normative significance of social relationships, Miller merely wants to claim that every competent member of our society intuitively sorts out questions of justice according to the sphere of social life to which he or she belongs. He therefore holds that we all possess a kind of shared grammar, a 'moral map', that – at adulthood at the latest – helps us to distinguish between different contexts of justice. But for

Miller, contrary to what is true in discourse ethics, these contexts indicate not various fields of application for one and the same procedure, but in fact distinct spheres of justice.[7] Each social sphere that he believes us capable of intuitively distinguishing has its own exclusive principle of justice. For the methodological aim that Miller pursues by reconstructing our sense of justice, it is almost imperative that the distinctions we make intuitively and daily between various spheres essentially coincide with the distinctions that people in fact make. Without such a vague, preliminary coincidence, Miller could not even want to grasp these reconstructed conceptions of justice as normative justifications of popular views on social justice. Therefore, it is ultimately not surprising that he also claims a differentiation of our intuitions of justice in three social spheres. On his account, the members of liberal-democratic societies intuitively separate their social world into three different contexts, which differ according to how narrow or ethically saturated their specific relationships of interaction are. Miller terms these relationships 'modes of human relationship', and distinguishes them as 'solidarity', 'instrumental associations' and 'citizenship'. While in the first sphere members of society relate to each other within a horizon of a shared 'ethics' of trust and solidarity, in the second sphere they each share an interest in their own respective advantage, and in the third sphere they share legal respect for the other's autonomy. According to Miller, part of the 'grammar' of our ideas about justice is also the fact that each of these forms of interaction is determined by the social validity of an independent principle that normatively regulates how the corresponding burdens and privileges are to be distributed. The dominant principle in the context of solidarity is the principle of need; the principle of desert dominates in 'instrumental associations'; and the principle of equality prevails in the civil sphere. In order to counter the astonishment that might arise at the fact that almost the same distinctions appear as in the empirical research, we must constantly keep in mind the status of these considerations. By claiming that each competent member of our societies intuitively recognizes three different spheres of justice, Miller aims to lay the basis for an independent, normative theory of justice, which, via the establishment of a 'reflective equilibrium', should be able to retrospectively justify ideas about justice observed in the empirical research.

But even after we have clarified this issue, Miller's merely reconstructive theory of justice still raises a few problems that are not easy to solve. He asks whether the close link between spheres of interaction and principles of distribution might not awaken suspicions of a certain circularity in his argumentation. If, after all, the different spheres of communication are characterized by a shared orientation towards the very same duties already contained in the respective normative principles, then the moral justification would coincide with the differentiation of the spheres and would thus lose its independence. For Hegelians, there would be no problem with such a fusion, since they would be convinced that the principles of social justice can only be derived from an analysis of the normative practices of the institutions of 'ethical life'.[8] But Miller, who has also been regarded as displaying Hegelian tendencies,[9] introduces the three normative principles of his theory independent of empirical patterns of interaction, thereby attempting to understand these principles as being justified in their own right. The formula that he chooses in order to take account of this independence is that subjects cannot make a 'logical' mistake when, within a certain sphere of communication, they bring to bear an alien principle. After all, he believes that the social practices which, taken together, constitute that sphere can be explained, at least rudimentarily, without taking into account the corresponding norms of justice. But it is not so clear whether Miller can actually claim such a 'logical' disjunction between practices and moral norms, because he almost always characterizes the three modes of interaction that he finds in liberal-democratic societies by using concepts that contain normative states of affairs, which are in turn borrowed from the corresponding principles of justice. In 'solidarity', feelings of mutual trust ensure that the 'neediness' of each member stands at the centre of attention; in 'instrumental associations' each member must make an individual 'contribution' to realizing the common goal; and 'citizenship' can only be defined by the rule of 'equal' rights and duties. In all three cases, the respective practice cannot be described without the use of categories that do not already refer to the corresponding norms of justice. For that reason, it is much more difficult than Miller claims to distinguish spheres of communication from moral norms in such a way that the principles of justice can assume an analytically independent position.

This is an important issue, because it touches on the methodological status of Miller's reconstructive theory of justice. If the three spheres of interaction are initially defined, so to speak, by the respective principles of justice, then no additional arguments are needed to justify why the corresponding principles should be valid in the spheres to which they are assigned. No theoretical gap arises for normative justifications to fill, because the different spheres would be constituted by the validity of the respective principles of justice. Miller's *de facto* approach of reconstructing the presup- positions of our practices would suffice to justify the thesis that the principles of equality, need and desert are normatively valid within their respective social spheres. If, by contrast, he does not want to assert such a seamless fusion of social practices and moral norms – that is, if he claims that the spheres of interaction are initially con- stituted independently of the corresponding principles of justice – then he must present additional normative arguments that could independently justify the dominance of these principles in these specific spheres. It is difficult to find any theoretical place within his study for such arguments. Therefore, Miller seems to move back and forth between two interpretations of his own procedure: on the one hand, he argues merely historically; on the other hand, he wants to add normative justifications. On the whole, therefore, his book remains undecided when it comes to justifying a theory of justice as a counterweight to the empirical research.

Closely connected to this first question is a second question, which Miller himself, however, does not pose. What is unclear about his argumentation is how he arrives at the claim that liberal- democratic societies should be characterized precisely by the three spheres of interaction that he describes. It is not that such a tripartite distinction does not seem somewhat plausible; a good number of classical theories of justice – although we might only think of Hegel – essentially draw the same boundaries between the three modes of social relationships upon which Miller bases his differentiations. But for all the care he takes to philosophically adopt the empirical material, he expends little effort in justifying the spheres between which he differentiates. The question as to what kinds of relation- ships of interaction can be distinguished in our societies needs to be answered by drawing upon social-theoretical arguments. Such patterns of interaction are not simply 'there', open to observation; rather they have a prior history and change both their normative character and their relation to each other over time. We can only put aside these empirical facts if we claim that there is a 'higher' sort of reason at work in the differentiation of these three spheres. But because Miller evades such considerations, and because perhaps he is not accustomed to thinking in terms of the history of philosophy, his tripartite distinction remains without justification and context (*begründungs- und bezugslos*).

This flaw becomes even more significant once we realize the nor- mative burden of justification that this differentiation must carry for Miller. After all, his distinction between three spheres of inter-action seems to provide the foundation for a theory of justice that justifies people's empirical judgements about justice. But to do so, the three patterns of social relationship must possess some kind of moral legitimacy on their own. It is not enough to claim their mere existence; rather, for each individual sphere it must be shown that there are good, normative reasons for how we encounter them in our intuitive social grammar. In other words, Miller would have to reach back beyond his own tripartite distinction in order to show that and how each individual sphere is morally or ethically justified. Only then could we exclude the possibility that we are defending a principle of justice linked to a certain sphere merely for historically contingent reasons. Throughout the course of his argumentation, it remains unclear whether Miller is aware of this necessity of justification. In any case, he seems to have a tendency to turn contingent empirical facts into the normative foundation for an entire theory of justice.

Conversely, these methodological concerns lose much of their weight once we have taken into account the true purpose of Mill-er's theory of justice. He is less concerned with illuminating the methodological procedure for justifying a theory of justice down to the last detail. Instead he puts all his effort into overthrowing the monism of currently prevalent theories of justice in order to restore a connection to political practice. At the heart of his theory we find the notion that our everyday beliefs about justice are char-acterized not by a single principle, but by three independent and self-standing principles. And perhaps there is no better way of defending this primary idea than taking our point of departure from the different modes of our social relationships.

III

The major achievement of Miller's book is doubtlessly his attempt to reintroduce two norms of justice – need and desert – that are in danger of disappearing from the horizon of more recent, procedur-alist theories of justice. It is in fact obvious that in certain social contexts, we have a tendency to distribute goods according to the criterion of individual need out of moral conviction. Here we only have to think of the context of the family or certain small groups, in which there are no moral doubts about the idea that those who are most hungry should receive priority in the distribution of por-tions. In the case that such a principle of unequal, need-based distribution has any place at all within a procedural theory of justice, it can only be justified as an agreed-upon exception from the principle of equality. All participants are thereby assumed to agree to unequal distribution in light of the particular circumstances, while preserving the condition of fundamental equality. Miller objects that the principle of need has an independent and original place in our beliefs about justice, one that is not owed to the 'parasitic' use of other principles. In a certain type of social relationship that is to be defined more closely, it is morally right and imperative that we treat each person according to his or her needs. Of course, the application of this principle requires a prior determination of what counts as a need and how the corresponding rule of distribution is to be defined. When it comes to the principle of need, Miller maintains that there are limiting conditions that prevent every arbitrary desire from being advanced as a reason for special treatment. These kinds of claims can only justify needs whose satisfaction is necessary for survival or for a sufficiently decent life as defined by the sociocultural norms of society. Therefore, the validity of the principle of needs is limited to social contexts in which solidarity prevails on the basis of shared values. Only in ethical communities in which the members agree upon what belongs to the domain of individual responsibility and what belongs to the domain of 'common fate' can the moral rule apply that each person be treated according to his or her needs. Such a principle, after all, presupposes that we all know the degree to which we as a collective are responsible for the satisfaction of each and every person's elementary needs.

In light of these limiting conditions, it can easily appear as if Miller is claiming that the principle of need is only valid in small groups. That this is not true, and that Miller even has much larger groups in mind, only becomes clear once we take account of another strand of his political philosophy. In a book entitled *On Nationality*, published four years prior to *Principles of Social Justice*, Miller undertook an attempt to give a positive slant to the notion of the nation-state.[10] Being sceptical of the tendency to regard the nation-state merely as a germ of aversive particularism, Miller sought to prove that feelings of national belonging are a necessary precondition for government measures of redistribution. This first attempt to describe the nation as a comprehensive community of solidarity was followed, five years later, by a second book with a similar thrust, except that now the concept of 'citizenship' stood at the centre of his argumentation.[11] The thesis he developed in this context was directed against the liberal conception according to which the demand of government neutrality requires abstaining from supporting certain particular forms of life or particular concepts of the good. Miller thus sought to show that such a limitation is absurd within the nation-state, because the latter must regard the upholding of a feeling of mutual trust and common identity as its essential task. Therefore it would be wrong to limit citizens' political activity to voting every few years. Instead there is the legitimate expectation that all members of society be able to actively participate in public discourse in order to contribute to the consensual solving of common problems.

This republican conception of citizenship, which of course has not been left uncontested,[12] represents the background against which we must understand Miller's treatment of the principle of need. He does not want to see the validity of this principle reduced to the domain of small groups, because he believes that even larger nation-states can, at least in principle, represent ethical communities. If that is the case and if solidarity exists among the members of a state who share a common ethos, then Miller believes they will assert the principle of need by giving priority to the needy (in the sense mentioned above) when it comes to distributing scarce goods. The example Miller uses in *Principles of Social Justice* to illustrate the status of this principle of justice is the system of health insurance. In national solidarity, the majority of contributors will agree to provide a significantly higher portion of the insurance volume to those in a position of particularly extreme need due to illnesses they have acquired through no fault of their own. The precondition for such a needs-based distribution is obvious, as Miller also makes clear: there must be a consensus among the citizens about where the border lies between needs that people have brought upon themselves and those for which they bear no liability.

Things are much different when it comes to the second principle of distribution that Miller proposes. In his view, the principle of desert neither depends on the presupposition of an ethical community nor does it require much effort in terms of finding a cultural consensus. Today, however, it is not at all easy to rehabilitate this principle, for a great number of theorists are fundamentally opposed to the idea that individual achievement can justify any sort of claims, instead viewing achievement as the product of a chance endowment of talents and skills. Highly influential in this regard are the arguments developed by Rawls in his *Theory of Justice*. After he had resolutely claimed that 'the initial endowment of natural assets and the contingencies of their growth and nurture in early life are arbitrary from a moral point of view',[13] it seemed almost impossible to reassert the principle of desert. This is the implicit consensus that Miller goes up against in his study; thus the defence of the principle of desert is such an essential component (Chapters 7–9) that it could be understood as the heart of his entire theoretical enterprise.

Miller is of course aware that the principle of desert is afflicted by a series of conceptual ambiguities that are a significant hindrance to its application. But in his view, it is absurd to take these complications as a pretext for completely dropping the principle of achievement-based distribution from the agenda of a theory of justice. Not only does empirical research demonstrate that the desert principle continues to play a crucial role in popular beliefs about justice, but he also showed, in certain spheres of society, that our intuitive understanding of the social gives priority to this principle. Finally, in the first part of his study, in which he lays the foundation for his approach, Miller has already outlined the place where this principle of distribution dominates. In all social relationships in which the members of society encounter each other in the production of goods and services, the normative principle of individual achievement is pre-eminent. The greatest difficulty thus consists in defining the concept of 'achievement' or 'desert' so as to obviate objections of pure accident or arbitrariness. Miller turns to this task in the seventh chapter of the book, shifting constantly between normative and conceptual arguments. When it comes to the concept of desert, he is convinced that one core element can be distilled from the variety of customary meanings, one that is untainted by arbitrary elements that cannot be ascribed to individual achievement. The point of departure for his considerations is the observation that 'desert' or 'achievement' expresses how, from the perspective of participants, we respond in so-called 'reactive attitudes' (Peter Strawson) to subjects who perform a certain task in a particularly exemplary fashion. The criteria for such positive judgements lie in the tasks themselves, which can be performed in a better or worse, more or less appropriate fashion. In addition, these judgements convey our belief that the subjects involved have done everything they can to perform the task especially well. If we combine these two elements, we see that judgements of desert represent moral expressions with which individual performances of particular tasks are deemed worthy of recognition; therefore, in Miller's view, these judgements provide reasons for why that subject should enjoy preferable treatment, advantages and privileges.

If we attempt to apply this form of judgement to society as a whole, then we will find what Miller calls the moral requirement of the principle of desert. When it comes to the distribution of goods, we cannot avoid giving preference to those who have performed important tasks in an especially skilful way. Certainly, the principle of desert cannot itself determine which tasks we take into account and which forms of compensation should be accorded. But as soon as an institutional order for making such decisions exists, to not remunerate the skilful performance of tasks we regard as important would be to violate the imperatives of justice. Furthermore, Miller makes clear that the application of the principle of desert always requires that we also bring to bear the 'principle of equivalence', which demands equal pay for equal labour. After all, to take achievement as a reason for according preferences in turn presupposes that everybody deserves to be awarded equal compensation for the equal performance of one and the same task. In Miller's view, there is no reason to combine the application of the principle of desert with the rule of equality. Beyond the threshold at which a person's subsistence is threatened, a pluralistic theory of justice justifies granting career positions and social status according to the criteria of individual skills and talents.

I have not dealt with much of what Miller additionally presents in order to give his conception of justice more contours. I have adequately discussed neither his thoughts on how the three principles of justice can complement one another, nor his attempt to clarify his relationship to proceduralism. But even this brief summary should suffice to prove the groundbreaking significance of his theory. With his proposal that we distinguish between three principles of social justice and assign them to various spheres of our society, Miller has shaken the foundations of prevailing, proceduralist theories of justice, thereby challenging us to reconsider our understanding of social justice.

Notes

1   David Miller, *Principles of Social Justice* (Cambridge, MA: Harvard University Press, 1999). [Tr.: This chapter was originally published as the introduction to the German translation of the book: *Grundsätze sozialer Gerechtigkeit* (Frankfurt/Main: Campus, 2008).]

2   Michael Walzer, *Spheres of Justice: A Defense of Pluralism and Equality* (New York: Basic Books, 1983).

3   Luc Boltanski and Laurent Thévenot, *On Justification: Economies of Worth*, trans. Catherine Porter (Princeton: Princeton University Press, 2010). See also Chapter 6 of this volume.

4   John Rawls, *A Theory of Justice* (Cambridge, MA: Harvard University Press, 1999).

5   This point is well developed in Adam Swift, 'Social Justice: Why Does It Matter What the People Think?', in Daniel A. Bell and Avner de-Shalit, eds, *Forms of Justice: Critical Perspectives on David Miller's Political Philosophy* (Lanham, MD: Rowman & Littlefield, 2003), pp. 13–28.

6   Rawls, *A Theory of Justice*, pp. 18, 42ff.

7   See Rainer Forst, *Contexts of Justice: Political Philosophy beyond Liberalism and Communitarianism* (Berkeley: University of California Press, 2002).

8   Axel Honneth, *Suffering from Indeterminacy: An Attempt at a Reactualization of Hegel's Philosophy of Right*, trans. Jack Ben-Levi (Amsterdam: Van Gorcum Ltd, 2000).

9   See Daniel A. Bell and Avner de-Shalit, 'Introduction', in Bell and de-Shalit, eds, *Forms of Justice*, p. 2.

10 David Miller, *On Nationality* (Oxford: Oxford University Press, 1995).

11 David Miller, *Citizenship and National Identity* (Cambridge: Polity Press, 2000).

12 See Erica Benner, 'The Liberal Limits of Republican National Identity', in Bell and de-Shalit, eds, *Forms of Justice*, pp. 205–26; Daniel Bell, 'Is Republican Citizenship Appropriate for the Modern World?', in ibid., pp. 227–47.

13 Rawls, *A Theory of Justice*, p. 274.

Part III

Social and Theoretical Applications

8

Recognition between States: On the Moral Substrate of International Relations

From an everyday, non-theoretical perspective, we seem to take for granted that state actors often insist that other states respect the community they represent, while suing for recognition with corresponding measures. In everyday discussion, we readily agree that the behaviour of Palestine's political leaders, for instance, cannot be understood without taking into account the striving for recognition; that Russia's government has been going to great lengths to compel Western countries to show more consideration for Russian interests; or that during the administration of George W. Bush, Western European governments used diplomatic relationships and manoeuvres to obtain renewed respect from their American ally.[1] At first sight, these applications of the category of recognition to international relations certainly do not seem surprising. After all, one of the more important motives behind the recent revival of Hegel's theory of recognition was the desire to return to a stronger moral vocabulary in analysing the comportment of collective agents and social groups, thereby extracting this behaviour from the dominant paradigm of purely purposive-rational, strategic action.[2]

But already in the *Philosophy of Right*, Hegel objected to applying the notion of a 'struggle for recognition' to international relations, at least in the case of 'civilized nations'. Instead, he sought to describe international relations in terms of the self-assertion of nation-states within the framework of universally accepted international law. He reserved the idea of a striving for recognition and respect for more underdeveloped and unrecognized nations, which have been unsuccessful in their efforts to attain honour and glory; meanwhile, the enlightened constitutional states of the West are solely guided by the aims of maximizing welfare and maintaining national security.[3] That is the image that the dominant theory of international relations has adopted over the last few decades. Without making any reference to Hegel, the theory maintains that from the moment of their internationally recognized independence, national governments essentially aim to assert themselves as nation-states and are thus mostly uninterested in matters of international respect and recognition. A significant gap therefore seems to lie between our everyday intuitions and the dominant theory, one that appears difficult to overcome. While in our more theoretical explanations of state comportment we accept that state activity is to be interpreted exclusively in terms of purposive rationality, our everyday intuitions also account for quasi-moral motifs such as a striving for recognition and violations of respect.

These intuitions, however, generally do not stand up to scientific models. The idea that state actors and governments are exclusively interested in collective self-assertion has so much suggestive power that we quickly abandon our everyday intuitions in favour of the standard scheme of purely material motives. From this perspective, what we once assumed to be acts fuelled by a feeling of being disrespected, or by a desire for recognition, now represents a merely symbolically concealed act motivated by national interest. The question this raises is, in the first instance, purely empirical and descriptive: is the dominant paradigm of purposive-rational behaviour an adequate model for explaining political tensions, conflicts and wars? From the perspective of our everyday intuitions, we would instead have to ask whether we need to consider more primary (*originär*) motives, such as the desire for recognition and respect, in order to explain foreign policy in general and international hostilities in particular. The answer to these questions has opaque normative implications that cannot be left out of the picture, for the more our explanations of international relations emphasize individual states' striving for recognition, the more it appears we will have to concede that states do not disregard the political reactions of their counterparts, and therefore have a latent awareness of the fact that their collective identity must be internationally acceptable. Even if this shift in our perspective cannot yield any immediate guidelines for action, it does strongly suggest that we should prefer 'soft power' to military force or 'hard power' in international conflicts.[4] The explanatory framework we choose therefore has a strong bearing on our prescriptions for how states should act in the case of international tensions, disagreements or conflicts. Depending on whether we emphasize the aspect of national self-assertion or the striving for international recognition, the normative horizon of our prescriptions will change accordingly.

In what follows, I will make some tentative, exploratory efforts to answer these questions. First, I explain why we should pay more attention to the dimension of recognition in international relations. This concerns the purely descriptive categorial means that are appropriate for describing international conflict and tensions (I). Second, I will touch on some of the normative consequences of this proposed paradigmatic shift in how we understand and explain international relations. Because of my lacking familiarity with the issue, I will have to restrict myself to some tentative considerations, which should nevertheless make apparent that by emphasizing the dimension of recognition in international relations, our moral perspective on world politics would be changed significantly (II).

I

The main difficulty we face in applying the category of recognition to international relations is revealed by the obstacles we run into on our search for an appropriate theoretical vocabulary. As soon as we try to give a name to the dimension of respect involved in state conduct, we find that the only terms at our disposal are too psychologically or intellectually laden. We speak, slightly awkwardly, of a striving for recognition or a need for respect, even though we know that such psychological concepts do not appropriately capture the issue at hand. As long as we only transfer the concept of recognition from the interpersonal level to the behaviour of social groups or movements, we do not seem to have any terminological problems. In this case, we view the collective identity of a given community as the higher-level equivalent of personal identity or relation-to-self. We therefore have a relatively clear picture about what is being fought over when individuals or groups engage in a struggle for recognition. Hence there has never been any problem with the notion of a 'politics of recognition' when it comes to the struggles of minorities for legal respect and social recognition for their collective identity. The starting point of these struggles consists in shared experiences of exclusion, indignity or disrespect, which motivates the members of such a group to band together and fight in solidarity for legal or cultural recognition.[5]

But such a conceptual transfer is much more difficult, and the conceptual problems much broader, once we switch from the level of group struggles to relationships between nation-states. Here we can no longer speak of collective identity, particularly because the obvious increase in ethnic and cultural subgroups has started to dispel permanently the illusion of a nationally homogeneous population. Even where, for historical reasons, the idea of the nation-state has been able to gain a toehold, the state apparatus cannot be viewed as the executive organ of a collective identity, because the tasks it carries out – providing for security, preserving power and ensuring economic coordination – obey their own set of rules (*eigengesetzlich*). Not only do the tasks of government change their form in accordance with various overall forms of political organization, but the manner in which they are described also changes according to the theory we employ. Depending on whether the function of the liberal-democratic state is regarded as consisting in the 'biopolitical' management of the population or in creating conditions of social justice compatible with the requirements of national security, we will find great differences in the description of the tasks of government. But even beyond differences pertaining to the form of government or the theoretical system of description, it remains true that the foreign-political function of the state cannot merely be viewed as a compliant agency charged with giving articulation to collective identity. Rather, the state is subject to forces and imperatives that derive from the tasks of preserving the borders, promoting economic well-being and maintaining political security. Therefore, we cannot simply transfer the concept of recognition and claim that wherever collective identities exist, there must also be a struggle for recognition. In the first instance, the functional imperatives of political control (*Steuerung*) and the preservation of power intervene between, on the one hand, the supposed need of a people to have their own, however fragmented, identity respected by foreign nation-states and, on the other hand, the actions of state actors. The psychological concepts we use when we speak of 'strivings', 'needs' and 'feelings' are thus inappropriate for describing international relations. State actors do not have mental attitudes, but represent authorities charged with carrying out politically determined tasks.

Now, on a theoretical level, there is a concept of 'recognition' that is applied to international relations as a matter of course. According to the statutes of international law, a politically organized community only comes into legal existence by virtue of being recognized by other internationally 'recognized' states. A major task of foreign policy thus consists in examining whether a certain community which regards itself as a state actually meets the generally defined prerequisites of a 'state'.[6] Hans Kelsen maintains that this act of legal recognition is a necessarily reciprocal act, because a newly recognized state can only be viewed as a full-fledged member of the international community if it recognizes the states that offer it recognition in turn. As long as a state fails to return the recognition extended to it, the birth of a state within the international community will remain incomplete, because that state will not yet have proven its competence as a member of the legal community of states.[7]

At the same time, however, Kelsen emphasizes that in acts of recognition between states, a government only officially takes note of or cognizes an empirical reality, rather than conveying its respect for that state. If a state recognizes another political community within the framework of international law, this only means that the recognizing state regards the recognized state as having fulfilled the conditions of statehood. This type of recognition, therefore, is not normative, but instead expresses a state's cognition of a given state of affairs: 'The legal act of recognition is the establishment of a fact; it is not the expression of a will. It is cognition rather than re-cognition.'[8] In order to speak of 'recognition' between states in the true sense of the term, Kelsen claims that there must be a certain amount of room for decision. This would not involve examining a *fait accompli* in order to perhaps draw the conclusion that a state deserves recognition; rather, a decision would have to be made as to whether more intense and friendly relations should be taken up. According to Kelsen, it is only at this second stage that we can justifiably speak of an act of recognition between states. This would refer not to the consequence of a state's cognition of an empirical fact, but to a government's free decision to enter into a positive relationship with another state. Kelsen terms these acts of recognition 'political' in order to emphasize their specificity. With a political act of recognition, a government expresses its intention to treat another state as an equal member of the international community. Even if Kelsen primarily focuses on the establishment of diplomatic relations and trade agreements, his conceptual proposal provides us with a key to pursuing the above-mentioned institutions on a theoretical level. Obviously, what we mean when we speak of recognition between states, of disrespect and indignity, lies on the same level that Kelsen has in mind when he speaks of 'political' acts of recognition.[9]

The first step we would have to take in order to get a better grasp of the issue consists in emphasizing the sources of legitimacy that bind the conduct of state actors. The latter cannot pursue foreign political objectives without considering whether the manner in which they do so conforms to the presumed expectations of the population. The manner in which a government defends the nation's security, political clout and economic prosperity must be made dependent upon the consent of the nation's citizens, if only to demonstrate the government's operational capacity. The necessity of legitimacy in foreign policy even holds true for non-democratic political systems. Even in authoritarian states or dictatorships, such as Iran or China, rulers and political elites are usually aware that their authority is wholly dependent on the degree to which the public consents to their actions. We can assume that the citizens of a state, regardless of the cultural, ethnic or religious differences that might divide them, are very keen on seeing their country accorded due respect and honour by other countries. The political representatives of other communities are to 'recognize' that upon which a community founds its self-image – the challenges it has overcome in the past, its power to resist authoritarian tendencies, its cultural achievements, and so on.[10] We must not make the mistake of immediately equating such desires with nationalism or feelings of supremacy. This is not only because the collective identity of a state-organized community can no longer found itself on historical or ethnic commonalities,[11] and not only because the processes of cultural globalization run counter to any such will to supremacy. Rather, the desire for international recognition of that which makes up a nation's self-respect is fundamentally directed towards the involvement, and not the exclusion, of other states. Mundane examples for such desires can be found in the often bemusing excitement that can envelop an entire population as soon as its team brings home a victory in an international sport event, or in the naïve pride with which a country's citizens attempt to draw the attention of visitors to cultural productions that honour the community's past. That is neither nationalism nor even patriotic love of the constitution (*Verfassungspatriotismus*), because it neither demonizes other peoples nor necessarily praises one's own democratic constitution. Instead, this represents a striving for a form of collective recognition, without which a collective identity could not be maintained in an unequivocal and unbroken fashion.

It is this kind of collective expectation on the part of a country's population that a state's political agents must respect in their foreign policies. In order to legitimate their own actions, they understand that they will have to appropriately display those features of their country that deserve recognition *while* carrying out their functionally defined tasks. Therefore, the collective striving for recognition is not just one particular function within the overall spectrum of a state's tasks; rather, it colours and underlies the way in which political agents fulfil the tasks assigned to them by the nation's constitution.

In order to understand the alternatives open to state actors in this context, we need to take another step in our analysis. We need to get a clear picture of the symbolic horizon of meaning that necessarily encompasses the entirety of state conduct. Political measures and actions have a whole series of meanings beyond their expressly formulated content, communicated through the manner of their implementation. This involves the use of certain easily understood metaphors, historical rituals, even the conscious manipulation of facial expressions and gestures at summits and other political events. These are all tools in the arsenal of symbols with which state actors can intentionally communicate messages that go beyond the 'official' content of their communiqués.[12] Presumably, much of what Kelsen terms 'political recognition' goes on in the symbolic staging of foreign policy. Statements intended to raise awareness for the collective identity of one's own country, or to express respect for the achievements of another country's population, are not normally an explicit part of a given political transaction, but are contained in the manner in which these transactions are concluded and presented. Of course, there will always be cases in which government representatives believe they are acting in accordance with the political mood of their home country when they explicitly express a certain measure of recognition for the culture of another nation's population. A striking example is President Obama's astounding speech at Cairo University in June 2009 before a large number of political and intellectual representatives of the Islamic world. From greeting the audience in Arabic to his repeated mentions of the cultural achievements of Islam, his entire speech sought to remove the impression of disdain in many Arab countries during the Bush years. But much less common are instances in which a political actor explicitly demands respect for the collective identity of his or her own nation's population. The desire to maintain the appearance that one's own nation is unaffected by another nation's opinions, the aim of avoiding public embarrassment, and the etiquette of diplomatic encounters – all that usually prevents a people's desire for recognition of its collective identity from being directly and openly expressed by its political representatives. This recognitional dimension of international relations is thus typically expressed indirectly and symbolically. Behaviour that serves to express a state's interest in self-assertion is staged so as to implicitly convey a finely calculated game in which respect and disrespect, desires for recognition and experiences of humiliation find expression.

Therefore, distinguishing a strategic dimension of self-assertion from a normative dimension of recognition is problematic. In their transactions with other states, political actors do not initially pursue purely purposive-rational aims such as preserving power and maximizing welfare, in order to subsequently grant or revoke recognition. Rather, states always define their interests within a horizon of normative expectations they presume their citizens to have in the form of diffuse desires for the recognition of their own collective identity or that of another collective. Therefore, it is wrong to initially assume a primary, isolated layer of purely strategic intentions and calculations. State actors cannot formulate such interests without considering the needs for recognition they can presume on the part of the fragile collective that is their own population, as well as the needs for moral reparations harboured by an equally porous foreign population. Because political representatives must preserve legitimacy by acting as interpreters of the experiences and desires of their own respective citizenry, all encounters and relationships between states stand under the moral pressure generated by a conflict over recognition. Issues of this kind – the need for an appropriate self-image in the eyes of the world, the defence against the shame of collective humiliation, and the desire to make reparations for unjust deeds – determine the execution of foreign policy to a degree that makes analytical differentiation impossible.

All this, however, relates solely to the descriptive level of the analysis of international relations. When it comes to explaining international relations, it is unwise to assume a certain bundle of interests that refer exclusively to a state's desire for self-assertion, in order to then subsequently add a diffuse 'need' for recognition. Rather, state actors define what they regard as necessary for the preservation of the country they represent in line with how they interpret the desires for recognition held by the citizenry. Naturally, rulers or state representatives have a certain amount of leeway in interpreting the smouldering, diverse and barely organized sentiments of the population in one direction or another: that is, in emphasizing either the conciliatory or the hostile elements of the public mood. Only in democratic states, in which the constitution itself is a principles-based interpretation of the nation-state's identity, are rulers compelled to obey certain guidelines while fulfilling the collective striving for recognition. But in no state can political actors simply ignore the population's demands on its collective identity, because this would mean risking the loyalty of the population. Therefore, when political agents interpret and execute the functions accorded to them, they must always consider the expectations of their citizens about the conduct of other states. Authors who, like Hegel, refuse to accept such a connection between foreign policy and collective strivings for identity in the case of civilized states do not have a clear grasp on the significance of the need to secure legitimacy. They believe instead that in explaining international relations, they can ignore moral demands emerging from collective identities, because they refuse to recognize that even modern, functionally differentiated states depend on the consent of the citizens.

If we look for illustrative examples in the recent past, we will find a number of both positive and negative cases. At the negative end of the spectrum, we would find National Socialism's policy of territorial expansion, which cannot be explained without reference to widespread feelings of collective humiliation among the German population owing to the Treaty of Versailles. These feelings even found their way into the definition of external enemies. In this case, it is almost impossible to examine Nazi foreign policy without referring to the successful attempt to take diffuse feelings among the population and concentrate them upon a feeling of national humiliation post-Versailles, thereby creating a justification for an aggressive policy of reparations and revenge.[13] At the other, positive, end of the spectrum, we could cite an example from the very recent past: the new American president's efforts at reconciliation with the rest of the world. We cannot explain these efforts adequately without seeing them as an attempt to overcome a widespread feeling of isolation and shame among the American population. Certainly, both examples are extreme cases of politically mediatized struggles for recognition. In the first case, political rulers formed a narrative of justification on the basis of a diffuse mood among the citizens, which allowed the rulers to engage in a campaign of conquest and revenge. In the second case, a democratically elected president with impressive rhetorical skills has interpreted the paralysing malaise of the majority in a way that allows him to justify reconciliatory gestures towards currently hostile governments. Both examples, as distinct as they might be, clearly illustrate that we cannot divorce a nation's foreign policy aims from the respective demands of the nation's collective identity. The manner in which states react to each other, and the kinds of relations they maintain with each other, derive from a fusion of interests and values brought about by both sides. This fusion consists in the disclosure of foreign policy goals from the perspective of the hypothetical community that joins together a population – interpreted as a collective that is striving for recognition. Therefore, psychological terminology has a place after all – not as an element of our theoretical language, but as one of the objects of that language in political reality. And within that reality, state actors must interpret the population's moods, making use of concepts related both to strivings for recognition and to historical humiliation.

At the same time, the moral spectrum illustrated by these two examples clearly demonstrates just how many directions the political mobilization of collective sentiments can take. The desire to have one's own collective identity be recognized by other peoples can be used to legitimize both an aggressive policy of conquest and a de-escalating policy of reconciliation. This raises questions that are no longer merely descriptive, but touch on the normative dimension of a theory of international relations.

II

In my opinion, we cannot further differentiate the type of recognition that plays a constitutive role in the dynamics of international relations. Unlike social groups or movements, whose own statements can be used to draw conclusions about the specific type of collectively desired recognition, national collectives are far too amorphous for us to be able to make comparable differentiations. Instead, we must content ourselves with the relatively vague assumption that the members of a nation-state generally have a diffuse interest in having their collective self-respect be respected by other states, and in receiving recognition for their common culture and history. Differentiations between various modes of recognition, such as are made in the realm of intersubjective relations,[14] seem inappropriate for entire populations. It is almost impossible to tell whether such populations are striving for signs of goodwill, legal equality or esteem in the eyes of the other side, because their individual members' motives are too diffuse, and because their aims are insufficiently integrated. In any case, such differentiations play a very marginal role when it comes to explaining international relations. What is decisive is not the type of recognition for which a certain population 'actually' strives, but how political actors and rulers interpret its respective moods. The sense of a collective 'We' among the population, which will always have an influence on the definition of foreign policy objectives, is not an empirical but a hypothetical quantity. It arises when disordered and presumed expectations and moods are formed into a collective narrative that makes a certain type of international stance appear justified in the light of past humiliations or desired recognition.[15]

Such narratives of justification give us a key to answering the normative questions that arise when it comes to shaping international relations.[16] After all, the shape of international relations determines the opportunities for changing these relations so as to reduce military conflict and improve prospects for peaceful cooperation. As soon as we turn away from the descriptive problems of a theory of international relations and turn towards the normative problems these relations entail, we must adopt a different perspective on actual conflicts in the world. We then ask no longer how to properly understand conflicts between states, but which measures would have to be taken in order to make such conflicts less likely, and to raise the chances for more peaceful international relations. This second category of questions, however, cannot be wholly separated from the first, because only an appropriate understanding of the causes of international conflict can enable us to envision solutions for overcoming the current state of affairs. The 'realism' of our normative considerations and utopias[17] will increase relative to the correctness of our hypotheses about the considerations that underlie how state actors and governments plan and calculate their relations with other states. The theoretical assumptions I developed in the first section of the essay play a key role at the juncture between empirical facticity and normative considerations. If it is true that states can only define their international relations with the help of narratives of justification that contain a credible and convincing interpretation of the population's interests in collective self-respect, then 'political' relations of recognition at the international level indirectly take on decisive importance as soon as we seek to reduce conflicts between states.

This basic normative idea results from the close connection between collective feelings, on the one hand, and political narratives of justification, on the other. State actors can only disclose and define foreign policy aims by viewing their citizens' elementary desires for security and prosperity in the light of interpretations that constitute a narrative synthesis of the diffuse expectations of the population. At the same time, very narrow limits are imposed on these interpretations, because a summarizing construction of collective feelings must prove to be a halfway appropriate and convincing interpretation of the citizenry's actual, if diffuse, expectations. Narratives intended to justify a hostile and aggressive foreign policy can remain intact only as long as the population has grounds for feeling that its collective self-respect has been violated or insulted by the conduct of other states. If there is no evidence for such disrespect, feelings of humiliation and degradation will not be able to spread among the fragmented public spheres in which citizens move, and the narratives in play will fast lose credibility and thus become incapable of playing this legitimizing role. What is true in the case of aggressive foreign policy can also apply to a policy of willing cooperation and reconciliation. A narrative interpretation that supports such conduct can only be upheld as long as the feeling of having one's own collective self-respect be disrespected by other states does not gain the upper hand. In both cases, the collective feelings of a population that follows the signals of other states with interest and suspicion will prove to be the decisive measure for the success of foreign-political narratives of justification. The greater the distance between the diffuse moods among the citizenry and the official justifications for political conduct, the more difficult it will be for state actors to maintain their foreign policy objectives. Therefore, perhaps we could say that states indirectly codetermine the foreign policy of other states, because the symbolic means with which they convey respect and recognition for other nations constitute an instrument for influencing the formation of public opinion and moods in other countries.

All these considerations have taken us a long way towards answering the normative questions at hand. We saw that the entirety of a state's foreign policy stems from a specific interpretation of interests and values. This interpretation must coordinate the functional requirements for maximizing security and prosperity with the public's expectations about other states' recognition of its own collective identity. For that reason, state actors or governments must base their conduct on narratives meant to justify, in light of historical events and episodes, pursuing the state's interests in an either cooperative or aggressive manner. At the same time, however, we saw that states also exercise an indirect influence on how other states legitimize their foreign policies, because they can influence the formation of public opinion and mood from abroad. The diverse tools used to signal recognition or disrespect constitute a means for casting doubt upon other states' narratives of justification by demonstrating a divergent view of those states' collective identity. These measures drive a wedge between the self-justifications of state actors and the political will-formation of the population; by means of credible expressions of respect and recognition, they attempt to convince another citizenry to mistrust its government's narratives of justification. Although the history of international relations is brimming with examples of such behaviour, they play a very marginal role in the theory. Because the latter interprets state activity largely as purposive-rational behaviour, it lacks the conceptual framework for according the affective dimension of international relations of recognition its proper place. On the normative level, this comes back to haunt the theory in the shape of a procedural lack of imagination about the chances for reducing hostile conflict and expanding relations of peaceful cooperation. The theory instead restricts itself to compromises and agreements under international law, even though the history of international conflict teaches us that collective feelings of recognition or humiliation by other states play a much more significant role.

The path for civilizing international relations lies primarily in sustained efforts at conveying respect and esteem for the collective identity of other countries. Even before legal agreements aimed at promoting peace can do their work, and even before the cultivation of diplomatic relations and economic agreements can reduce international tensions, we need publicly visible signals that the history and culture of other nations are worth being heard among the cacophony of the world's peoples. Only by means of such recognition, which goes over the heads of government representatives and political agents, can we ensure that the citizens of another state no longer believe the demonization practised by political elites, and that they can begin to trust that the other side respects them. The history of international relations contains enough examples to prove that a violation of this normative principle only raises the danger of international conflict, while demonstrable respect for this principle has reduced the potential for such conflicts. Willy Brandt's famous 'Warschauer Kniefall', his act of kneeling before the monument to the martyrs of the Warsaw Ghetto Uprising, was an internationally perceptible gesture that made it nearly impossible for the Polish government to revive formerly prevalent prejudice and resentment about the Federal Republic of Germany.[18] Europe's (and especially Germany's) ignoring of the harsh and determined struggle of the Serbs against the Nazis prepared the way for a fatal policy of overly hasty international recognition of individual ex-Yugoslavian states (Croatia, Kosovo), which drove Serbia's government into increasing isolation and thereby ultimately strengthened ultra-nationalistic narratives among the Serbian public.[19] The lack of sympathy, and perhaps even a total absence of solidarity, on the part of internationally dominant states for the demeaning situation of the Palestinian population continues to fuel a situation in which the local ruling elites' fantasy of taking revenge on Israel finds collective support among the lower, impoverished classes.[20]

We could easily extend this list of examples. We might think of the constant stream of new members joining Islamist terrorist organizations over recent years in order to get a sense of the effects of a policy that fails to extend recognition to other peoples, an act of recognition that would go over the heads of state authorities. The first step towards reconciliation between states, towards developing peaceful and cooperative relations, will always consist in using the soft power of respect and esteem, which signals to a foreign citizenry that its cultural achievements are in no way inferior, and that it can count on others' sympathy for its sufferings. The more explicitly we demonstrate such recognition, the more visible these demonstrations will be to other peoples, and the more we can cast doubt on demonizations serving to justify hostile reactions. The best means a state has at its disposal for counteracting demonization and resentment on the part of other nation-states consists in globally visible and clear signals of willingness to include other citizenries in the international moral community.

Certainly, such symbols of political recognition are not enough to create a solid basis for international cooperation. We need to follow up on efforts to overcome rejectionist attitudes arising from experiences of collective humiliation, to undermine historically grounded and yet long-exploited demonizations, by taking steps towards contractual agreements that secure peaceful relations and long-term arrangements on how to coordinate efforts to meet common challenges. On the basis of that cooperation, more stable networks of transnational communities can arise,[21] such as we might find in the process of European integration.[22] But before such a decentring of state politics can take place, different citizenries must have the experience of recognizing each other's cultural productions and historical achievements, both of which make up the conditions of their collective self-respect. A political theory that fails to gain conceptual access to these affective roots of transnational confidence-building will also be unable to appropriately conceive of the normative conditions for civilizing world politics. Therefore, it is time that we view international relations in a new light – one that differs from the view of Hegel and the political realists following in his wake.

Notes

1 I have taken these examples from Reinhard Wolf, 'Respekt: Ein unterschätzter Faktor in den internationalen Beziehungen', *Zeitschrift für Internationale Beziehungen*, vol. 15, no.1 (2008), pp. 5–42.

2 See Axel Honneth, *The Struggle for Recognition: The Moral Grammar of Social Conflicts*, trans. Joel Anderson (Cambridge: Polity, 1995), ch. 8.

3 G.W.F. Hegel, *Elements of the Philosophy of Right*, trans. H.B. Nisbet (Cambridge: Cambridge University Press, 1991), §§ 338–52.

4 These terms stem from Joseph Nye, *Soft Power: The Means to Success in World Politics* (New York: Public Affairs, 2004).

5 See Charles Taylor, ed., *Multiculturalism* (Princeton: Princeton University Press, 1994); Jürgen Habermas, 'Struggles for Recognition in the Democratic Constitutional State', in ibid., pp. 107–48; Axel Honneth, 'Redistribution as Recognition: A Response to Nancy Fraser', in Nancy Fraser and Axel Honneth, *Redistribution or Recognition? A Political–Philosophical Exchange* (London and New York: Verso, 2003), pp. 110–97.

6 See Hans Kelsen, 'Recognition in International Law: Theoretical Observations', *The American Journal of International Law*, vol. 35, no. 4 (October 1941), pp. 605–17.

7 Ibid., p. 609.

8 Ibid., p. 608.

9 On this perspective within the theory of international relations, see Wolf, 'Respekt'; Jürgen Hacke, 'The Frankfurt School and International Relations: On the Centrality of Recognition', *Review of International Studies*, vol. 31 (2005), pp. 181–94.

10 See John Rawls, *The Law of Peoples* (Cambridge, MA: Harvard University Press, 2001).

11 See Jürgen Habermas, 'Historical Consciousness and Post-Traditional Identity: Remarks on the Federal Republic's Orientation to the West', *Acta Sociologica*, vol. 31, no. 1 (1988), pp. 3–13.

12 Murray Edelman, *The Symbolic Uses of Politics* (Urbana: University of Illinois Press, 1964). For a critique of this book, see Axel Honneth and Rainer Paris, 'Zur Interaktionsanalyse von Politik', *Leviathan*, vol. 7, no. 1 (1979), pp. 138–42.

13 See Patrick Cohrs, *The Unfinished Peace after World War I: America, Britain and the Stabilization of Europe, 1919–1932* (Cambridge: Cambridge University Press, 2006). (I owe this reference to Volker Heins.)

14 See *The Struggle for Recognition*, ch. 5.

15 For the logic of such constructions, see Benedict Anderson, *Imagined Communities: Reflections on the Origin and Spread of Nationalism* (London: Verso, 1983).

16 On the concept of 'narratives of justification', see Rainer Forst and Klaus Günther, 'Über die Dynamik normativer Konflikte: Jürgen Habermas' Philosophie im Lichte eines aktuellen Forschungsprogramms', *Forschung Frankfurt*, vol. 2 (2009), pp. 23–7.

17 See Rawls, *The Law of Peoples*, § 1.

18 For an analysis, see Christoph Schneider, *Der Warschauer Kniefall: Ritual, Ereignis und Erzählung* (Konstanz: UVK Verlagsgesellschaft, 2006); Michael Wolffsohn and Thomas Brechenmacher, *Denkmalsturz? Brandts Kniefall* (Munich: Olzog, 2005).

19 Despite all the idiosyncrasy and hyperbole of Peter Handke's statements on the wars in the former Yugoslavia, his critique of Western Europe's lack of respect for the sufferings of the Serbian population is nevertheless compelling.

20 See 'Suicide Bombers: Dignity, Despair and the Need for Hope. An Interview with Eyad El Sarraj', *Journal of Palestine Studies*, vol. 31, no. 4 (2002), pp. 71–6. (I owe this reference to José Brunner.)

21 See Horst Brunkhorst, 'Demokratie in der globalen Rechtsgenossenschaft – Einige Überlegungen zur posstaatlichen Verfassung der Weltgesellschaft', *Zeitschrift für Soziologie. Sonderheft 'Weltgesellschaft'* (2005), pp. 330–47.

22 Maurizio Bach, ed., *Die Europäisierung nationaler Gesellschaften* (Wiesbaden: Westdeutscher Verlag, 2000).

9

Organized Self-Realization: Paradoxes of Individualization

From its beginnings in the late nineteenth century, sociology, to the extent that it takes the form of a theory of society, has always regarded itself as a discourse on the symptomatic transformation processes of modern societies. In this context, two concepts inherited from classical social philosophy stood at its disposal: first, there is 'rationalization', a term Max Weber used to indicate the gradual expansion of the criteria of purposive rationality to social spheres that still remained under the sway of traditional modes of integration via shared value attachments and affectivity; second, 'individualization' has been used, for example by Durkheim, to describe the process of an increasing and irreversible liberation of the members of society from traditional attachments and stereotypical constraints, thus allowing them to attain greater autonomy and freedom of choice. On the basis of these two concepts, the development of modern societies has often been understood as a process in which rationalization and increasing individualization become institutionally interwoven to an ever greater extent. Despite the significant insights brought about by this conceptual pairing, from the beginning both categories have been attended by problems on multiple levels. With regard to rationalization, it is unclear whether the unified standard of the effectiveness of technical regulations is really what allows us to speak of institutional rationalization in areas as diverse as the organization of the economy, political institutions and our individual and family lives. Regardless of how the processes of institutional transformation in these individual spheres are analysed, it is at least questionable whether they can all be sensibly understood according to the single criterion of increasing purposive rationality. Of course, just as controversial is the use that Durkheim makes of the category of socially induced individualization. In a somewhat similar way to Hegel, he derives an increase in individual choice (*Gestaltungsmöglichkeiten*) from functional differentiation. Even Weber mentions at one point that 'the expression individualism includes the most heterogeneous things imaginable'.[1] From the start the central problem consists in determining the extent to which the description of the pluralization of individual roles, attachments and affiliations can be connected to an increase in personal autonomy. We could probably name a number of criteria for this second aspect – the increase in individual capacities for action and abilities for reflection – which would be open to a certain kind of external observation; but regardless of how we might answer such questions, it seems certain that the individualization of our lives is an easily observable and thus objective process, while the claim about the autonomization of the subject ultimately remains tied to the perspective of partners in interaction. Therefore, the concept of individualization, the second element of the sociological diagnosis of modernity, houses a precarious ambivalence, because it refers both to the external fact of increasing personal qualities and the 'inner' fact of the subject's increasing individual achievements. The structural particularities marking the current process of individualization determined by both these poles constitute the focus of this chapter. Before we proceed, however, some preliminary conceptual clarifications are in order, for the topic is somewhat more multilayered than it would appear at first sight.

I

The sociologist Georg Simmel early on developed a sense for the conceptual distinctions required by his own discipline were it to dissolve the ambiguities in the concept of individualization. More than any other author in the generation of sociology's founders, Simmel was aware of the fundamental difference between the mere fact of increasing personal qualities – i.e. the pluralization of lifestyles made possible by the modern money economy – and the increase in personal autonomy. Although the anonymization of social relationships in urban areas also leads to a dissolution of group affiliations and thus to increased choice, in his view this does not at all imply an increase in individual freedom, for the latter requires the 'sustaining support' of other subjects.[2] But Simmel did more than give an early warning about the need to differentiate between social individualization and increased freedom in order to deliver a proper diagnosis of modern capitalism. He also caused even further complications for sociology's concept of individual-ization by uncovering two further layers of meaning. First, as the analyses in *The Philosophy of Money* make clear, Simmel claims that the empirical processes of pluralization of choice are accompanied by the danger of an impoverishment of social contacts, an increase in intersubjective indifference. Therefore, there is a third element that needs to be differentiated within the concept of individualiza-tion, one that refers to a tendency to isolate the individual subject within a growing network of anonymizing social contacts. This is also a tendency that Simmel claims can only be described from the perspective of an observer. He thus refers not to a process of increas-ing loneliness or isolation felt or suffered, but to the objective fact of increasing concentration on merely individual interests, inde-pendently of others.

More importantly, Simmel recognizes two different aspects in the idea of an increase in freedom, which lead him to further differenti-ate the concept of individualism.[3] He starts by making a distinction with regard to the aim of the second pole of individualization, i.e. autonomization. On the one hand, according to his conception of Latin civilization, the *telos* of the formation of inner freedom refers to an autonomous articulation of beliefs and intentions that can in principle be shared by all humans. This is an individualism of equality, for it refers to the enabling of the individual's capacity for reflection, a defining characteristic of the human species. On the other hand, this notion of autonomy is confronted with a second kind of individualism rooted in German Romanticism, in which the aim of increasing individual freedom is the development of those unique, unmistakeable qualities that distinguish individual subjects. Here we would have to speak of a qualitative individu-alism in the tradition of Herder, Schleiermacher, Nietzsche and Kierkegaard, one which focuses entirely on the articulation of an authentic personality. For Simmel, therefore, the individual increase in freedom runs in both directions: towards an increase in autonomy and towards a growth in authenticity. Between these two poles, there are a variety of tensions that cannot be easily recti-fied in modernity. If we summarize Simmel's sociological investi-gations, we see that he distinguishes between four phenomena to which the concept of individualization could refer: alongside the individualization of lifestyles, which appears to be an empirical fact, there is also the growing isolation of acting subjects, as well as either an increase in the capacity for reflection or an increase in individual authenticity. The difficulty for sociological diagnosis consists in keeping these four developmental processes separate, such that reciprocal connections cannot arise in the first place.

This enormous wealth of meaning could be what has led, over the past hundred years, to entirely different interpretations of individualization in modern societies. In his historical survey, Markus Schroer offers an instructive distinction between three different currents in the evaluation of the process of increasing individuality. On the one side, the growing ascription of individuality by education, administration and the culture industry is described as an advance in discipline from which a peculiar form of conformist individualism has emerged, weakening the individual's reflexive powers of resistance. On the other side, following the tradition of Durkheim and Parsons, detraditionalization and functional pluralization are interpreted as a chance for increasing individuality, which liberates our ability to lead conscious, reflective and self-responsible lives. And in between these two currents, there is a third theoretical school that views the process of individualization as ambiguous, entailing both the emancipation of the individual from traditional attachments and a background increase in conformity.[4] If we turn to the present, the already confusing picture becomes even more complicated. In addition to the three interpretive perspectives described by Schroer, recent accounts view the process of individualization either as an intensification of individual phenomena or as a completely changed structural pattern. In the tradition of communitarianism, for instance, we find a sociological attentiveness to the aspect of individualization that Simmel described as an increase in indifference: because, owing to increased mobility and more frequent career changes, subjects abandon relationships ever more frequently, they are regarded as being only marginally capable of forming attachments, instead developing an increasingly egocentric attitude towards their partners in interaction.[5] While investigations into the cultural consequences of virtualizing social communication point in the same direction,[6] Charles Taylor's recent observations on modernity touch on another topic raised by Simmel: according to Taylor, the romantic ideal of authenticity has become so trivialized that it has lost its dialogical, communitarian aspects and has led to a merely egocentric perspective of self-discovery.[7] Finally, we should mention those empirical studies that refer to the institutional patterns of expectations that turn the development of lived originality into a demand on subjects: more and more, and especially when it comes to skilled labour, the presentation of an 'authentic self' has become a necessity, and it is difficult to distinguish between a 'true' process of self-discovery and one that is merely stylized, even for those involved.[8]

We could surely add a few more observations to this list of new phenomena in the far-reaching sphere of individualization. Especially in social psychology and media sociology, we find recent analyses that could expand the spectrum of processes of individuation and autonomization opened up by Simmel. But even this brief sketch suffices to present the full extent of the difficulty faced by a discussion of the process of individualization. There are too many social appearances, too many radical changes that concern some aspect of individualization for us to be able to point out a clearly outlined pattern of development. When I nevertheless speak of such a schema in the concept of paradox, then I do so only with the methodological reservation that I am presenting only one possible interpretation among many other views that are just as legitimate. The thesis I want to argue for here is that claims to individual self-realization, which have rapidly grown as a result of an historically unique combination of very different processes of individualization in Western societies over the last thirty or forty years, have become such a strongly institutionalized pattern of expectations for social reproduction that they have lost their inner *telos* and instead become a basis for legitimizing the system. The result of this paradoxical transformation, in which those processes that once promised an increase in freedom have now become ideologies of deinstitutionalization, is the emergence of a number of individual symptoms of inner emptiness, the feeling of being superfluous and meaningless. In order to justify this claim, I will proceed in three steps. First, I will attempt to describe the 'elective affinity' that emerged during the 1960s and 1970s in the Western developed countries between entirely independent processes of individualization, such that we could speak of a new form of individualism (II). Next, I will reconstruct the social processes through which, in the following decades, these individual claims, via institutional and organizational acts of conformity, were transformed into institutionalized patterns of expectations that encounter subjects as external demands. Here as well, I will have to restrict myself to a few major trends (III). Finally, in the third step, I will list the social-psychological and clinical indicators suggesting that the paradoxical transformation of the process of individualization threatens to lead to a variety of new forms of social suffering, both material and psychological. This prospect will then allow me to conclude with a surprisingly topical quote by Simmel (IV).

II

Today, from a distance of some forty years, we can easily describe the social and cultural upheavals in Western post-war societies as a process in which diverse and divergent individualizing tendencies were intertwined. So it is not entirely wrong to speak with Ulrich Beck or Anthony Giddens of a new, late modern stage of conscious individualism.[9] Of course, in order to make such a diagnosis we need to be wholly aware of the fact that this emerging form of individuality is not the result of a virtually linear increase, but the outcome of a process of mutual intensification between two wholly separate developmental dynamics. What has happened here can best be described in the words of Max Weber as the confluence of material, social and intellectual processes of transformation that shares, in a kind of 'elective affinity', so many common features that they were capable of bringing forth a new form of individualism.[10] The material foundations for this individualist push stem from a series of socio-structural processes of development, which, operating in conjunction, have led to a pluralization of individual ways of life that can be recounted in a purely descriptive manner. The disproportionate growth of income and free time allowed for the gradual expansion of our individual options, while conversely reducing the influence of class-specific milieus. The expansion of the service sector in the capitalist countries of the West brought about a broad process of social upward mobility through which people's lives became increasingly diverse. And with the expansion of education throughout the West roughly fifteen years after the end of the Second World War, career options multiplied as well, further contributing to a differentiation between people's life plans. By the time of the student uprisings in the late 1960s, the population had already become far more pluralistic and diverse in terms of biographical development and forms of life than had been the case ten years prior.

In addition to the objective tendencies towards an increase in the range of options, there are indicators that offer at least vague signs that individuals' capacity for autonomy, which can ultimately only be grasped in a performative sense, rose in the same period. It would therefore have been astounding if the expansion of educational opportunities had not been accompanied by a substantial increase in chances for individual self-realization and reflection.[11] The dissolution of class-specific milieus emerging on the basis of the reform of the education system, as well as through the reconstruction of urban areas, might have done its part to expand individuals' horizons of conceivable life-paths and thus also increase their options for experimentation. Referring to tendencies towards an intensifying crisis of adolescence, empirical studies show that in the early 1970s the general potential for autonomous identity formation had risen considerably.[12] But whatever the individual social causes, it seems clear that within only two decades, forms of life had become strongly individualized: members of Western societies were compelled, urged or encouraged, for the sake of their own future, to place themselves at the centre of their own life plans and lives.

But all of these socio-structural transformation processes would not have sufficed to lead to a truly new form of individualism had they not been accompanied by other, more social and cultural transformations and attitude changes. Although we could say that without the objective expansion of individual options the new cultural ideals would not have had a chance to establish themselves, the roots of these ideals lie in entirely separate regions. Rising incomes accompanying post-war economic growth were what allowed possibilities for moderately luxurious consumption, but the specific significance that individuals increasingly attached to this process derived from wholly different, cultural sources. According to Colin Campbell, the need to find an increase in one's own *joie de vivre* by consuming cultural products not necessary for survival derives from religious, mostly Protestant undercurrents in which, as an alternative to the Calvinist work ethic, the extraordinary state of affective arousal was interpreted as a sign of the goodness and grace of God. Once the religious roots of this desire for imaginary stimulation had been extinguished as a result of sentimentalism and the Romantic ethic, it could become a normative spark for massive investment in consumer goods that increase the feeling of intensity, lending the mundane consumerism of the post-war era its specific character as an anchor for identity.[13] What is true of consumerism in particular also seems to apply to a number of different behavioural changes. In general, the dismantling of rigid demands on individual behaviour does not simply lead to the formation of a new ideal type of personality, but increases broadly the chance to acquire cultural traditions previously reserved for a few minorities, which only secondarily motivated the development of changed patterns of identity. The socio-structural processes of transformation that increasingly place individuals at the centre of their own life plans enabled the widespread acceptance of interpretive schemes with largely Romantic origins, passed down through small, sect-like groups, which cast life as a process of experimental self-realization.

A good example of this 'elective affinity' and linkage between social change and cultural transformation is that process of behavioural change referred to in hindsight as the 'sexual revolution'. After all, the dissolution of conventional roles, which became possible in the course of the pluralization of lifestyles in the 1960s, did not by itself suggest the revaluation of sexuality as a preferred field for experimenting with one's own individuality. Instead, what was needed was a broad acceptance of an already-existing, albeit minority, cultural ideal whereby humans were interpreted primarily as 'subjects of desire' (Foucault); a style of comportment could then be formed in which constant promiscuous experimentation could be experienced as an expression of individual self-realization. Furthermore, perhaps the most crucial medium for the dissemination of these traditional interpretive patterns was the reception of certain novels, such as those by Hermann Hesse or Henry Miller, as well as the emergence of rock music. The normative gaps that sprang up as a result of these newly developed, socio-structurally enabled freedoms were almost exclusively filled by the acceptance of quasi-Romantic traditions that encouraged people to experience their own biography as a process of tentatively realizing the core of their own, unique personality. In this way, the confluence of socio-structural individualization and the Romantic ideal of authenticity produced what could be described as the compact structure of a new kind of individualism. Further accelerated by the multiplication of social relationships, subjects increasingly lost their willingness to grasp their own life as a linear process of identity development, at the end of which stood their career roles and the gender-specific division of labour in the family. In place of the relatively stiff schema of identity upon which Parsons bases his theory, the opening up of new options – through membership in various social milieus, stronger contacts with lifestyles previously considered to be strange and foreign, and the acceptance of Romantic patterns of interpretation – led to a tendency to view diverse possibilities of identity as material for experimental self-realization. In Simmel's terms, a 'qualitative' kind of individualism arose: subjects experimented with various forms of existence in order to realize the core of their own self in the light of their experiences, a core that distinguishes them from all others. The continuation of this nascent process of transformation consists in the fact that key social organizations creatively adapt to this new ideal of behaviour in order to turn it into a profile of existence that serves to increase social effectiveness; the ideal thus forms the basis for legitimizing more far-reaching processes of reorganization.

III

In the mid-1970s, the social process of transformation I have just described as the confluence of material and intellectual developments led Daniel Bell to draw sweeping conclusions about growing contradictions within capitalism.[14] Bell mainly based his theory on cultural upheavals in the aftermath of the student movement, claiming that a new, hedonistic everyday morality had arisen, one that would necessarily come into conflict with the economic requirements of capitalism. The values of aesthetic creativity and sensuous impulsiveness, which he believed had spread beyond the subcultures of the artistic avant-garde and penetrated the behavioural orientations of a large portion of the population, represented an ever-greater hindrance to the formation of the work ethic still needed to preserve economic efficiency. Even from our current vantage point, we can say with certainty that this sociological prognosis has not been borne out; the new 'qualitative' individualism, which can easily be discerned in Bell's description of the hedonistic character-type, has not had a negative impact on the productivity of capitalist economic enterprise. It is true that the growing demand for self-realization and experimental identity-seeking have left their mark on growing divorce rates, falling birth rates and changes in the structure of the family.[15] According to Anthony Giddens, parent–child relationships have become increasingly fractured and short-lived, because they have become more and more like 'pure' relationships in which mutual attachment only feeds on the fleeting material of one's own feelings and inclinations.[16] Increasingly prevalent is also the tendency to spend a great deal of energy on so-called 'hobbies', which are experienced no longer as rest and recuperation from the working week, but as an experimental attempt to define one's own self.[17] Finally, the consumption of luxury goods has grown significantly over the last few decades with the familiar differences in social strata, because such consumption is viewed as an opportunity, at least for a short period, to aesthetically represent identities in flux.[18] Nevertheless, all these developmental tendencies, which undoubtedly point in the direction of an 'individualism of irreplaceability' (*Individualismus der Unverwechselbarkeit*) (Simmel), in no way conflict with the functional requirements of the capitalist economy; on the contrary, we cannot entirely avoid the impression that they have become a productive force, albeit one that is peculiarly misused for capitalist modernization.

Even the processes of transformation that thereby came into view cannot be understood as a mere outflow of a single developmental process; nor does it seem appropriate to conceive of them as intentionally connected chains of actions – that is, consciously effected reactions. Instead, the notion of transformational processes joined in 'elective affinity' seems more plausible for explaining why the demand for self-realization since the last third of the twentieth century has been increasingly reformulated as an institutional demand. At first hesitantly, then more and more intensely, individuals are expected to present themselves as biographically flexible subjects willing to change continuously in order to succeed in their careers or in society.[19] Electronic media have certainly had a pioneering role in this process of redirection; their increased significance in everyday life now makes a much stronger contribution to sustaining the stylistic ideal of an original, creative life. Even though, as Adorno presumed,[20] individuals are usually sceptical about the ways of life presented in the media, it is possible that the ideal of self-realization is experienced as a more subtle demand on the formation of our own subjectivity.[21] The border between reality and fiction might be blurry in certain individual cases, thus creating a subconscious tendency to search for one's self in those places where television or cinema presumes its idols to be. Perhaps, therefore, we could say that there is a certain tendency to follow standardized patterns of identity-seeking, in order to in fact experimentally discover the core of one's own personality.

The marketing strategies developed by the consumer industry over recent decades in order to accelerate sales have probably also had a comparable effect. Here we see a tendency to advertise with the promise that by buying this or that good, consumers can acquire an aesthetic means for presenting and increasing the originality of their chosen lifestyles.[22] Instrumentalizing the demand for self-realization in this way has led to the emergence of an accelerating spiral of stylistic innovation and response, because every new self-image is quickly turned into the encoded content of the next marketing strategy. By now, we might even get the impression that the relation of dependency has been reversed, since the fashion and consumer industries seem capable of propagating images of authentic living worthy of imitation, which guide subjects in their search for identity. The attempt to achieve self-realization in the course of one's own life gets subtly organized by the cultural offers that the advertising industry makes to individuals – with a calculated sensitivity for differences in age, social gender and rank.

However, doubtlessly more important than these effects, whose social reach also seems questionable, is the restructuring of the production and services sector that occurred in the 1980s. What happened in this era has been described economically as a dismantling of Fordist production methods, but what is decisive for our purposes is the entirely new conception of working subjects that has accompanied it. The latter are addressed no longer institutionally as employees but as creative 'entrepreneurs' or self-employed persons.[23] When theorists now speak of a 'normative subjectification of labour'[24] and an increased esteem for individual labour,[25] then this first of all means that workers' intellectual initiative has been increasingly called upon in the organization of production and services. New management concepts, such as levelling hierarchies, encouraging teamwork, team-autonomy and self-direction, are to accommodate demands for self-realization on the part of employees seeking opportunities to autonomously contribute and sell (*Entäußerung*) the skills they have learned. But it has soon become clear that the new, post-Taylorist entrepreneurial strategies have had an entirely different effect, making labour more and more conceivable as a 'vocation', in turn allowing wholly different expectations of workers: their motivation should be tailored intrinsically to the activities demanded of them; they must be willing to present every change in their job description as a product of their own decision, and their active involvement must be dedicated to the good of the entire company. This is how, in the span of only three decades, a new system of demands has been established, allowing employment to be made dependent on a convincing presentation of a desire for self-realization in the workplace. This inversion in turn has created the space for justifying measures of deregulation with reference to the obsolescence of status and

seniority in the workplace, given employees' growing willingness
to take on individual responsibility. The pressure this puts on both
'white-collar' and 'blue-collar' workers assumes an extremely paradoxical form: employees, for the sake of their own future careers,
must construct their own job history according to the pattern of
self-realization, even though they most likely only desire a measure
of social and economic security.[26]

It would probably be not entirely wrong to see in these processes
a tendency to transform increased demands for self-realization into
a productive force in the capitalist economy. Subjects' inclination to
view their lives more and more as an experimental search for their
own identity not only serves as a basis for legitimizing a series of
measures aimed at economic restructuring, the goal of which is to
deregulate industry and the service sector;[27] this new individualism is also used as a production factor directly: on the basis of these
seemingly changed needs on the part of workers, the latter are to
display more active involvement, flexibility and initiative than
would have been the case in a socially regulated kind of capitalism. However, to me it seems misleading to interpret this tendency
as an intentional strategy employed by clever and cooperative
managers as a response to the 'hedonistic' critique of capitalism
that emerged in the 1960s. The 'new spirit of capitalism', investigated by Luc Boltanski and Ève Chiapello in a fascinating study
by the same name,[28] instead seems to be the unintended result of
a number of different, connected processes, each of which has its
own history and developmental dynamic. If we take the structural
transformations in the field of electronic media, the advertising
industry and the sphere of production, and add in the increase
in diffuse, everyday expectations of individual self-realization, then
we will arrive at the same conclusion as Boltanski and Chiapello
in their own investigation: the processes of instrumentalization,
standardization and fictionalization have turned the individualism
of self-realization, which has been gradually developing over the
last half-century, into an emotionally barren system of demands
within which individuals today seem more likely to suffer than to
prosper.

IV

With the institutional changes that Western capitalism has undergone over the past thirty years, self-realization, once a relevant

ideal to be strived for, has developed into an ideology and a productive force in a deregulated economic system. The demands that
subjects voiced once they began to interpret their lives as an experimental process of identity-seeking have now returned to them as
diffuse external demands, compelling them – implicitly or explicitly – to keep their biographical aims and options open. This transformation of ideals into constraints, and claims into external
demands, has given rise to forms of social discontent and suffering
previously unknown in Western societies, at least as mass phenomena. To be sure, this is not true of the everyday malaise that Bourdieu
and his colleagues sought to grasp in *The Weight of the World*:[29]
when deregulation and unemployment create a growing class of
permanently superfluous people; when international corporations
operating across borders keep an eye out for constantly new forms
of labour contracts that elude government regulation; when immi-
grant workers from poor countries come to occupy Western cities
in their search for job opportunities; the same forms of unprotected
labour present at the birth of capitalist industrialization return:
temporary work, part-time work and working at home.[30] The
growing flexibility of the labour market, the creeping commercialization of society as a whole, both of which have been justified in
a fragile manner by invoking this new individualism, have caused
the 'social question' to become a challenge once again – a question
that, in the second half of the twentieth century, was thought to
have been successfully taken care of in the nineteenth century.

But below this threshold of visibility, other forms of social suffering have spread over the last few decades; in a certain sense, they
are without precedent in the history of capitalist societies. They are
much less accessible to empirical observation because they exist in
the sphere of psychological illness, and thus there are only clinical
indicators available to detect them. In an impressive study bearing
the title *The Weariness of the Self*,[31] French sociologist Alain Ehrenberg concludes on the basis of the clinical material that we are now
encountering a rapid rise in depression. A growing number of
therapeutic findings, along with the unprecedented trend towards
the use of pharmaceutical anti-depressants, indicate that depres-
sion-related illnesses are displacing neurosis. According to Ehrenberg, the key to explaining this widespread clinical illness is the
idea that individuals have become psychologically overwhelmed
by the diffuse demand that they must be themselves. The permanent compulsion to draw on one's own inner life to find the material needed for authentic self-realization demands from subjects

a constant form of introspection that at some point has to come up empty. And the point at which psychological experiences no longer point the way forward, even with the strongest of efforts, is where Ehrenberg marks the moment at which depression begins. It might be that the point at which the ideal of self-realization passes over into compulsion marks the historical threshold at which the experience of emptiness has become common to a growing part of the population. Compelled from all sides to remain open to the psychological impulses of authentic identity-seeking, subjects are faced with the alternative of feigning authenticity or fleeing into depression; they are forced to choose between staging originality for strategic reasons and pathologically shutting down (*krankhafte Verstummung*). Given the perspicacity with which Simmel observed the social and cultural transformations of his time, it is not surprising that his *Philosophy of Money* contains a precognition of this situation. On the ideal of self-realization he writes:

> It is true he [the peasant at the end of the Middle Ages] gained freedom, but only freedom *from* something, not liberty *to do* something. Apparently, he gained freedom to do anything – because it was purely negative – but in fact he was without any directive, without any definite and determining content. Such freedom favours that emptiness and instability that allows one to give full rein to every accidental, whimsical and tempting impulse. Such freedom may be compared with the fate of the insecure person who has forsworn his Gods and whose newly acquired 'freedom' only provides the opportunity for making an idol out of any fleeting value.[32]

Notes

1   Max Weber, *The Protestant Ethic and the Spirit of Capitalism*, trans. Talcott Parsons (Mineola, NY: Dover Publications, 1958), p. 222, n. 22.
2   Georg Simmel, 'Individualismus', in *Schriften zur Soziologie: Eine Auswahl*, eds Heinz-Jürgen Dahme and Otthein Rammstedt (Frankfurt/Main: Suhrkamp, 1983), pp. 267–74.
3   Ibid.
4   Markus Schroer, *Das Individuum in der Gesellschaft* (Frankfurt/Main: Suhrkamp, 2001).
5   Robert D. Putnam, *Bowling Alone: The Collapse and Revival of American Community* (New York: Simon & Schuster, 2000).

6   Andreas Wittel, 'Towards a Network Sociability', *Theory, Culture and Society*, vol. 18, no. 6 (2001), pp. 51–76; Hubert L. Dreyfus, *On the Internet* (London: Routledge, 2001).

7   Charles Taylor, *The Ethics of Authenticity* (Cambridge, MA: Harvard University Press, 1992).

8   Martin Baethge, 'Arbeit, Vergesellschaftung, Identität: Zur zunehmenden normativen Subjektivierung der Arbeit', *Soziale Welt*, vol. 42 (1991), pp. 6–19; Hermann Kocyba, 'Der Preis der Anerkennung: Von der tayloristischen Missachtung zur strategischen Instrumentalisierung der Subjektivität der Arbeitenden', in Ursula Holtgrewe, Stephan Voswinkel and Gabriele Wagner, eds, *Anerkennung und Arbeit* (Konstanz: UVK, 2000), pp. 127–40.

9   Ulrich Beck, *Risk Society: Towards a New Modernity*, trans. Mark Ritter (London: Sage, 1992); Anthony Giddens, *Modernity and Self-Identity: Self and Society in the Late Modern Age* (Cambridge: Polity, 1991).

10 Weber, *The Protestant Ethic and the Spirit of Capitalism*.

11 Jürgen Habermas, *Theory of Communicative Action*, vol. 2: *Lifeworld and System: A Critique of Functionalist Reason*, trans. Thomas McCarthy (Cambridge: Polity, 1987).

12 Rainer Döbert and Gertrud Nunner-Winkler, *Adoleszenzkrise und Identitätsbildung* (Frankfurt/Main: Suhrkamp, 1975).

13 Colin Campbell, *The Romantic Ethic and the Spirit of Modern Consumerism* (Oxford: Blackwell, 1987).

14 Daniel Bell, *The Cultural Contradictions of Capitalism* (New York: Basic Books, 1976).

15 Kurt Lüscher, Franz Schultheis and Michael Wehrspaun, eds, *Die postmoderne Familie* (Konstanz: UVK, 1990); Hartmut Tyrell, 'Ehe und Familie – Institutionalisierung und Deinstitutionalisierung', in ibid., pp. 145–56.

16 Giddens, *Modernity and Self-Identity*, ch. 3.

17 See Dean MacCannell, 'Staged Authenticity: Arrangements of Social Space in Tourist Settings', *American Journal of Sociology*, vol. 79, no. 3 (1973), pp. 589–603.

18 Eva Illouz, *Consuming the Romantic Utopia: Love and the Cultural Contradictions of Capitalism* (Berkeley: University of California Press, 1997).

19 Richard Sennett, *The Corrosion of Character* (New York: W. & W. Norton, 1998); Sighard Neckel, 'Identität als Ware: Die Marktwirtschaft im Sozialen', in *Die Macht der Unterscheidung: Essays zur Kultursoziologie der modernen Gesellschaft* (Frankfurt/Main: Campus, 2000), pp. 37–47.

20 Theodor W. Adorno, 'Freizeit', in *Gesammelte Schriften*, vol. 10.2 (Frankfurt/Main: Suhrkamp, 1977), pp. 645–55.
21 John B. Thompson, *The Media and Modernity: A Social Theory of the Media* (Stanford: Stanford University Press, 1995), ch. 7.
22 Rob Shields, ed., *Lifestyle Shopping: The Subject of Consumption* (London: Routledge, 1992).
23 Günter Voss and Hans Pongratz, 'Der Arbeitskraftunternehmer: Eine neue Grundform der Ware Arbeitskraft?', *Kölner Zeitschrift für Soziologie und Sozialpsychologie*, vol. 50 (1998), pp. 131–58.
24 Baethge, 'Arbeit, Vergesellschaftung, Identität'.
25 Kocyba, 'Der Preis der Anerkennung'.
26 Johann Behrens, '"Selbstverwirklichung" oder: Vom Verblassen aller Alternativen zur Berufsarbeit: Umfragen und Fallstudien zur Krise der Arbeit in Familie und Erwerbsarbeit', in Hans-Joachim Hoffmann-Novotny and Friedhelm Gehrmann, eds, *Ansprüche an die Arbeit: Umfragedaten und Interpretationen* (Frankfurt/Main: Campus, 1984), pp. 117–35; Sennett, *The Corrosion of Character*.
27 Robert Castel, *From Manual Workers to Wage Laborers: Transformation of the Social Question*, trans. and ed. Richard Boyd (New Brunswick, NJ: Transaction Publishers, 2003).
28 Luc Boltanksi and Ève Chiapello, *The New Spirit of Capitalism*, trans. Gregory Elliott (London: Verso, 2007).
29 Pierre Bourdieu et al., *The Weight of the World: Social Suffering in Contemporary Society* (Cambridge: Polity, 1999).
30 Castel, *From Manual Workers to Wage Laborers*.
31 Alain Ehrenberg, *The Weariness of the Self: Diagnosing the History of Depression in the Contemporary Age*, trans. Enrico Caouette et al. (Montreal: McGill-Queens University Press, 2010).
32 Georg Simmel, *The Philosophy of Money*, trans. Tom Bottomore and David Frisby (London: Routledge, 1990), p. 402.

10

Paradoxes of Capitalist Modernization: A Research Programme*

Over the last 150 years it has become natural to analyse the development of capitalist societies by means of a schema in which a positively construed process of rationalization or emancipation runs again and again into contradiction with the delaying, blocking or even colonizing structural relations of the economy. In the course of time the shape of what is meant by processes of rationalization or emancipation has indeed been progressively enriched; however, the idea of a structural restriction by the capitalist system is always retained. Even if one counts on the internal logic of the communicative rationalization of the lifeworld, the leading developmental schema is still growing opposition to the world of economic functional laws that take on a life of their own. Anyone who sets out to investigate the new transformations of Western capitalist societies today will quickly run up against the deficits of this long-serving model. Not only can the borders between culture and the economy, lifeworld and system, no longer be unambiguously determined, but today what counts as progress is more contested than ever before. What is confusing – indeed, perplexing – about the contemporary situation may be that, while the normative principles of past decades still possess a performative currency, beneath the surface they seem to have lost their emancipatory meaning or been transformed; in many instances they have become mere legitimizing concepts for a new level of capitalist expansion. In the following we seek to pursue this transformed, opaque form of capitalist 'modernization' by replacing the old schema of

*With Martin Hartmann.

contradiction with that of paradoxical development. By this we have in mind the peculiar fact that today much of the normative progress of the last decades has been turned into its opposite, a culture that decreases solidarity and independence, and, under the pressure of a neoliberal de-domestification of capitalism, has become a mechanism of social integration.

I   Normative potentials of capitalist societies

The starting point of our analysis is the historical period twenty years after the end of the Second World War in which a state-regulated capitalism emerged in the developed countries of the West that, owing to its counter-cyclical social and economic policies, was able to create a welfare-state arrangement. In this phase, which bore the marks of a social-democratic regime even where Social Democratic parties did not attain a governing majority,[1] not only were the conditions for effective forms of equal opportunity significantly improved in the realms of education, social policy and labour policy, but in all key areas the normative integration of capitalist societies showed moral progress far beyond what had previously been taken to be compatible with the basic requirements of capitalism. To get an overview of these developmental processes, it makes sense first of all to enumerate the central spheres that together from the beginning brought about the normative integration of capitalism. Here we loosely follow Parsons' picture of the evolution of modern societies, but give his impressive sketch a recognition-theoretical interpretation in order to do justice to the interactive and justificatory character of the normative spheres.[2] With Parsons it can be said that in modern societies the establishment of a capitalist economic system only succeeded because the following principles were simultaneously institutionalized: (1) 'individualism' as a leading personal idea; (2) an egalitarian conception of justice as a legal form of government; and (3) the idea of achievement as the basis for assigning status. We supplement these assumptions by further supposing that (4) with the romantic idea of love a utopian vanishing point emerged that allowed members of society increasingly subject to economic pressures to preserve the vision of an emotional transcendence of day-to-day instrumentalism.[3]

Now, each of the spheres – which naturally should be thought of not as spatially demarcated areas but as social forms of moral knowledge[4] – possesses a normative potential, since the idea that underlies them always contains more legitimizable claims and obligations than are realized in the facticity of social reality. It is true that Parsons only worked out this tension between reality and the normative idea, between facts and norms, for the two dimensions of modern law and the achievement principle, but it can likewise call our attention to the modern principles of individualism and love. Accordingly, Western capitalist society should be understood as a highly dynamic social order whose capacity for self-transformation arises not only out of the imperatives of the constant realization of capital, but also from the institutionalized normative surplus that stems from its new, emerging spheres of recognition. By calling upon the moral ideals that constitutively underlie them, members of society can always assert and prosecute legitimizable claims that point beyond the established social order. In particular, this means that subjects can:

1 assert the normative promise of institutionalized individualism by experimentally referring to aspects of their autonomy or facets of their authenticity that have not so far found appropriate recognition in the social culture;
2 enforce the modern legal order's idea of equality by pointing to their membership or structural aspects of their life circumstances in order to be treated as equals among equals;
3 assert the normative implications of the modern achievement principle by referring to the actual value of their labour for social reproduction in order to attain greater social esteem and the material compensation connected to it; and, finally,
4 enforce the moral promise of romantic love by calling attention to needs or wishes that the institutionalized practice of intimate relationships has hitherto failed to meet with appropriate sensitivity and responsiveness.

Parsons already showed that in modern society the normative surplus of such institutionalized norms of justice possesses a transformative potential above all because they make the given reality appear as a moral situation of discrimination that cannot be legitimized.[5] From this we can gather that there are at least four spheres of recognition in which subjects can experience social relations as morally unjustified discrimination or exclusion. Now, the margin that exists for articulating the normative surplus is determined by the political extent to which capitalist imperatives are neutralized:

the more the state is in a position to check the accumulation tendencies of capital by means of regulatory social and economic policy, the greater the opportunity for members of society to assert, and sometimes institutionally implement, the moral potentials in the four spheres. It therefore seems to us justified to understand the social-democratic era as a phase in the development of capitalist societies marked by an exceptional degree of normative progress. In all four spheres, moral developments emerged that pointed towards an expansion of the respective recognition norms.

II   Moral progress in the social-democratic era

It is not difficult to cite evidence of moral progress in the four spheres during this period. The social-democratic arrangement established in nearly all capitalist countries since the late 1960s allowed either the increase or the generalization of norms that had been institutionalized in the culture of capitalism with a corresponding normative surplus.

   1   Under the combined influence of socioeconomic and cultural transformations, in the social-democratic era institutionalized individualism grew into the idea of experimental self-realization, at the centre of which is the idea of a lifelong testing of new forms of authentic existence. The disproportional growth of incomes and free time, on the one hand, and the rapid spread of romantic life-ideals, on the other, allowed a growing part of the population to interpret their lives no longer as fixed and linear processes of sequentially assuming professional and familial roles, but as opportunities for the experimental realization of their own personalities.[6] If 'individualism' had formerly been an ideal of leading an autonomous life largely reserved for the upper classes, now, in the new, augmented version of the ideal of authenticity, it took hold of the majority of the population.
   2   In no other domain was moral progress clearer in the twenty years of the social-democratic era than in the sphere of the modern legal order. Not only, under pressure from those affected, were forms of legal discrimination that had prohibited, sanctioned or made taboo the practices of cultural or sexual minorities abolished, but also in many areas, new freedoms and social rights (labour, criminal and family law) were created that enhanced the economic and social preconditions for the development of individual auton-

omy. Parallel to the expansion of subjective rights there was also a generalization of legal equality; for the first time, either previously excluded groups (foreigners) came to enjoy citizen rights or cultural minorities obtained new special rights (cultural rights). All in all, it can probably be said that in this phase the legal autonomy of all members of society was better protected than in all previous periods of capitalism.

3   Moral progress also took place in this period with reference to the modern achievement principle, as the women's movement succeeded in calling its masculine-industrial construction into question on a large scale. Even if these protests and claims did not lead directly to institutional success, tendencies nevertheless emerged to thematize child-rearing as well as housework as valuable contributions to social reproduction that should be valued as 'achievements' (*Leistungen*) and find corresponding material recognition. In the same period, however, there were also various educational reforms that shared the aim of improving the conditions for equal social opportunity. With the attempt to increase the permeability of educational institutions and dismantle barriers based on origins, there was greater scope for individuals to successfully take part in the competition for achievement (*Leistungswettbewerb*).

4   Finally, in this phase, intimate relationships were freed from the last vestiges of external social or economic steering. Not least connected to the general rise in incomes, subjects could be left completely to their own feelings in their search for a partner. With this establishment of 'pure relationships',[7] not only did social mobility in marriage increase, so did the deinstitutionalization of the nuclear family. Intimate relationships were entered into for their emotional value, and no longer for lifelong security or progeny.

III   The neoliberal revolution

Having portrayed the normative achievements of the social-democratic era, we must now address the economic developments that, particularly since the beginning of the 1980s, contributed to delegitimizing state-regulated capitalism in its different integrative functions. We collect these developments under the heading of the 'neoliberal revolution'. This term refers, first, to a transformation of economic processes themselves, often confirmed by industrial sociology, but also to the increasing expansion of evaluative standards, tied to 'new' economic organizational structures, into spheres of action that, in the social-democratic era, could still restrict or at least channel unmediated economic pressures in light of the normative principles discussed above.

From this double perspective, capitalism can be described, on the one hand, as an economic system that follows its own laws of motion and, as Parsons always emphasized,[8] is in its own way normatively integrated; but also, on the other hand, as a social system that continually forces social-political institutions to adapt to transformed economic structures. Here we use the concept of the neoliberal revolution to describe all the processes that (1) so weaken (welfare-)state steering activities that safeguards can no longer be guaranteed at post-war levels. Especially in connection with globalization research, the factors are now analysed that lead to the weakening of welfare regimes guaranteed by the nation-state (even if the concept of 'globalization' is not uncontested[9]). Terminologically, in this context one occasionally speaks of 'disorganized capitalism', often blamed especially on the growing power of global firms, the internationalization of financial flows and the fading of class-cultural ties, which have weakened the social-democratic model of political organization.[10] From a firm-internal perspective, the neoliberal revolution can be described (2) by the spread of shareholder-oriented management, where the influence of shareholders on the firm grows to precisely the extent that that of other groups with a stake in the firm dwindles: 'The share price reflects the firm's value through the lenses of the shareholders and is blind to the firm's value for all other groups involved: for workers, banks, the region, the state, suppliers, purchasers and consumers.'[11] This has been called 'shareholder capitalism'. For our purposes, what is particularly central is the transformation of contemporary capitalism (3) that concerns what Luc Boltanski and Ève Chiapello, with reference to Max Weber, call the 'spirit' of capitalism. The starting point of these reflections is the assumption that capitalist practices require justification, that they cannot mobilize sufficient motivational resources by themselves. Following Boltanski and Chiapello's analysis, while between 1930 and 1960 the large company offered its employees long-term career opportunities and under some circumstances even a protected social environment by means of worker apartments, holiday centres and training structures, contemporary capitalism can be described as 'project-oriented'. In the framework of a project-oriented 'order of justification' or 'polity' (*cité par projets*), the more valuable people are those who can engage in new projects with great personal application and flexibility, who possess good networking skills and act autonomously as well as faithfully.[12] Terminologically, in this context one speaks of 'new' or 'flexible' capitalism. The most important criterion for describing this new capitalism is no longer the ability to efficiently fulfil hierarchically determined parameters within a large enterprise; it is the readiness to show initiative and bring one's own abilities and emotional resources to bear in the service of individualized projects. In this way, the worker becomes an 'entreployee' or himself an entrepreneur; no longer induced to participate in capitalist practices by external compulsion or incentives, he is in a sense self-motivated.[13] It is above all this 'network capitalism' and its inherent principles that are responsible for the trends we will discuss in section V under the heading of desolidarization.

Our thesis is that this 'new', 'disorganized', shareholder value-oriented capitalism affects in one way or another the normatively structured spheres of action distinguished above, bringing about developments that lead to the reversal of these institutionalized normative achievements. What is essential for the influence of contemporary capitalism on these spheres is the fact that this influence cannot be understood as a colonizing attack of capitalist imperatives on the action model of the lifeworld. As is well known, the description of economic action as a merely instrumentally oriented activity has been repeatedly criticized for its neglect of its internal normative aspects. But apart from this systematic point, our sketch of contemporary capitalism shows the continuing validity of the statement that 'capitalist societies were always dependent on cultural boundary conditions that they could not reproduce themselves'.[14] When Jürgen Habermas formulated this sentence in his study of the 'legitimation problems of late capitalism' at the beginning of the 1970s, it was connected to the diagnostic thesis that the traditional motivational resources of capitalist action ('citizen' and 'familial-professional privatism') would be eroded by the attainments of the welfare state; the contradiction between capital and labour, which continued to pervade late capitalist societies, would be robbed of its legitimizing garb in the light of a morality that is critically oriented towards increasingly universalistic criteria. On this interpretation, late capitalist society is contradictory in terms both of 'latent' class antagonisms[15] as well as of a logic of development that leads the detraditionalizing tendencies of welfare-state capitalism to self-destructively expose the inequalities and injustices typical of this stage of capitalism.

It is easy to see that contemporary capitalism has succeeded in mobilizing new motivational resources – both on the basis of the critique made by welfare-state agents themselves and with reference to the critical objections to Taylorist or Fordist work structures. In other words, the 'new' capitalism can only be so successful and counteract the political neutralization of the imperatives connected with it because, from the perspective of influential interest groups, it at least appears as an integrative model in its own right that contributes to maintaining some of the institutionalized achievements of the social-democratic era under changed socioeconomic conditions, recasting them in a modernized form. It is precisely this tendency towards a normatively charged economization of social contexts that produces some of the paradoxical effects treated in the fifth section of this chapter, since they are now as it were encouraged or legitimized in the name of normative principles fundamental to the Western self-understanding. Behind these reflections is the assumption that the contradictions and insecurities of the 'new' capitalism map onto spheres of action that are removed from capitalist imperatives or structured by solidarity. Thus, in an often complicated and paradoxical way, they contribute to the erosion of the emancipatory norms and values articulated and institutionalized in these spheres. These contradictions – and this may already be a central paradox of the current period – are of course often no longer even perceived as those of capitalism as such, since subjects have 'learned' in their role as entreployees to assume responsibility for their own fate.

IV   On the concept of paradox[16]

Here it will be helpful to delimit more precisely the concept of paradox. It should have become clear from what has been said so far that we are introducing the concept of paradox not in opposition to that of contradiction, but rather as an explication of a *specific* structure of contradiction. Many experiential situations now described as contradictory have their starting point in the practical conversion of normative intentions. A contradiction is paradoxical when, precisely through the attempt to realize such an intention, the probability of realizing it is decreased.[17] In especially striking cases, the attempt to realize an intention creates conditions that run counter to it. In order to be able to confirm such paradoxical effects, on this thesis, we must draw on a normative vocabulary by means of which these effects can be referred to particular 'original' intentions. In the context of our reflections, this function is fulfilled by the four normative spheres mentioned above, which must of course be interpreted as the always open-ended results of social struggles within whose framework subjects seek the recognition or appreciation of their personal characteristics, rights, achievements or emotional needs. However, these struggles for recognition or appreciation do not of themselves or necessarily produce paradoxical effects. Rather, all the transformative processes collected here under the term 'neoliberal revolution' serve as a structural condition of these struggles and thereby modify their form as well as their consequences. Under the growing pressure of capitalist imperatives, on this assumption, the institutionalized interpretive models of individualism, law, achievement and love are transformed in what can only be called a paradoxical way.

There are three points connected with a transformation of the 'classical' concept of contradiction into the concept of 'paradoxical' contradiction.

(a)   First, talk of paradoxical contradictions must do without a clear juxtaposition of progressive and regressive elements of social development. Paradoxical effects are distinguished precisely by the fact that within them positive and negative moments are mixed, that in complex ways improvements of a situation go along with deteriorations. Some of the contradictions we thematize have precisely this structure: under the influence of expanding capitalism, elements of an emancipatory vocabulary or a transformation of social institutions undertaken with emancipatory intent lose their original content and thus in complex ways promote precisely the utility-based logics of action they were meant to contain. Here it is not a matter of denying the diagnosability of pathological or negative social conditions; it is rather that the description or deciphering of these conditions cannot do without reference to concepts that originally had an emancipatory content.

(b)   Beyond this, talk of 'paradoxical' contradictions must get by without the model of *self-destructive* economic processes characteristic of descriptions of 'late capitalist' social formations. The assumption that, under the influence of a universalistic morality and a welfare-state-induced erosion of traditional justifications of inequality, the inequalities connected to capitalist models would lose legitimacy implies, as indicated, the assumption that capitalism would not be able to recruit new legitimations for inequality. Talk of the 'paradoxical' contradictions of capitalism, in contrast,

implies the image of an 'ethicized' capitalism that has managed, with
reference to an available vocabulary of normative self-description,
to formulate new justifications for social inequality, injustice or
discrimination.

(c)   The model of 'paradoxical' contradictions finally dispenses
with a class-theoretical reconstruction of social conflicts. This is in
no way to deny the possibility of identifying some of the class- or
milieu-specific negative consequences of the 'new' capitalism. But,
on the one hand, this identification is made more difficult by the fact
that many modes of experiencing capitalism typically described
as paradoxical affect higher-level employees; while, on the other
hand, we have already indicated the extent, paradoxical in itself, to
which subjects are now ready or required, despite growing social
interdependence, to perceive their behaviour as individualized. As
a result of both factors, theories of contradiction, which juxtapose
collective subjects, are robbed of their empirical reference point and
thereby it becomes more difficult to identify progressive and 'reac-
tionary' subjects.

This general talk of the paradoxical contradictions of capitalism
must now be filled in and expanded in many places in order to
claim greater plausibility. The capitalist 'pressure' described has
different effects on different spheres of action. But what may be
central here is that the structure of the 'new' capitalism is already
contradictory in itself and that these contradictions are carried into
non-economic spheres of action. Paradoxical effects then result precisely when subjects in these spheres continue to see themselves in
light of their characteristic norms (and this as it were with assent
to a capitalism that is also normatively flexibilized). But this need
not be the structure that characterizes all the relevant paradoxical
contradictions. How exactly a paradoxical contradiction can be
reconstructed must in a certain way be investigated from case to
case. The thesis put forth here is only that the structure of contemporary capitalism produces paradoxical contradictions to a significant extent, so that the concept is a suitable instrument of general
explanation.

V   Paradoxes of capitalist modernization

As mentioned, our general thesis is that the neoliberal restructuring
of the capitalist economic system exerts a pressure to adapt that
does not undo the previously enumerated progressive processes,

but permanently transforms their function or significance. Within the framework of the new organizational form of capitalism, what could previously be analysed as an unambiguous rise in the sphere of individual autonomy assumes the shape of unreasonable demands, discipline or insecurity, which, taken together, have the effect of social desolidarization. What this means specifically will be elucidated in conclusion by means of the differentiated spheres of action.

1   The normative progress signified by the social generalization of romantically charged individualism in the social-democratic era, which led to an increase of biographical freedom, has in a peculiar way turned into its opposite under the pressure of the neoliberal restructuring of capitalism. It is not that the new interpretive model has simply lost its power in the lifeworld, let alone been dissolved with regard to increased demands for flexibility; rather, it still possesses an undiminished significance that shapes the self-understandings of many members of society. But in the last twenty years its meaning has imperceptibly changed; it has crept into economic processes as a professional and behavioural requirement. Today, the appeal to the idea that subjects understand their occupations not as fulfilling social duties, but rather as revisable steps in their experimental self-realization, justifies dismantling the privilege of membership in a firm, dissolving legal status guarantees and expecting increased flexibility. Moreover, to a growing extent the qualifications for well-paid jobs in the manufacturing and service sectors incorporate extra-functional demands for creative and biographical indeterminacy. This normative interpretive transformation of romantic individualism, which is starting to become an ideology and a productive factor of the new capitalism, accompanies desolidarizing tendencies insofar as employees are less and less in a position to develop longer-term connections with firms or colleagues. Furthermore, the changed demands require one to remain so open with regard to choice of location, use of time and type of activity that friendships, love relationships and even families are exposed to a high degree of pressure. In any case, network capitalism is characterized by tendencies towards an unlimited demand for subjective action capacities that blur the borders between the private and the professional-public sphere. 'Entreployees' are expected not only to dutifully fulfil externally given production quotas, but also to bring communicative and emotional skills and resources to bear in order to meet project goals

they are more or less responsible for setting. This dedifferentiation (*Entgrenzung*) of work-related efforts entails softening the separation of private and professional spheres of action[18] and, relatedly, mobilizes informal, 'lifeworld' skills for professional goals (economic rationality, it could be said, is now being 'colonized' by the lifeworld).[19] Beyond this, network capitalism is colonizing spheres of action that were previously distant from utility, thereby introducing the principles of achievement and exchange into the field of asymmetrical reciprocity structured by solidarity. The consequences of this informalization of the economic and economization of the informal are multifarious and cannot be discussed in detail here. However, three phenomena can be briefly enumerated.

First, when informal, emotional skills are included in utility-based work processes and economic imperatives intrude into informal relations, it becomes increasingly difficult for subjects to distinguish clearly between instrumental and non-instrumental aspects of intersubjective relationships. In other words, in network capitalism, friendship-like relations are established also with a view to instrumental interests, while instrumental relationships are repeatedly transformed into friendship-like relations. In this respect, unclear intermediate forms of friendships/instrumental relationships are common. These are felt as ambiguous by subjects themselves, since the 'true' intentions with which others encounter us can scarcely be discerned.

In addition, subjects in network capitalism are in a certain way called upon to pursue their 'authentic' interests more in professional contexts. At the same time, however, project-based workplaces reward 'flat' personalities that can respond flexibly to new challenges. Here, too, we consequently find a field in which the originally emancipatory significance of the ideal of authenticity has been transformed into an instrument for legitimizing capitalist arrangements. As an example of the difficulty of recognizing the particular contributions of employees within the firm, we can cite the fact that project-based work situations have hardly any recall of individual work achievements (we assume here without further discussion that demands for authenticity as a rule can only unfold when they are recognized). Employees' contributions are accordingly decreasingly appreciated in their individual aspects:

> In flexible organizations the memory of past services is very short, which leads to a thoroughly predictable instability of hierarchies: the person is no longer appreciated as such, but rather with a

view to her skills here and now. Correspondingly, in these organizations, there is no longer any place for the specific obligations that, for example, arise from the appreciation of (an employee's) past achievements, be it only via the detour of age or length of service.[20]

Finally, the blending of private and public, informal and formal, skills and resources reduces the value of the more or less objective criteria by means of which subjects could measure the value of their qualifications and contributions. The ability, for example, to build and stabilize relationships can only with difficulty be cast in the form of a reference or a degree. Moreover, networks tend to create local reputations whose value is hard to assess outside the network.[21] It may be this uncertainty about the social value of some qualifications and abilities, which will be thematized again below, that increasingly leads subjects to seek recognition of their ostensibly distinctive achievements and attributes in struggles for attention outside the real professional sphere (and thus, for example, on innumerable exhibitionistic television talkshows).[22]

2　The attainments of the social-democratic era cited above consisted in the ongoing establishment and expansion of civil liberties and political rights of participation. With these measures, on the one hand, the realm of individual autonomy was enlarged (e.g. beyond contractual freedom), while, on the other hand, prohibitions on discrimination sought to avoid cases of unequal treatment, which are still entirely possible on the basis of bourgeois civil rights. Political participation rights finally served to prevent illegimate domination and, in T.H. Marshall's view, provided the precondition for the *de facto* realization of bourgeois civil liberties in the first place. Now, especially important for our reflections is the category of social status rights, which in Marshall's famous essay on 'Citizenship and Social Class' make up citizen status in combination with bourgeois civil rights and political participation rights. The welfare state's institutionalization of social status rights serves at the same time as a confession that political rights, but also other rights of social participation, can only be realized in fact under conditions of minimal material provision. In Marshall's essay it was thus precisely social status rights that created 'a universal right to real income which is not proportionate to the market value of the claimant'.[23] Only when subjects had at their disposal a measure of material provision independent of their achievement were they put in a position to participate in basic social institutions and practices in a more or less equal way. In this context, two aspects should be emphasized. First is the insight into the conditionality of rights connected to citizen status.[24] The assumption is that civil and political participation rights can only be realized if subjects have disposal over a certain standard of living they cannot always establish by themselves. Second, and relatedly, social status to a certain extent frees subjects from having to assume sole responsibility for their life situations. The institutionalization of welfare-state support accompanies the acknowledgement that in complex societies social inequalities are connected to different starting conditions, the precise character of which is hardly under subjects' control. In this sense, social rights have an empowering and an unburdening status.

Looking at contemporary society, erosive tendencies can now be seen in both respects. In the course of the transformation of welfare-state agencies, in part social rights are massively cut, but in part they are also transformed into economized social services on which claims are again dependent on the material resources of the clientele. Likewise, within this transformation we can discern a remoralization of entitlements and a paternalization of welfare-state provisions. Those who want to enjoy welfare-state benefits must do something in return – for instance, in the case of unemployment, be prepared to take any job they are offered – that only then qualifies them as justified claimants. There is a threat of paternalism wherever eligibility in principle for social services, and consequently the ability to claim benefits, is systematically undermined by a discourse of responsibility. The less possible it is to perceive welfare-state benefits as rights claims, the greater the danger that these benefits will be handed over to the arbitrariness of an unburdened bureaucracy or the unpredictable ability of civil society organizations to call sufficient public attention and generosity to their plight.[25] Primarily, however, the discourse of self-responsibility tends to remove attention from welfare-state agencies altogether. As Klaus Günther has shown, this discourse then disregards the extent to which the ascription of individual responsibility depends upon internal and external preconditions that must be given for subjects to be justifiably treated as responsible for their deeds or omissions.[26] If responsibility is assigned without considering these preconditions, it is transformed into an 'imperative' that takes on paradoxical features precisely when, in an increasingly complex society, subjects can hardly any longer assume responsibility in the full sense of the word for many aspects of their existence.[27] The imperative character of assigned responsibility is thus reinforced to the extent that individuals must assume responsibility for states of affairs for which they are not in fact responsible. This paradox is heightened by the fact that the conception of responsibility originally possessed thoroughly emancipatory features. For it was the critique of an impersonal welfare bureaucracy that led to the demand for provision that was nearer to its clients, thereby creating a domain in which subjects no longer needed to be seen only as the passive recipients of social transfers. Even before a serious discussion of the appropriate balance between the preconditions of responsible action and the scope of meaningful initiative could get under way, however, a vehement discourse of responsibility broke into public debate, suggesting that the extent of personal responsibility for the social circumstances of one's actions was greater than had previously been assumed.

What emerges here is a disruption, which accompanies the spread of network capitalist structures, of the uncommonly effective picture of a community of responsibility – mostly constituted by the nation-state – which makes it possible to make greater redistributive sacrifices generally reasonable by appeal to membership in a political or cultural community. Now, to the extent that the image of a society pervaded by networks takes hold as a fundamental means of societal self-description, other images of the social whole lose influence. Like all models of social solidarity, however, a framework is required 'in which a relationship between the misfortune of those who suffer and the good fortune of the prosperous can be established'.[28] In network capitalism, on this thesis, citizens tend to perceive their efforts, successes and failures as individualized, so that a reference to the greater whole scarcely seems possible any longer. On the one hand, the consequences for subjects can be designated by the paradoxical concept of the compulsion to responsibility; on the other hand, they can be grasped in psychological terms: the greater the responsibility individuals must assume for their life situations, the greater the danger the demands will be excessive. Alain Ehrenberg has accordingly put forth the thesis that the number of depressive illnesses increases with feelings of dissatisfaction resulting from greater demands for responsibility. 'The depressed person', writes Ehrenberg, 'is in a state of breakdown' – the depressive is a person who believes that he or she has failed, not one who has broken the rules or been cheated out of an existing legal benefit.[29]

3   While in feudal or premodern societies status was distributed above all according to ascriptive features (birth, origin), modern

industrial societies can be characterized by the decomposition of
the ascriptive assignment of status in favour of universalistic criteria. Parsons in particular showed that with the increasing professionalization of social status politics, an achievement principle
gained importance which is in principle universalistically structured, since no one could be excluded from the efforts connected to
this principle on the basis of birth or origin alone.[30] It is not difficult
to recognize that the achievement principle therefore possessed an
emancipatory content: the larger the realm in which subjects can
succeed on the basis of their efforts alone, the greater the realm
of equal opportunity of participation in social status positions.
Looking at the economy, for instance, processes like the 'differentiation between households and employing organizations' typical
of modern industrial society, as well as the 'progressive attenuation
of owners' control of economic organizations' to the benefit of a
growing class of salaried employees, can be identified as phases of
a systematic spread of achievement-based fields of activity.[31] The
pushing back of the familial form of management that had long distinguished smaller businesses by modern management methods
(and the corresponding educated manager class) also contributed
to replacing the model of personal dependency predominant in
family businesses with more impersonal and thus less arbitrary or
paternalistic relations.[32] Now, there can be absolutely no doubt that
the achievement principle cursorily sketched here was already the
object of serious social-scientific critique. Parsons himself pointed
out that the central assumption in early capitalism – that the individual could enter as an equal into the system of market competition on the basis of his innate abilities alone – quickly proved to be
illusory. With the spread of educational institutions after the Second
World War came the insight that abilities relevant for participation
in the market could only be 'mediated through a complex series of
stages in the socialization process'.[33] Of course, this interpretation
only points to preconditions, recognized in the social-democratic
era, for equal participation in achievement-oriented market competition. More important are all the forms of criticism that suspected
the status of the achievement principle as a general social ordering
principle of being an ideology, since it tends systematically and with
reference to a normative argumentative arsenal to justify inequalities and thereby to disavow 'alternative models of social production and distribution', for instance those that avoid reference to the
achievement principle.[34] Beyond this, to this day there are good
empirical arguments that, especially in the realm of senior manage-

ment, origin or class-specific *habitus* trumps the characteristics that depend upon achievement, so that we can by no means speak of a full overcoming of ascriptive status distributions.[35] These critical models did not, however, undermine the legitimizing power of the achievement principle. On the contrary, recent research shows that this principle continues to exert consciousness-shaping influence as a normative expectation and thus to serve as an evaluative standard for the judgement of structures of social distribution and reward.[36] Of course, part of the critique of the achievement principle can also be interpreted as evidence of an unsatisfactory or overly restrictive translation of the universalistic criteria connected with it. In other words, the emancipatory content of the achievement principle is usually adhered to precisely when it is criticized.

Along with the consistently positive role the achievement principle thus continues to play as a general idea of social ordering, there is another political and economic discourse within whose framework the semantics of achievement attains increasing prominence ('Achievement should pay again'). Now, taken together, the two states of affairs could, on this thesis, then assume paradoxical features if it could be shown that the achievement principle loses its last remnants of reality precisely in the economic realm as a whole. There are various circumstances that in this context involve what should here be characterized as 'achievement insecurity'. For one thing, tendencies can already be identified in the empirical rise of achievement justice as a phenomenon to allow market success as the sole criterion for rewarding achievement. In other words, only those who deploy their labour-power for the production of products or services that can be sold on the market earn their keep in the literal sense. From this perspective, the market appears as an 'unavoidable authority for evaluating achievement'.[37] All achievements that cannot be converted into profits in the way described must then be uncertain. The thesis that the achievement principle *marketizes* (*vermarktlichen*) itself in this way has been the basis of social-theoretical diagnoses of the present independent of particular empirical judgements. Sighard Neckel and Kai Dröge, for instance, assume that markets in themselves are exclusively interested in economic results that remain 'at the same time "blind" and "neutral"' with respect to the way they come about.[38] To the extent, then, that societies are 'marketized', factors like accident, inheritance or luck come into question as legitimate criteria for the distribution of material or symbolic goods. It is certainly still too early to conclusively judge whether the 'marketization' of evaluative criteria observable in particular fields will stabilize more broadly as a normative framework of expectations, which may also entail that factors like accident, luck or inheritance are not meaningfully included in a generally acceptable structure for justifying social inequality. But there undoubtedly seems to be a general insecurity about the value and status of one's own achievements that is reinforced by the already enumerated characteristics of project-oriented capitalism. Thus, it is frequently unclear, to mention again the important point here, whether a working relationship is initiated on the basis of objective criteria or personal inclination; this is connected to the general difficulty of objectifying the skills that are decisive for network capitalism (e.g. the ability to build relationships, to generate trust, flexibility, etc.). Finally, the gains for one's reputation connected with the pursuit of a project hardly correspond to the 'national equivalents' of a reference or a diploma and thus remain in a certain sense internal to the project.[39] Taking these factors together, it quickly becomes clear why contemporary subjects have difficulty attaining certainty about the 'true' value of their contributions and achievements. But if the practical content of the achievement principle changes in this way, prevailing contemporary political and economic discussions about achievement are transformed from a means of potential emancipation into a tool that, like the discourse of responsibility, serves to undermine aspects of social welfare freed from achievement, as well as to suggest the possibility of partaking of status where it in fact does not exist.

4   The idea that arose on the threshold of the nineteenth century, opposing romantic love to the instrumental world of exchange relations, was probably always a typical product of bourgeois illusion.[40] Indeed, at the historical moment when the first signs of the beginnings of secularization seemed to multiply, couple relationships were affectively experienced as outfitted with all the experiential qualities that had previously been reserved for the transgressive experience of the 'saint'. Early on, however, a sober sense for social advantage surreptitiously intruded into the counter-world of the symbiotic union of man and wife, ensuring that longer-term relationships or marriages usually occurred only between members of the same social class. But its delimitation from the 'cold' sphere of economic relations only finally collapsed when, with the social spread of the romantic love ideal, social practices arose that made the initiation and maintenance of couple relationships ever more dependent on consumption. Since the beginning of the twentieth

century, as Eva Illouz has convincingly shown, love was increasingly 'reified' and commercialized as subjects used consumer items and luxury goods to give their affective relationships symbolic expression and to ritually mark themselves off from the social environment.[41] Nevertheless, in these processes of growing commercialization, as Illouz also observes, subjects, despite their ensnarement in economic practices, preserved the ability to keep their feelings free from strategic utility considerations. With almost virtuosic skill, they rather seemed able to employ the consumption of goods to protect 'pure' relationships still based only on emotional inclination from quickly deteriorating and, at least for a certain time, to make them last. To this extent, the provisional obligations that entered into intimate relationships as a recognition norm with the rise of the romantic love ideal remain peculiarly in force with the economization of love practices. Indeed, we are convinced that, owing to the women's movement in the social-democratic era, they ensured that couple relationships took on more the character of a partnership and that the unequal distribution of housework and childcare was increasingly perceived as a moral challenge on the masculine side as well.

In the 1980s and 1990s, however, tendencies emerged that threaten to dissolve this precarious integration of consumption and feeling by giving rise to a new form of consumer rationality in love. For one thing, owing to the unlimited work typical of the network structure of the new capitalism, longer-term love and intimate relationships are exposed to considerably more pressure; today, growing demands on time resources, increased mobility demands and the constant expectation of greater responsibility and emotional engagement at work make it more and more difficult to bring into the private domain that creative virtuosity that is necessary to maintain 'pure' relationships founded on inclination alone. However, it is not only these structural pressures that are to blame for the tendential erosion of the consumption-saturated practice of romantic love. Rather, the new 'spirit' of capitalism, which transfers the entrepreneurial idea of calculative action to subjects' self-relations, penetrates into the capillaries of intimate relationships, so that the model of utility-oriented calculation begins to predominate. This means less that today intimate relationships are increasingly taken up after sober calculation of their utility in terms of pleasure and enjoyment; what rather seems to be emerging as a new model of behaviour is the tendency to calculate the long-term chances of such love relationships according to their compatibility with the future mobility demands of a career path that can only be planned in the short term. If so, this would mean that what now dominates the innermost core of love would be something that has long had a place in consumer practices, but has never overwhelmed the power of feelings: economic rationality. Until now, this was something partners took into account together to make their precarious relationships last, but now they are becoming a tool they apply to evaluate one another as partners.

Notes

These reflections further specify a research programme that is to serve as a theoretical framework for empirical projects at the Frankfurt Institute for Social Research. The first outlines of this research project are to be found in Axel Honneth, ed., *Befreiung aus der Mündigkeit: Paradoxien des gegenwärtigen Kapitalismus* (Frankfurt/Main: Campus, 2002). This chapter was first published as 'Paradoxien des Kapitalismus', *Berliner Debatte Initial*, vol. 15, no. 1 (2004), pp. 4–17. The publishers would like to acknowledge permission to reproduce 'Paradoxes of Capitalism' in *Constellations*, Volume 13, Issue 1, 2006, 41–58. © Blackwell Publishing Ltd., 2006. This material is reproduced with permission of John Wiley & Sons, Inc.

1   Ralf Dahrendorf, 'Das 20. Jahrhundert – Bilanz und Hoffnung', in Dieter Wild, ed., *Spiegel des 20. Jahrhunderts* (Hamburg: Hoffman & Campe, 1999), p. 18.
2   Talcott Parsons, *The System of Modern Societies* (Englewood Cliffs, NJ: Prentice Hall, 1971), chs 5 and 6.
3   Eva Illouz, *Consuming the Romantic Utopia: Love and the Contradictions of Modern Capitalism* (Berkeley: University of California Press, 1997).
4   Axel Honneth, 'Redistribution as Recognition: A Response to Nancy Fraser', in Nancy Fraser and Axel Honneth, *Redistribution or Recognition? A Political–Philosophical Exchange* (London and New York: Verso, 2003), pp. 110–97.
5   Parsons, *The System of Modern Societies*, p. 80.
6   See Chapter 9 in the current volume.
7   Anthony Giddens, *The Transformation of Intimacy: Sexuality, Love and Eroticism in Modern Societies* (Cambridge: Polity, 1993), ch. 4.
8   Talcott Parsons, 'The Motivation of Economic Activities', in *Essays in Sociological Theory* (New York: Free Press, 1954), pp. 50–68.

9 Michael Zürn, *Regieren jenseits des Nationalstaates* (Frankfurt/Main: Suhrkamp, 2003), pp. 64ff.

10 Scott Lash and John Urry, *The End of Organized Capitalism* (Madison: University of Wisconsin Press, 1987), ch. 7.

11 Martin Höpner, *Wer beherrscht die Unternehmen? Shareholder Value, Managerherrschaft und Mitbestimmung in Deutschland* (Frankfurt/Main: Campus, 2003), p. 15.

12 Luc Boltanski and Ève Chiapello, *The New Spirit of Capitalism*, trans. Gregory Elliott (London: Verso, 2007).

13 Hans J. Pongratz and Günter Voss, *Arbeitskraftunternehmer: Erwerbsorientierung in entgrenzten Arbeitsformen* (Berlin: edition sigma, 2003).

14 Jürgen Habermas, *Legitimation Crisis*, trans. Thomas McCarthy (Boston: Beacon, 1975), pp. 175ff.

15 Ibid., pp. 93–4.

16 See also Martin Hartmann, 'Widersprüche, Ambivalenzen, Paradoxien: Begriffliche Wandlungen in der neueren Gesellschaftstheorie', in Honneth, ed., *Befreiung aus der Mündigkeit*, pp. 221–51.

17 Anthony Giddens, *The Constitution of Society: Outline of the Theory of Structuration* (Cambridge: Polity, 1984), p. 313.

18 Arlie Russel Hochschild, *The Time Bind: When Work Becomes Home and Home Becomes Work* (New York: Henry Holt, 1997).

19 See Nick Kratzer, *Arbeitskraft in Entgrenzung: Grenzenlose Anforderungen, erweiterte Spielräume, begrenzte Ressourcen* (Berlin: edition sigma, 2003), pp. 236–9. Kratzer writes in this context of a 'weak' side of post-Taylorist rationalization (p. 236).

20 Nicolas Dodier, *Les Hommes et les machines: La conscience collective dans les sociétés techicisées* (Paris: Métailié, 1995), pp. 341–2. See also Kai Dröge and Irene Somm, 'Spurlose Leistung, Zeit, Status und Reziprozität im flexiblem Kapitalismus', *bios*, vol. 18 (2005), pp. 368–74.

21 Boltanski and Chiapello, *The New Spirit of Capitalism*, p. 430.

22 Alain Ehrenberg, *L'individu incertain* (Paris: Calmann-Levy, 1995), pp. 175ff.

23 T.H. Marshall, 'Citizenship and Social Class', in T.H. Marshall and Tom Bottomore, *Citizenship and Social Class* (London: Pluto, 1992), p. 28.

24 See Georg Vobruba, 'Freiheit: Autonomiegewinne der Leute im Wohlfahrtsstaat', in Stephan Lessenich, ed., *Wohlfahrtsstaatliche Grundbegriffe: Historische und aktuelle Diskurse* (Frankfurt/Main: Campus, 2003), p. 141.

25   Nikolas Rose uses the concept 'remoralization' above all with a view to the benefits given by civil associations operating beyond the state and the market, since these help only certain personality profiles. See *Powers of Freedom: Reframing Political Thought* (Cambridge: Cambridge University Press, 1999), p. 265.

26   Klaus Günther, 'Zwischen Ermächtigung und Disziplinierung: Verantwortung im gegenwärtigen Kapitalismus', in Honneth, ed., *Befreiung aus der Mündigkeit*, pp. 117–39.

27   Ibid., p.128.

28   Boltanski and Chiapello, *The New Spirit of Capitalism*, p. 379.

29   Alain Ehrenberg, *The Weariness of the Self: Diagnosing the History of Depression in the Contemporary Age*, trans. Enrico Caouette et al. (Montreal: McGill-Queens University Press, 2010), p. xvi.

30   Parsons, *System of Modern Societies*, p. 110.

31   Ibid., pp. 108, 106.

32   Boltanski and Chiapello, *The New Spirit of Capitalism*, p. 17.

33   Parsons, *System of Modern Societies*, p. 97.

34   Claus Offe, *Leistungsprinzip und industrielle Arbeit: Mechanismen der Statusverteilung in Arbeitsorganisationen der industriellen Leistungsgesellschaft* (Frankfurt/Main and Cologne: Europäische Verlagsanstalt, 1970), p. 9.

35   Michael Hartmann, *Der Mythos von den Leistungseliten: Spitzen-karrieren und soziale Herkunft in Wirtschaft, Politik, Justiz und Wissenschaft* (Frankfurt/Main: Campus, 2002).

36   Sighard Neckel, Kai Dröge and Irene Somm, 'Welche Leistung, welche Leistungsgerechtigkeit? Soziologische Konzepte, nor-mative Fragen und einige empirische Befunde', in Peter A. Berger and Volker H. Schmidt, eds, *Welche Gleichheit, welche Ungleichheit? Grundlagen der Ungleichheitsforschung* (Wiesbaden: VS, 2004), pp. 137–64.

37   Ibid.

38   Sighard Neckel and Kai Dröge, 'Die Verdienste und ihr Preis: Leistung in der Marktgesellschaft', in Honneth, ed., *Befreiung aus der Mündigkeit*, p. 105.

39   Boltanski and Chiapello, *The New Spirit of Capitalism*, p. 430.

40   Niklas Luhmann, *Love as Passion: The Codification of Intimacy* (Cambridge: Polity, 1986).

41   Illouz, *Consuming the Romantic Utopia*.

Part IV

Psychoanalytical Ramifications

11

The Work of Negativity: A Recognition-Theoretical Revision of Psychoanalysis

With a topic as complex as the role of 'negativity' within psychoanalysis, it is best to present a few theses that convey one's own beliefs as concisely as possible. I will proceed in three steps: I begin by outlining the reasons why Critical Theory is dependent on psychoanalysis (I); I move on to discuss the necessity of opening Critical Theory to object relations theory, contrary to the accusation of revisionism advanced by former representatives of the Frankfurt School (II); and I finish by considering whether the price for this paradigm shift is too high, because it removes 'negativity', the real 'spur' for Freud's work, from the psychoanalytical approach. In this final step, I also discuss the problem underlying the title of this brief essay. But before that, a detour through these first two steps is needed in order to explicate the importance of inquiring into the power of 'the negative'.[1]

I

There are at least two reasons why a critical theory of society in the tradition of the Frankfurt School continues to have a close connection to psychoanalytical theory. But this connection cannot be justified merely by pointing to the transmission of the works of Adorno and Marcuse. From our current vantage point, there is something coincidental about the cooperation between Critical Theory and psychoanalysis, envisaged by Horkheimer and brought about by Fromm. At the time there was a broad current of attempts to integrate Marxism and psychoanalysis, with the main purpose of supplementing the social-theoretical core of historical materialism with a psychological theory that could explain the absence of revolutionary uprising: that is, the degree of social integration. Psychoanalysis was a logical candidate, because it seemed capable of clarifying the psychic, unconscious attachments that prevented oppressed subjects from perceiving what was in their rational interest. Already after the end of fascism, and certainly after the (partial) return of the members of the Institute for Social Research to the newly founded Federal Republic of Germany, the social-cultural situation had changed dramatically; it was no longer the psychological integration of the proletariat that needed to be explained, but the peculiar apathy and failure to resist on the part of the whole population. Here as well, psychoanalysis seemed to be an appropriate complementary theoretical strategy, because, in connection with assumptions about the decline of the capitalist market economy, it offered the prospect of interpreting subjects' loss of identity (*Ich-Verlust*), the 'crisis' of the individual, as the psychological result of the loss of paternal authority. Since that time, the dramatic changes in contemporary experience have also extinguished the primary evidence of the necessity of integrating psychoanalysis and a critical theory of society. At a time when the lifeworld is being rapidly detraditionalized and subjects appear to be willingly undergoing a process of individualization and autonomization, it no longer seems clear which aim a critical theory of society, equipped with psychoanalytical concepts, would actually pursue. The desire to fuse these two theories together is often merely the expression of an orthodoxy hostile to experimentation – a thoughtless rejection of conceptual innovations. The interdisciplinary shape a critical theory of society should take is no longer a settled matter, but varies according to the basic concepts employed and the issue to be explained. Therefore, it was only logical that when it came to developing his theory of communicative action, Habermas would abandon psychoanalysis and replace it with a form of development psychology inspired by Piaget and Kohlberg; in conceptual agreement with his own major concepts, this was to determine the chances for establishing a post-conventional moral consciousness.

It is this internal historicity of Critical Theory that constantly demands that we inquire into the special position of psychoanalysis within Critical Theory. With the exception of the historical tradition, about which there is a good deal of contingency in terms of time (1920s and 1930s) and place (Frankfurt am Main), nothing seems to necessitate integrating these two theoretical approaches. Unlike Habermas, however, I believe that there are a number of good reasons that make a critical theory of society dependent on psychoanalysis (in the broadest sense of the term). The two reasons I will name both relate to the conception of the subject put forth by psychoanalytical theory.

(a)   A critical theory of society needs, on the normative level, a concept of the human being that is as realistic and close to the phenomena as possible; it should be able to accord an appropriate place to individuals' unconscious, non-rational attachments. Without taking into account such unconscious motives and affects, the theory runs the danger of succumbing to moral idealism, demanding too much rationality of individuals. Even today, psychoanalysis in all its variations represents the theory that pays most attention to the constitutive boundaries of human rationality. Whether in the form of suppressed instinctual fantasies, largely unconscious attachments or uncontrollable constellations of affects, the theory always takes into account human beings' unconscious drives, which impose certain, nearly inevitable restrictions on rational deliberation. To defend against the illusions that accompany notions of a morality of reason (*Vernunftmoral*), Critical Theory must be supplemented by a kind of moral psychology guided by psychoanalytical insights. According to this view, humans are conceived of as beings who would be overwhelmed by the strict obligation to be unbiased, because this would ignore the existential foundations of one's life. At the normative level, therefore, psychoanalysis plays the same role for Critical Theory that Horkheimer accorded to 'materialism': it recognizes that humans are tied, through unconscious drives or attachments, to their own, unique lives in a way that every principled morality of reason must take into account.

(b)   But it is not only at the normative level that a critical theory of society needs to be supplemented by psychoanalysis; this is just as true of the explanatory level, as psychoanalysis can best account for the unconscious (*reflexionsentzogen*) motives of human action. This line of argumentation runs parallel to the one that is advanced with regard to the idealistic tendencies of a morality of reason. Social occurrences can be appropriately explained by grasping them, beyond their articulation by subjects, as the outcome of actions in which unconscious drives or needs for attachment have left their mark. At a very fundamental level, we should expect that within the social world, there will be affects and motives that are inaccessible to consciousness. In order to be able to take account of the opaque, unconscious motives expressed in anxiety, longings for attachment, desires for togetherness and fantasies of submission, we need a psychological theory of the subject, a theory of socialization that takes sufficient account of the genesis of unconscious affects in our individual biographies. I do not yet see any other theory better suited to this demand than some version of psychoanalysis.

The question at this point, however, is which of the many variants of psychoanalysis can best fulfil this task. In my view the answer will depend on which variant can best take account of the socialization milieu of society as a whole. This criterion could also be defined by saying that the best candidate for a psychological supplement to Critical Theory will be that current of psychoanalysis whose basic concepts allow a relatively seamless translation into social-theoretical categories. In the next step, I will name the reasons why we should view object relations theory as the most suitable variant of psychoanalysis for the task at hand.

II

I begin by briefly presenting the major thesis of object relations theory, before outlining the reasons that make this theory especially suited for an interdisciplinary linkage with a critical theory of society. Of course, I would also like to demonstrate that the efforts undertaken thirty years ago by Alfred Lorenzer and Jürgen Habermas to revise Critical Theory have not gone far enough, because they place intersubjectivism only at the methodological level of the psychoanalytical approach, rather than grouping it among the basic concepts of the attendant theory of socialization. Object relations theory deduces, on the basis of the therapeutic analysis of relationship disorders, the conditions that could lead to the successful formation of affective bonds with other persons. But before psychoanalysis could concentrate on the interpersonal aspects of human action, a series of theoretical impulses was needed, one capable of undermining the orthodox conception of the development of children's drives. For Freud and his immediate successors, children's partners in interaction are, in the first instance, only significant to the extent that they appear as objects for the libidinous projections arising out of the intrapsychic conflict between unconscious urges and a gradually developing ego. Beyond this derivative, secondary role, the mother alone could be viewed as a caretaker, because the child's fear of losing the mother in the phase of psychological helplessness was regarded as the cause of all mature variants of such feelings. After thus anchoring an image of children's psychological development according to which their relations to other persons are a mere function in the development of libidinous urges, the empirical investigations undertaken by René Spitz raised some initial doubts. His observations showed that the withholding of maternal affection can lead to serious behavioural disorders, even if all of the child's other bodily needs are satisfied. These initial indications of the independent significance of emotional bonds in early child development, as Morris Eagle shows in his overview entitled *Recent Developments in Psychoanalysis*,[2] would soon be reinforced by the results of a series of further investigations: ethological experiments managed to show that the bonds between baby apes and their so-called surrogate mothers cannot derive from the experience of having their biological urges satisfied, but must instead stem from the experience of 'contact pleasure' (*Kontaktbehagen*). John Bowlby's groundbreaking studies found that human infants, already in their first few months of life, develop an active readiness for interpersonal closeness, thus laying the basis for all later forms of emotional bonds. Daniel Stern, encouraged by the research of Spitz and Bowlby, managed to deliver convincing evidence that the interaction between mother and child is a highly complex process in which both sides train each other's capacity for sharing feelings and sentiments.

This must have appeared highly confusing in post-war Britain and the USA, where psychoanalysis was still open to research. After all, unlike Freud's id–ego model, this research appeared to point to the lasting significance of early, pre-speech experiences of interaction: if the process of socialization was largely dependent on children's experiences in their affective dealings with their primary caretakers, then the orthodox notion that psychological development consists in a sequence of organizational forms of the 'monological' relationship between libidinous urges and the capacity of the ego was invalid. The conceptual framework of psychoanalysis needed to be fundamentally expanded, adding the independent dimension of social interactions within which children learn to view themselves as independent subjects through emotional relationships with other persons. This theoretical conclusion

corresponded to the psychotherapeutical finding that a growing
number of patients suffered from psychic illnesses traceable not to
intrapsychic conflicts between ego and id, but solely to interpersonal disorders owing to weaning. These pathologies, expressed in
symptoms of borderline personality disorder and narcissism, compelled therapists to resort increasingly to explanatory approaches
that were irreconcilable with orthodox notions, seeking to give the
mutual attachments between children and their caretakers an independent meaning.

The psychoanalytical theory of object relations represents the
first attempt at a conceptual answer to the various challenges outlined by these few indications. Generalizing somewhat, we could
say that the child's psychic process of socialization is very different
from how Freud and his students saw it. The structure of intrapsychic agencies (*Instanzen*) – that is, what we philosophically term
the subject's relation-to-self – represents a process in which children gradually internalize the patterns of interaction they learn
in their successive encounters with their mother, father, siblings
and, finally, peers. The organization of the psyche thus occurs
as an interactive process in which the maturing subject learns to
recognize the independence of objectively existing relations of
interaction only by mirroring them intrapsychically, in order to
give rise to a variety of different internal agencies.

This makes clear why object relations theory represents a suitable discipline for cooperating with a critical theory of society. By
grasping the structure of the psyche – what Eric Fromm termed
character formation – as the expression of typified patterns of
interaction, we can easily draw a connection to a theory of society
that, for its part, is interested in the social formation of relations of
interaction. For Fromm, the spectrum of social reality that could
be included in psychoanalytical theory initially seemed extremely
thin; it was limited to paternal behaviour, as this was considered to
be responsible for the fixation on a particular stage of psychosexual
development.[3] But in object relations theory, society appears in all
the patterns of interaction into which children are successively integrated over the course of their development, and with which they
gradually learn to cope. Each of the child's object relations, each
of his or her stabilizing interactions with a concrete or generalized
other, has a socially typified form; this form, even in the agencies
the child has internalized, mirrors social relations of interaction. In
the third step, I discuss the extent to which this link to object relations theory might represent a danger to Critical Theory, robbing it

of the psychoanalytical impulse of negativity. At least that is how Adorno viewed the matter.

III

After what has been said so far, it might seem that the socialization of children through the internalization of patterns of interaction is relatively free of conflict, leaving no scars or injuries on the individual's psychic structure. Even if this model of socialization is supplemented with a correspondingly reformulated theory of drives, in which the latter are understood as impulses for forming psychic agencies,[4] this does not seem to have any significant impact on this harmony. Therefore, we could object that this concept underestimates the negative forces – be they in the form of the death drive or an endogenous tendency for aggression – that are, after all, constantly at the centre of orthodox psychoanalysis. By linking up with object relations theory, Critical Theory would lose the knowledge of the constitutional non-conformity of human beings, which Adorno always took to be the central contribution of psychoanalysis. If I am right, the question comes down to the following: must we conceive of this negative force – or perhaps we should say: the psychic tendency for transgression, the psychic fragmentation of human beings – as an element of our drives, or can we view it as an inevitable result of our socialization, a process of internalization? This question is so crucial because it determines the critical potential of object relations theory. After all, Winnicott's concept of transitional objects, for example, concedes that children are injured by the compulsion to recognize an independent world of interaction in a way that is difficult to compensate; it affects us throughout our lives as a tendency to restore symbiotic unity. Such an urge can even be understood, in line with Cornelius Castoriadis, as an inner-psychic source of strength, which constantly requires subjects to repeatedly transgress the boundaries of the ego and search for new, expanded forms of interaction.[5] What distinguishes this view from the orthodox conception is essentially that dynamic negativity is understood not as a part of our drive nature, but as an inevitable result of our socialization. The difference between these two conceptions in terms of both the normative and the explanatory role of psychoanalysis in Critical Theory is rather insignificant; in both cases, subjects are only capable of a fragmented form of intersubjectivity, because they are overwhelmed by the independence of a world of interaction that they cannot control. Both versions of psychoanalysis address the unconsciously working desires for attachment, longing for submission or fantasies of conquering that we would have to account for both normatively and explanatorily. Therefore, despite all doubts about the empirical accuracy of assuming endogenous aggressive tendencies,[6] it seems wise to abstain from an overly strong theory of drives. The critical intention of a theory of society will suffer little by abstaining from the assumption that humans are constitutionally equipped with a death drive or aggression drive.

Notes

1 Joel Whitebook, 'Mutual Recognition and the Work of the Negative', in William Rehg and James Bohman, eds, *Pluralism and the Pragmatic Turn: The Transformation of Critical Theory. Essays in Honor of Thomas McCarthy* (Cambridge, MA and London: MIT Press, 2001), pp. 257–91; see also my detailed discussion of Joel Whitebook in Chapter 13 of the current volume; Reimut Reiche, 'Subjekt, Patient, Aussenwelt', *Psyche*, vol. 53 (1999), pp. 572–96.

2 Morris Eagle, *Recent Developments in Psychoanalysis: A Critical Evaluation* (Cambridge, MA: Harvard University Press, 1989).

3 See Gunzelin Schmid Noerr, 'Zwischen Sozialpsychologie und Ethik: Erich Fromm und die "Frankfurter Schule"', in Institut für Sozialforschung, ed., *Mitteilungen*, vol. 11 (Frankfurt/Main: Institut für Sozialforschung, 2000), pp. 7–40.

4 See, for instance, Hans W. Loewald, 'Triebtheorie, Objektbildung und psychische Strukturbildung', in *Psychoanalyse: Aufsätze aus den Jahren 1951–1979* (Stuttgart: Klett-Cotta, 1986), pp. 193–205.

5 Cornelius Castoriadis, *The Imaginary Institution of Society* (Cambridge, MA: MIT Press, 1987).

6 See Martin Dornes, *Die frühe Kindheit: Entwicklungspsychologie der ersten Lebensjahre* (Frankfurt/Main: Fischer, 1997), ch. 9.

12

The I in We: Recognition as a Driving Force of Group Formation

Although the concept of the 'group' is highly plastic and applicable to very different social phenomena, each historical epoch picks out, from this variety of appearances, individual and especially striking features in order to construct its own image of what constitutes a group. These constructions reflect the fears and hopes, concerns and expectations that motivate individuals, through contemporary experiences of coming together, to form relatively stable and continuous associations. Even a cursory glance at the turbulent history of the twentieth century reveals the diversity of the associations linked, under the pressure of certain quickly generalized experiences, to the emergence and dissemination of social groups. Initially, the experience of anonymous, obedient large groups captured the attention of society so completely that from Freud to Canetti and Adorno, the concept of the group is almost entirely defined by the image of the regressive masses.[1] Later, following the Second World War, this negative conception was often transferred to the category of 'gangs' – small groups of violent youths. The popular use of the term reflected the fears of the growing affluent society in the face of the losers it had produced.[2] However, part of the history of such social images of groups during the twentieth century is the fact that, parallel to these negative stylizations, positive conceptions also emerge, reflecting hopes about the beneficial effects of social groups. After American social psychology discovered the civilizing function of sports teams and neighbourhood associations,[3] and following Piaget's pioneering study on the moral development of children, which demonstrated the role of peer groups in the process of socialization,[4] there was a rapid spread of excessive expectations on primary social groups; the latter came to be regarded as an obvious guarantor of harmonious social relationships. Today, thanks to the popularization of communitarianism, the notion of cultural community has replaced the group ideal. In this community's milieu, characterized by common values, individuals are to be capable of developing and reinforcing their own personality, something they would be incapable of doing within merely legal relationships.[5]

As different as these historical types of group formation might be, they are largely similar in terms of their formal tendency to pick out just one possible feature of social association and stylize it as the definitive one. In negative conceptions of group formation, those features that are more regressive and threaten individuality were generalized; as a result, out of the variety of social appearances of groups, ultimately only the dull masses remained. In positive conceptions, by contrast, those elements that are more civilizing and reinforce the individual were so idealized that the dangers of losing autonomy subtly disappeared from view. With such one-sided perspectives, these theories have influenced, not uncommonly, our everyday consciousness by contributing to the formation of social mythologies soon to be found in literature and the media. The dominant images of the effects of social groups were drawn from the selective plundering of scientific theories, which, through a process of methodological abstraction, had concentrated on certain particular features of social groups. Nevertheless, this process gave rise to the danger of a closed circuit; these everyday mythologies had a retroactive effect on the same scientific research from which they had drawn the material used for their popularized generalization. Researchers paradoxically became the victims of social mythologies they had unwillingly helped produce by intentionally taking a one-sided approach to a single aspect of a social phenomenon. In the research on group formation, the twentieth century witnessed a number of such uncontrolled retroactive effects of popularized social images on theoretical work. Even today there is a tendency to emphasize either the regressive features of groups or those features that promote autonomy, without taking into account the fact that both are rooted in one and the same mechanism. Unfortunately, therefore, psychoanalysis is dominated by a negative image of the group, which the Freudian tradition explains as the result of a drive to compensate for a weak ego. Psychoanalysis focuses accordingly on the regressive processes that reactivate primitive layers of the individual psyche within the life of the group. Sociology and political science, by contrast, retain an exceedingly positive image of the group, characterized by the appearance of cultural community: language, tradition and the values of integrated groups, large or small. This current is correspondingly more interested in processes through which collective identities, which provide individuals with psychic security and integrity, are formed in the shape of deviations from dominant value systems.

These 'reciprocal blind spots' result in the fact that both currents of research are incapable of recognizing how much their own object domain is marked by the other respective tendency. Just as psychoanalysis refuses to admit that involvement in social groups strengthens the ego, sociological group research is largely unaware of the dangers facing individuals in collective experience as the result of an unconscious reactivation of earlier object relations. But an even more serious flaw lies in the fact that these one-sided stylizations seem to prevent a basic conceptual link between both disciplines. The motives that each side views as decisive for group formation are so far apart that they appear to be dealing with two entirely different social phenomena. The only way of coping with this danger today is to locate the categorial starting point for the explanation of social groups in a terminology that, at the first stage, is neutral towards both the negative and the positive alternatives. In order to do so, groups should be understood, whatever their size or type, as a social mechanism that serves the interests or needs of the individual by helping him or her achieve personal stability and growth (*Erweiterung*). However, depending on the type of social ties and later social experiences, this striving for support within the group can take on various forms that codetermine the extent of the unconscious 'subject matter' (*Thematik*) in the group. In this essay, I will resort to the concept of 'recognition' in order to develop such a unified categorial structure. The first step will be to briefly present the premise that individuals' dependency on experiences of social recognition explain why they seek membership in various forms of social associations. Each form of recognition that individuals rely upon in the course of their development corresponds analytically to another form of sought-after group membership (I). However, this initial premise entails an abstraction, because it sets aside the individual's need for 'fusion', which usually has an impact on the life of the group. Therefore, drawing on Winnicott, the second step will be to attempt to correct this idealized image of the group by discussing the regressive tendencies that often codetermine group experiences (II). But this is still not sufficient for adapting the concept of 'the group' entirely to social reality. The behaviour of the group can obviously be influenced by unconscious projections and fantasies, which lead to the pathologization of communication processes and carry destructive consequences in their wake (III). Therefore, the idea is to take back, step by step, the idealizations that underlie the initial premise of a harmonic absorption (*Aufgehen*) of the 'I' into the 'We' of the group.

I

The thoughts I will present on various forms of group formation are based on a recognition-theoretical concept of the development of human sociality and personality. By synthesizing the results of object relations theory and American social psychology in the tradition of Mead, I assume that subjects' 'I-'formation takes place in stages of internalizing social responses characterized by intersubjective recognition. By gradually relating the approval, encouragement and affirmation of their partners in interaction to their own, still unorganized experiences, small children learn to cultivate an inner core personality (*Persönlichkeitskern*) consisting of layers of a positive relation-to-self.[6] We can further differentiate this socializing process by analytically distinguishing between various stages of such a relation-to-self, with the subject's capacity for autonomy increasing at each stage. As the number of interaction partners grows, recognitional behaviour, which enables maturing children to become aware of their own abilities and rights, becomes more complex and demanding. Given this premise, it seems unproblematic to assume the existence of an initial stage of children's relation-to-self at which they learn to grasp their needs and desires as an articulable part of their own person. With a serendipitous concept that Erik H. Erikson has made fruitful for psychoanalysis, we can use the term 'self-confidence' to depict this kind of elementary security about the value of one's own needs.[7]

If the formation of this kind of self-confidence occurs through the successful internalization of the stable care provided by one's primary caretaker, usually the mother or the father, attaining the second stage already requires an expansion of the network of significant partners in interaction. Children must learn to go beyond self-confidence and acquire an additional form of positive relation-to-self that consists in the elementary consciousness of being regarded by others as a responsible (*zurechnungsfähig*) individual.

By resorting to observations we owe to both George Herbert Mead and Jean Piaget, we can presume that this stage consists in the internalization of the experience of playing with other children. Children develop initial, germinating forms of self-respect by experiencing themselves at play as an interaction partner whose judgement is regarded as valuable or reliable.[8] Of course, what also plays a role in this process is the experience of being increasingly respected by other members of the family as a subject whose beliefs are no longer wholly irrelevant for common decision-making. Finally, the third stage in the development of autonomy is not subsequent to the conclusion of the second stage, but occurs in parallel. After all, the intersubjective experiences that children must have in order to ultimately arrive at an awareness of the value of their own physical and mental abilities will generally already have taken place within the period in which they acquire initial forms of self-respect in interaction with a weakly generalized other.[9] In the main, this distinction between three stages of positive relation-to-self – self-confidence, self-respect and self-esteem – should not be understood in the strong sense of an ontogenetic sequence; rather, we can safely assume that all three forms of relation-to-self can develop in unison through the internalization of parental care, and are only experienced later as distinct aspects in one's life by gradually differentiating various partners in interaction.

The model of human socialization that emerges from these considerations implies an interweaving of individuation and socialization, which already allows us to make inferences about the role of social groups in individual maturation. As I have claimed above, the internalization of gradually differentiating recognitional behaviour leads to the development of a complex relation-to-self, through which children gradually learn to regard themselves as competent members of their social surroundings. The process of autonomization is tied to the process of socialization, because the only subjects who will be able to fulfil socially expected norms are those who have made these norms the practical core of their own understanding-of-self. But in order to preserve and even expand these forms of a positive relation-to-self, subjects need membership in social groups that represent a kind of mirror for original recognitional behaviour. The experience that one's own needs, judgement and, above all, skills are regarded as valuable is one that subjects must constantly renew and re-concretize so that they do not lose their strength and vitality in the anonymity of a generalized other. The group allows adults to re-experience the direct recognitional behaviour – still communicated by gestures and words – they once experienced during childhood in the affirmative reactions of their concrete caretakers – at least in fortunate cases.[10] Therefore, I believe we are justified in assuming that subjects have a very normal and even natural need to be recognized as members in social groups in which they can receive constant affirmation of their needs, judgement and various skills in direct interaction with others.

Of course, we can distinguish these groups according to which form of positive relation-to-self experiences a kind of re-concretized recognition in them. In order to maintain and perhaps even strengthen their self-confidence, subjects need to receive constant, reliable affection, which for the most part they encounter in relationships of friendship and love. Here we cannot speak of groups in the strict sense of the term, since the intersubjectivity sought after instead takes on a dyadic form which, in a balance between affiliation and disaffiliation, seems to be modelled on the structure of early symbiosis. In any case, it would not be too risky to assume that adults have an impulse to become conscious of the value of their own needs within intimate, often sexual experiences of togetherness. And because a single experience of love is not enough to sustain self-confidence over the span of a lifetime, subjects are generally dependent upon the repetition of symbiosis-like experiences of recognition.[11] Things are different when it comes to the kind of positive relation-to-self that I have termed 'self-respect'. Normally, subjects learn by the end of adolescence to detach their confidence in the value of their own judgement from the concrete approval they have previously received within their peer group. Perhaps even the gradual adoption of the role of a citizen suffices to permanently and psychologically establish a feeling of self-respect, henceforth allowing subjects to act independently of direct approval and affirmation. But such a fortunate outcome is extremely rare; in general, the experience of civil duties and, above all, rights remains too abstract to deliver the required degree of self-respect. Therefore, it is especially when subjects are denied the status of legal persons that they rely on social groups to offer a kind of compensatory respect. Such groups, to use a term coined by Richard Sennett, constitute 'countercultures of respect', in which group-specific codes of responsibility and respect prevail.[12] Only rarely do these gangs exceed a size that still allows direct interaction, since, after all, they must help individuals become aware of the value of their own judgement through the gestures and expressions of encouragement. Once a group grows and face-to-face interactions are no longer possible, it becomes a social movement in which alternative norms of respect become a generalized medium. In such anonymous large groups, collectively shared symbols and rituals replace concrete gestures of recognition, but they must retain enough symbiotic power to give members, even from a distance, compensatory respect.

But without a doubt, the most fertile ground for group formation is the layer of personality development above described as 'self-esteem'. After all, the feeling that one's own skills are valuable to others requires lifelong affirmation if it is to avoid becoming weak and feeble. Successful socialization lays the psychological basis early for this kind of positive relation-to-self, because parents, siblings or peers normally give clear signals that the growing subject possesses a certain bundle of valuable talents or skills; but after the subject has entered school and, above all, a career, the number of people upon whose esteem one's own self-esteem depends grows considerably. As a response to this increased vulnerability, the desire for concrete approval and affirmation grows. In the need to directly experience the esteem of one's peers lies *one*, if not *the*, central motive behind group formation today. With the pluralization of values and the emergence of the most diverse sub-milieus, this tendency is probably stronger than ever, because there are hardly any more unified, social standards that could anonymously inform individuals about the value of their own achievements. Today, we can barely grasp the number of organized or informal groups whose existence is exclusively dedicated to practising certain aspects of value and which allow members to receive mutual approval of their own skills and talents. And the competition that normally takes place within and even between such groups is merely an expression of the fact that this kind of esteem presupposes a position within a hierarchy.

This brief overview of the connection between the need for recognition and group formation might give the impression that all these groups are free of unconscious dynamics. The purpose of group life seems to be so transparent to all members and so committed to mental health that unconscious forces and impulses have no influence. However, this initial conception is only the result of a methodological fiction whose purpose was, in the first instance, to give an isolated view of the entirely innocent and virtually natural motives behind group formation. The scenery changes decisively once we turn to a deep layer of the desire for recognition that lies beyond the control of individual subjects. According to Winnicott, children are overwhelmed to a certain extent by their detachment from the early childhood symbiosis that represented the first step of the recognition of the independence of the other. Therefore, subjects retain, into late adulthood, the impulse to sporadically regress to a state of affiliation and fusion (*Verschmelzung*) in which they can experience themselves as being one with other subjects. This tendency, as I will claim in a second step of my argument, is typical of all forms of group life. But the fact that these are unconscious impulses does not mean that we are dealing with regression in a pathological sense.

II

The reason that Winnicott offers for his main premise is not hard to comprehend, even if there have been a number of recent objections to it. In his argument, this theorist of object relations merely draws the consequence from his thesis that we experience a symbiotic unity at the beginning of our lives. If it is true that small children only learn to organize their mental capacities by internalizing an early pattern of interaction through the stable care provided by the mother (or another primary caretaker), then this phase must be preceded by an experience of unity, a lack of separation between the subject and reality. Here we cannot speak of an other who is experienced as being independent of oneself. In this earliest phase, for which psychoanalysis offers a variety of more or less adequate concepts, ranging from 'primary narcissism' to 'symbiosis', infants regard their own impulses and drives as being so completely fused to reactions of satisfaction on the part of their primary caretaker that there can be no gap in their affective experience between their own self and reality.[13] Therefore, it is not only for the sake of mere survival that newborn children, because of their helplessness (*Mängellage*), are completely dependent upon the care of their primary caretakers. In a more profound experiential sense, they are in no way separated from the satisfying reactions of others. Winnicott is so convinced of the key inner psychological significance of this initial experience of symbiosis not only for small children, but in principle for adults as well, that in essence he dedicates his psychoanalytical work to explaining the mechanisms that allow us to master the gradual realization of an independent reality in early childhood. But we must also emphasize that Winnicott is interested not in the cognitive creation of a schema of objective, independent reality, but in the mechanisms through which children manage to recognize affectively the reality of a caretaker who is independent of their own desires. The hypothesis that Winnicott uses to explain this decisive step in children's learning process is the fantastic notion of 'transitional objects', of which I can only give a brief summary.[14] In their highly affective relation to the objects in their immediate surroundings, be they parts of a toy, the corner of a blanket or their own thumb, infants construct, generally with the implicit approval of their caretaker, an independent sphere of reality that belongs neither merely to their inner experience nor to the world of objective circumstances. On the contrary, the particularity of such an 'intermediate' zone of experience is the fact that it is grasped by all involved as an ontological sphere in which there is no question about its reality.

If we also take into account the phase of development in which children discover such intermediate objects of relation, then it seems we could presume that these objects are substitutes for the mother, who has been lost to external reality. Because these objects have a kind of hybrid nature, children can use them, before the eyes of their parents, to continue to experience their initial fantasies of symbiosis beyond the experience of separation, while at the same time creatively exploring these experiences in reality. What emerges from this playful and experimental use of objects, however, is that the function of transitional objects cannot merely be reduced to symbiotically playing the role of a mother as experienced in the initial state of fusion. Children after all do not merely relate to these objects in symbiotic tenderness, but also expose them to repeated attacks and attempts at destruction. Winnicott thus concludes that these transitional objects are ontological links between the primary experience of fusion and the experience of separation. In the playful use of affective objects, children repeatedly attempt to symbolically bridge the painful gap between internal and external reality. The fact that this is also tied to the beginning of an intersubjectively accepted illusion moves Winnicott to even go one step further and make a consequential claim: because the formation of this ontological transitional sphere derives from attempts to solve a problem humans are faced with throughout their lives, this sphere is the origin of all the interests that adults later develop in cultural objectifications (*Objektivationen*). With a certain sense of speculative daring, Winnicott writes:

> It is assumed here that the task of reality-acceptance is never completed, that no human being is free from the strain of relating

inner and outer reality, and that relief from this strain is provided by an intermediate area of experience which is not challenged (arts, religion, etc.). This intermediate area is in direct continuity with the play area of the small child who is 'lost' in play.[15]

Thus the notion of 'transitional objects' leads to the idea that humans have a lifelong tendency to sporadically fall back behind previously erected boundaries of identity (*Ich-Grenzen*) in order to cope with their growing distance from the original state of symbiosis. Strangely enough, Winnicott does not count the intersubjective life of the group among the areas of experience that allow us to get relief through regression. And yet it would have made sense to interpret certain periods in the course of group life according to the same pattern he discovers in the cultural spheres of art and religion. Even when during shared activity the mental distance between the members of the group begins to disappear and a feeling of affective concordance grows, the pressure for each person involved to accept external reality as an independent entity seems to suddenly decrease. Everyone is familiar with the difficulty of separating oneself from a group after having spent a few hours or days in a state of intensive togetherness. The difficulty of coping with the experience of separation does not relate so much to the individual members of the group, or to the productive outcome of the joint activity, but solely to the peculiar state of limbo in which the previously existing limits separating us from others are temporarily lowered. Therefore, Winnicott's fascinating observation can be expanded to include, alongside art and religion, the intersubjectivity of groups as an area of experience that dissolves the borders between internal and external reality. And if we take his reference to the origin of these intermediary zones of childlike play, we could even say that the experience of fusion in a group is, for adults, the most direct reflection of their early childhood experiences.

The consequence of expanding Winnicott's diagnosis in this way is that the intersubjective life of the group is generally marked by regularly occurring, episodic states that lead to a more or less intense fusion between the group members. Although the spectrum of such collective experiences can be extremely broad, they all take on the same form: a gradual increase, a sudden climax and a subsequent denouement in the unity of the group. Whether in the sublimated form of completely absorbed and ecstatically experienced cooperation, in the much more exhilarating feeling of being a part of a celebrating crowd, in football stadiums, at a rock concert or in the isolation of a working group that has lost the sense of time and is 'lost' as if at play – all these moments in the life of the group are marked by the tendency of an almost orgiastic fusion, which Durkheim termed 'collective effervescence'.[16] This is not, however, an unconscious theme that could give rise to group conflicts linked to primitive drives; rather, the irregularly renewed fusion feeds a common feeling of sharing norms of respect or values in the light of which subjects can grant each other recognition.

Now that we have claimed that adult subjects will normally feel an impulse to join groups in which the value of their own personality is reflected in an experiential way, we can go one step further: because the same subjects who depend on the confirmation of their self-value in the group are also driven by the need to find relief by regressing back beyond previously constructed boundaries of identity, intersubjective life in the group will constantly be marked by tendencies towards fusion. But the regressive surges that normally accompany such experiences of fusion are not an indicator of pathological re-primitivization, but an expression of having regained mental vitality; every social group, provided it fulfils the function of re-concretizing intersubjective recognition, must affirm in states of unleashed togetherness precisely those values and norms to which subjects owe the affirmation of their self-value. Therefore, the error of traditional psychoanalysis consists in fully equating these 'healthy' symptoms of regression with those in which primitive energies, when reactivated within the group, threaten individual identity.[17] Of course, these pathologies of group life do exist, but they are not to be equated with the periodic fusions through which a group renews its own culture of recognition.

With that I come to the third and shortest step in my argument. In a certain sense, even these last considerations are the product of a methodological abstraction. After all, even after taking account of regressive tendencies, I have treated social groups as if they were always free of themes and conflicts that possess a conspicuous and even pathological character. It is true that most of the conflicts that typically arise within groups are closer to consciousness and can easily be reconstructed rationally. In general, they derive from the need to interpret and hierarchically organize the individual accomplishments that subjects must be able to demonstrate in order to be counted among the recognized members of the group. The fact that hard-fought hierarchies emerging within the group can lead to rivalries, which in turn can foster partial alliances and factions, means that these fragmentations can ultimately produce mental

dynamics that can get so far out of control that they attain a scale
that is not only painful for individuals, but even threatens their
identity. However, this is not the kind of conflict we mean when we
speak of the pathology of a group; these conflicts have a rational
kernel inasmuch as they result from the fact that individual achievements can be hierarchically organized, which can in turn lead to a
flooding of group life with strategic attitudes, resentment and envy.
And of course, the compulsion to detach from the state of fusion
in the group can, in the case of individual members, always lead
to defensive reactions and tendencies of denial, because it is not
always easy to accept one's independence from others. Nevertheless, even these individual difficulties of adjustment can only lead
to the pathologization of the entire group if there are not enough
members who provide entirely inconspicuous and virtually nor-
malized, quasi-therapeutic aid.

III

In his writings on group psychology, Freud often suggests that
group life as such is responsible for the regressions that motivate
group members to submit to a leadership figure they imagine to
be omnipotent. Not the individual's psychological defects, but the
beguiling atmosphere of anonymous large groups is what causes
the individual to lose control, turning early childhood projections
into a driving force of social activity.[18] Adorno as well, for reasons
that certainly relate to his experience of national-socialist masses,
long clung to such a conception. In his essays on social psychology,
the notion that subjects within the group have little control over
their psychological energies plays a decisive role.[19] It was not until
a few years after his return from exile that he apparently changed
his mind. In the *Soziologische Exkurse* that he composed together
with Horkheimer, we find under the heading of 'group' a sentence
that largely accommodates the views expressed here: 'The obvious
precondition for all humanity is the intimate closeness to other
persons, and therefore membership in groups that enable immediate human contact.'[20] According to this definition, the psychological milieu of the group itself cannot be what leads to pathological
symptoms of a willingness to obey; on the contrary, individual
personality disorders within the group must combine in such an
unfortunate way that the interaction of the group as a whole
is burdened with a conflict in which all individuals regressively

participate. Contrary to Freud and some of his followers, group processes do not 'generally' represent, as Kernberg claims, a threat to personal identity.[21] Such threatening developments only come about once reactivated primitive energies on the part of individual members flow together, forming a current that tears away individuals' capacity for control. Among the individual currents that can thereby play a dynamic role, I would like to pick out two that appear to me to be especially influential.

What may first of all be responsible for group pathologies is the accumulation of a personality type which, owing to incomplete processes of separation, remains at the stage of primitive idealizations. Individuals of this type, perhaps paired with 'ochnophile' reactions, as Balint has described them,[22] tend to fearfully cling to a beloved object they believe to be omnipotent. If members with this psychological profile exceed a certain number beyond which the civilizing influence of the others becomes reduced or insignificant, the group as a whole can develop, as if by contagion, pathological forms of behaviour: members experience an idealized leader as all-powerful and all-knowing, while they regard themselves as inadequate, immature or incompetent. If the leader does not constantly correspond to this ideal, they will react with denial or devaluation, immediately followed by the search for a replacement leader. In his illuminating typology, Wilfred Bion referred to groups of this type as 'dependency groups' (*Abhängigkeitsgruppen*).[23] Of course, they can in no way provide members with an experiential and dense culture of recognition.

A second form of group pathology can result from the summation of a personality type which, owing to early experiences of disrespect or neglect, possesses an almost uncontrollable capacity for aggression.[24] They will tend to project their destructive fantasies upon their surroundings, seeing themselves constantly surrounded and threatened by external enemies. If such fantasies take hold of the rest of the group through a process of communicative amplification and stimulation, without the more mature members being able to contribute to realistic readjustment, the group will quickly develop a collective pathological style. Because the group members cannot tolerate any contestation of the ideologies they have developed to support their paranoid fantasies, they will tend to split into subgroups; togetherness and closeness can then only be restored by means of a collective denial of internal enmities, which in turn increases the aggression externally directed towards the enemy. According to Bion, distrust, struggle and the fear of annihilation are the essential basic features of such pathological associations, which he attempts to characterize as 'fight–flight' groups.[25] They too, of course, are extremely far removed from groups that derive from individuals' need for personal forms of recognition.

These two patterns of group pathology certainly do not exhaust the spectrum of potential group disorders. Bion cites at least one other basic form which he takes to be a clinical disorder.[26] Yet my purpose here has been not to give an exhaustive overview, but instead – by demonstrating negative deviations – to once again prove the claim at the centre of my argumentation: the 'I' seeks the 'We' of shared group experience, because even after maturity, we are dependent on forms of social recognition imbued with direct encouragement and affirmation. Neither self-respect nor self-esteem can be maintained without the supportive experience of practising shared values in the group. Therefore, far from constituting a threat to personal identity, groups are, to take a phrase from Adorno, a primary 'source of humanity'. The pathologizations that we repeatedly observe in the life of the group are, conversely, caused by the infiltration of individual personality disorders. Therefore, social groups are always as good or as bad as the prevailing conditions of socialization.

Notes

1   Sigmund Freud, 'Group Psychology and the Analysis of the Ego', in *The Standard Edition of the Complete Psychological Works of Sigmund Freud*, vol. XVIII, ed. James Strachey (London: Hogarth Press, 1981), pp. 67–143; Elias Canetti, *Crowds and Power*, trans. Carol Stewart (New York: Farrar, Straus and Giroux, 1962); Theodor W. Adorno, 'Freudian Theory and the Pattern of Fascist Propaganda', in *The Culture Industry: Selected Essays on Mass Culture*, ed. J.M. Bernstein (London: Routledge, 1991), pp. 132–57. On the significance of the concept of the masses within German sociology, see Helmuth Berking, *Masse und Geist: Studien zur Soziologie in der Weimarer Republik* (Berlin: Wissenschasftlicher Autoren-Verlag, 1984).
2   The subject of gangs, which goes back to Frederic M. Thrasher's classic study *The Gang: A Study of 1313 Gangs in Chicago* (Chicago: New Chicago School Press, 2000), was picked up again in 1950s Germany and discussed under the term *Halbstarken*. See Heinz

Kluth, 'Die "Halbstarken" – Legende oder Wirklichkeit?', *Deutsche Jugend* (November 1956), pp. 495–502.

3 See Charles Cooley, *Social Organization* (New York: Charles Scribner's Sons, 1963).

4 Jean Piaget, *The Moral Judgement of the Child*, trans. Marjorie Gabain (New York: Free Press, 1997).

5 See Michael Sandel, *Liberalism and the Limits of Justice* (Cambridge: Cambridge University Press, 1982). For a psychoanalytically inspired critique of the idealizations of communitarianism, see Hinrich Fink-Eitel, 'Gemeinschaft als Macht: Zur Kritik des Kommunitarismus', in Micha Brumlik and Hauke Brunkhorst, eds, *Gemeinschaft und Gerechtigkeit* (Frankfurt/Main: Fischer, 1993), pp. 306–22.

6 Axel Honneth, 'Objektbeziehungstheorie und postmoderne Identität: Über das vermeintliche Veralten der Psychoanalyse', in *Unsichtbarkeit: Stationen einer Theorie der Intersubjektivität* (Frankfurt/Main: Suhrkamp, 2003), pp. 138–61.

7 Erik H. Erikson, *Identity and the Life Cycle* (London and New York: W.W. Norton & Company, 1980), pp. 51ff.

8 George H. Mead, *Mind, Self, and Society* (Chicago: University of Chicago Press, 1967).

9 John E. Mack and Steven L. Ablon, eds, *The Development and Sustenance of Self-Esteem in Childhood* (New York: International Universities Press, 1983).

10 Owen Flanagan, *Varieties of Moral Personality: Ethics and Psychological Realism* (Cambridge, MA: Harvard University Press, 1991), part II.

11 Axel Honneth, *The Struggle for Recognition: The Moral Grammar of Social Conflicts*, trans. Joel Anderson (Cambridge: Polity, 1995), ch. 5.

12 Richard Sennett and Jonathan Cobb, *The Hidden Injuries of Class* (Cambridge, MA: Harvard University Press, 1972), pp. 79–89; see the example offered by Phillippe Bourgois, *In Search of Respect: Selling Crack in El Barrio* (Cambridge: Cambridge University Press, 1995).

13 Donald W. Winnicott, *Maturational Processes and the Facilitating Environment* (London and New York: Karnac, 1984).

14 See Donald W. Winnicott, *Playing and Reality* (New York: Tavistock Publications, 1971), ch. 1.

15 Ibid., p. 18.

16 Émile Durkheim, *The Elementary Forms of Religious Life*, trans. Carol Cosman (Oxford: Oxford University Press, 2001); Hans Joas, *The*

Genesis of Values, trans. Gregory Moore (Cambridge: Polity, 2000), ch. 4.

17 Axel Honneth, 'Anxiety and Politics: The Strengths and Weaknesses of Franz Neumann's Diagnosis of a Social Pathology', in *Pathologies of Reason*, trans. James Ingram (New York: Columbia University Press, 2009), ch. 8.

18 Freud, 'Group Psychology and the Analysis of the Ego'.

19 Adorno, 'Freudian Theory and the Pattern of Fascist Propaganda'.

20 Institut für Sozialforschung, *Soziologische Exkurse: Nach Vorträgen und Diskussionen* (Frankfurt/Main: Institut für Sozialforschung, 1956), ch. IV, p. 64.

21 Otto F. Kernberg, *Ideology, Conflict and Leadership in Groups and Organizations* (New Haven: Yale University Press, 1998), part I, ch. 1.

22 Michael Balint, *Angstlust und Regression* (Stuttgart: Klett-Cotta, 1994), ch. 2.

23 Wilfred Bion, *Experiences in Groups* (London: Tavistock, 1961), ch. 2.

24 See Ferdinand Sutterlütty, *Gewaltkarrieren: Jugendliche im Kreislauf von Gewalt und Missachtung* (Frankfurt/Main: Campus, 2002).

25 Bion, *Experiences in Groups*, ch. 2.

26 Ibid., ch. 6.

13

Facets of the Presocial Self: Rejoinder to Joel Whitebook

In his essay on 'Mutual Recognition and the Work of the Negative', Joel Whitebook relies on a number of classical theoretical approaches to outline his thesis, which represents a strong objection to the so-called 'Habermasians'. He claims that the intersubjective, socialization-theoretical turn in Critical Theory abandons the idea of the non-conformism of the individual subject in relation to reality, and thus betrays the motif of 'negativity' from Hobbes all the way through to the work of Freud.[1] Even if Whitebook does not draw this comparison himself, the intention and execution of his argument strongly resemble the critique that Marcuse and Adorno, over fifty years ago, advanced against 'revisions' in psychoanalysis. At that time, it was the renouncing of the Freudian drive theory that served as proof of a turn to conformism,[2] while today, abandoning the notion that subjects have an asocial tendency counts as an indicator of a conformist tendency in Critical Theory. Of course, this assessment is based on a certain idea about the tasks of a critical theory of society, one that is anything but self-evident and thus requires independent justification. Why should a critical theory of society only be considered 'critical' if its socialization-theoretical premises assume that there is a structural conflict between the individual and the social order, expressing itself in the 'negativity' of the subject? But in this rejoinder, I want to bracket out this metatheoretical problem and instead focus on the point that is most important to Whitebook. The key question is whether and how we should assume human beings to have a presocial nature that can count as a source of ineradicable 'negativity'. Of course, I can only speak for myself and cannot outline the position of all those whom Whitebook labels, somewhat vaguely, as 'Habermasians'. My aim is a discussion with a long-time friend with whom I share an orientation towards the tradition of Critical Theory, but with whom I apparently no longer share a common conception of the theoretical means for updating this theory.

I

After an initial reading of his essay, the central aim that Whitebook pursues on very different levels of his argumentation seems clear. Once humans, in the course of the intersubjective turn in Critical Theory, are viewed as owing their subjectivity entirely to the social process of recognition, there remains no theoretical space for hypotheses about the presocial constitution of the subject. This also eliminates the possibility of seeing a quasi-natural force of negativity in the human individual, one that is responsible for nonconformism, resistance and revolt – without any societal influence. As appealing as this thesis might appear at first sight, under closer examination it falls into various pieces, each of which requires independent treatment. It seems to me that in the course of his argumentation, Whitebook presents three very different views on what genetically precedes processes of recognition, thus representing a presocial potential for negativity. In order to simplify matters, I will label these three alternatives according to the names of the classic works that Whitebook uses as theoretical references for his argument. The text presents in sequence the leitmotifs of Hobbes, Kant and Freud in order to draw attention to a 'presocial' layer in individual subjects, which the intersubjective turn in Critical Theory threatens to lose sight of.

(a)   Like Hobbes, Whitebook assumes that humans are naturally aggressive and have a fundamentally hostile stance towards each other, which cannot be wholly controlled or overcome by any form of socialization. He claims, referring to the institutionalization of the capitalist market economy, that modern societies have managed to produce a social institution in which humans' capacity for aggression can be expressed in a relatively socially tolerable manner, without entirely losing its destructive force. I seriously doubt that Hobbes' political anthropology can be understood as the claim that humans have an inborn capacity for aggression; in my view he claims *solely* that individual subjects have a natural impulse for self-preservation that can be expressed in very different needs, while aggression might be a psychological by-product of the struggle of all against all, a struggle that results from the general opacity of others' motives.[3] But for our purposes, it might be acceptable to assume that social theory in the tradition of Hobbes entertains the premise that humans, owing to a natural aggressiveness, are hostile towards each other. What the theory of recognition would therefore lose sight of is the human capacity for aggression, which, as a presocial relic, could not be removed by any form of socialization, no matter how successful.

(b)   Following Kant, Whitebook surprisingly also assumes humans to have another presocial potential, which he describes as a kind of original reflexivity on the part of the individual. Here we see a confluence of two currents in the recent debate on the concept of subjectivity, and it is not clear to me how they can be systematically linked. On the one hand, Whitebook refers to the extremely complex debate between Jürgen Habermas and Dieter Henrich, taking the side of Henrich and claiming that intersubjectivism must assume that subjects have an 'initial intuition of the self', if it is to give a cogent explanation of the possibility of self-consciousness. After all, how else could we justify the fact that individuals must always already have understood themselves as addressees of the recognition of their partners in interaction, if we do not assume them to have an antecedent and rudimentary intuition of the self?[4] On the other hand, Whitebook draws on Mark Sacks, who seeks to revive Kant's transcendental subjectivism by arguing that individual subjects can only be understood as being capable of taking up a critical and detached stance towards their social surroundings if we do not interpret their capacity for reflection solely as the product of socialization through recognition. After all, if the self was nothing but the product of a socializing interaction, we could not determine the origin of its conscious reflective capacity, its ability to detach itself from its social circumstances.[5] The difference between these two lines of argumentation consists in the fact that, in the first case, a pre-reflective intuition of self and, in the second case, an initial capacity for reflection are asserted against any notion of intersubjectivity.

(c)   Finally, drawing on Freud, Whitebook assumes that humans have an ontogenetically initial phase in which they strive for omnipotence; the particularity of this phase is the absence of any idea of an objective reality that is beyond our control. In the earliest phase of childhood, at least that is the claim of psychoanalytical theories of narcissism or symbiosis, children can separate neither themselves from their surroundings nor their caretakers from other objects. Instead they encounter reality in a kind of hallucinatory state, experiencing it as the material of their own intentions (*Verfügungsmasse*). However, we do not arrive at Whitebook's central thesis until we see the relics from such an omnipotent phase at work in adults, thus viewing the striving for omnipotence as constitutive for human subjects: individuals retain a presocial relic inasmuch as they preserve a tendency for omnipotent fantasies throughout their lives; this tendency is developed prior to all experiences of social recognition and remains resistant to them. What the intersubjective turn loses sight of is this measure of reality-denial, the 'irrationality' of individual subjects that stems from the persistent influence of an early-childhood striving for omnipotence.

In my view the problem with Whitebook's approach is the fact that he seeks to employ all three motifs at once, without sufficiently inquiring into their internal reconcilability. Before I examine the cogency of his individual objections (III), I first want to examine the consistency of his own argumentation. A good starting point lies in the question of how these three theoretical motifs relate to each other when they are reformulated using the contemporary terminology of basic psychoanalytical discourse (II).

II

For each of the three theoretical complexes that Whitebook employs in his critique of intersubjectivism, we can find equivalents in the current debate on the relationship between psychoanalysis and research on early childhood development. By translating these older ideas into the vocabulary of this more current research, it is easier to identify the dispute between Whitebook and myself. Furthermore, by updating these ideas, it becomes more apparent that Whitebook runs the danger of asserting two irreconcilable premises.

Whitebook's first objection consists in the claim that humans have an inborn capacity for aggression, which intersubjectivism loses sight of owing to the fact it leaves no space for destructive tendencies in the process of mutual recognition. This Hobbesian notion of intersubjective hostility has had a long history within psychoanalysis.[6] After Freud revised his initial version of drive theory and claimed, apparently influenced by the First World War, the existence of a life drive and a death drive, the idea quickly spread throughout the field of psychoanalysis that alongside the sex drive, there must be a second bodily drive responsible for subjects' aggressive and destructive tendencies. Today, we can continue the discussion over whether we have to assume that humans have a capacity for aggression with reference to empirical observations in experimental child psychology. The majority of the findings in this field suggest that aggressive behaviour on the part of small children – primitive expressions of anger and hostility – are to be understood not as endogenous drives, but as a reaction to unpleasant experiences. The older children become, the easier it is to interpret their aggressive tendencies as reactive efforts to cope with failures and injuries that have their source in social relationships. These primarily include traumatic experiences, such as physical or sexual abuse, but also frustrations stemming from neglect. However we might interpret these findings, whether we see them as indicators of a genetic capacity for aggression or merely as a secondary, reactive way of coping, there is little reason to assume a genetic aggressive drive. Even Winnicott, who is a 'Kleinian' in a certain sense, understood children's destructive tendencies as expressions of a kind of ontological experimentation meant to test out the independence of the world.[7]

This last point gives us an opportunity to jump to Whitebook's third objection, before examining his complex second argument. By claiming that at the beginning of each person's individual development there is a phase of imagined omnipotence, Whitebook touches on an especially controversial topic between representatives of psychoanalysis and research on infant development. Building upon the theoretical speculations of Freud, who spoke of 'primary narcissism', within the psychoanalytical movement there developed a tendency to simply assume an initial phase in which children entertain fantasies of omnipotence. Cognitively incapable of distinguishing between themselves and their environment, infants experience all elements of their perceivable environment as being fused with their own activities, posing no resistance and standing at their disposal. Even object relations theory, which, contrary to Freudian orthodoxy, emphasized the crucial importance of interaction with a primary caretaker, largely retained this description of the initial childhood phase. Although it spoke mostly of initial 'symbiosis' rather than 'primary narcissism', children were still regarded as experiencing this state of fusion with the mother as a 'grandiose' expansion of their own power.[8]

It was above all Daniel Stern's synthesis of experimental investigations that put a major dent in this conception of an initial phase
of omnipotence by showing that even in the first months after birth,
children develop an elementary sense of self.[9] The psychoanalytical hypothesis that small children cannot initially distinguish their
own self from their environment could no longer be so easily maintained; this empirically undermined the entire idea of an initial
phase of imagined omnipotence. Ever since that time, the discussion has essentially focused on the question as to which corrections
need to be made to the assumption of primary symbiosis in order to
reconcile it with the empirical finding that infants have an elementary sense of self. The term 'symbiosis' is now used to refer not to a
cognitive but to an affective state; instead of being conceived of as
an entire phase, it is now regarded merely as an interim period of
symbiotic experience.[10] But wherever these theoretical adjustments
might lead, it is now clear that the classic idea of an initial phase of
infant fantasies of omnipotence is irreconcilable with experimentally proven findings of an early sense of self.

So it is all the more surprising that Whitebook simply places
both theses alongside each other, without paying any attention to
whether they are reconcilable or not. His third objection against
intersubjectivism consists in asserting an initial, presocial intuition of self, such as Stern proposed in his concept of the infant's
early sense of self. Even if Stern's thesis is meant as an empirical
claim, whereas Henrich's considerations aim to provide a conceptual or transcendental determination, the empirical finding can, in
a certain way, be used as evidence for the plausibility of the philosophical claim: humans must have a genetic intuition of a 'core self'
and a 'core other' before 'creating an interpersonal world'.[11] But
Stern's argument is primarily aimed not against intersubjectivism,
into which he in fact seeks to inject more clarity, but instead against
the psychoanalytical tradition for its clinging to the idea of an initial
state of 'fusion': this thesis, the assumption of a primary state of
unity between self and world, is irreconcilable with the empirical
finding that infants, already after a few weeks, have a rudimentary
capacity for distinguishing between self and other and for perceiving the intentionality of the other. The conclusion, therefore, that
Stern draws on the basis of his experimental inquiries is the following: '[The evidence] suggests that the capacity to have merger- or
fusion-like experiences as described in psychoanalysis is secondary
to and dependent upon an already existing sense of self and other.'[12]
However, this is precisely the consequence about which Whitebook

seems to be uncertain. On the one hand, he objects to intersubjectivism by pointing to an initial intuition of self; on the other hand, he retains the assumption of a presocial state of cognitive unity between self and world. Either infants are inclined, because of their experiences of fusion, to states of imagined omnipotence, or they already possess an elemental sense of self, which would leave little to no psychological room for fantasies of omnipotence.

The matter is even more complicated, because Whitebook takes Henrich's thesis of an initial intuition of self and projects onto it the claim that subjects must be capable of conscious reflection prior to any social interaction. Apart from the fact that Henrich conceptually seeks to avoid such a claim by speaking of an 'intuition' rather than 'consciousness' of self – that is, by claiming a quasi-affective state of consciousness rather than a relation of knowledge – Whitebook ascribes a fourth quality to presocial subjects that seems to overwhelm them once and for all. The subject that genetically exists prior to any social interaction and recognition is defined not only as being naturally equipped with a need for aggression, possessed by a delusion of omnipotence and a capacity for distinguishing between self and world, but also as possessing the capacity for conscious reflection (*Reflexivität*) that we often describe with the term consciousness-of-self (*Selbstbewusstsein*). This last claim doubtlessly stems from a development-psychological reinterpretation of a thesis that, in the first instance, was only intended to be a 'transcendental' claim: what Mark Sacks had in mind was the conceptual compulsion to conceive of individual subjects as being independent of all social conventions and expectations of recognition in order to be able to view them as rational and responsible (*begründungsfähig*) beings. If the subject merely came about by adopting social expectations of behaviour, then it couldn't contemplate the kind of beliefs that are necessary for examining given norms and claims individually. But contrary to Sacks, this claim should not be stylized into a general objection against the kind of intersubjectivism that would only be incapable of taking into account the individual's capacity for reflection if it identified the mechanism by which we take up the perspective of the other (Mead) or acquire a linguistic form of life (Wittgenstein) with a complete adoption of corresponding *substantive* beliefs. For Mead and Habermas, subjects only acquire the ability to distinguish their own beliefs from those of their partners in interaction and to assert the individual core of their personality by *formally* acquiring a social perspective or an intersubjectively shared language.[13] But above all, one should not conflate Sacks' objection with the implausible claim that subjects have their own set of beliefs prior to all social interaction. This would give the odd impression that we are not only intuitively familiar with our own intentional states at an early age, but also possess knowledge that we could articulate about these states prior to learning a language through intersubjective interaction. Therefore, the claim that subjects possess a kind of reflexivity prior to social interaction is appropriate only as an indication of a structural fact, not as a basis for development-psychological reconstructions. Since the writings of Dewey, Mead, Wittgenstein and Habermas, there can be no doubt that we only acquire the capacity for rational justification of our beliefs and judgements through symbolically mediated interaction. But this must not be equated with the assumption that individual subjects are only made up of the beliefs, desires and intentions they have learned by adopting the perspective of their partners in interaction. Individuals acquire individuality as mature persons to the degree that they are capable of articulating their own impulses and views through the medium of an intersubjectively shared, general vocabulary.

But of course, this is not the objection that Whitebook ultimately intends to present in his essay. He himself concedes that the idea of an ontogenetic process of individualization within an intersubjective framework is unproblematic. But if we attempt to extract the rational essence of Whitebook's objections not from the content of his relatively disconnected theses, but from the overall affect of the text, then we run into a problem that represents a significant challenge for intersubjectivism. At first sight, it is not very clear how we are to conceive of the element of dissent and resistance within individual subjects if they owe their identity and personality structure entirely to a process of social recognition. As Whitebook seems to ask throughout his many irreconcilable theses, do we not have to assume that individuals have some indestructible trace of antisocial impulsiveness if we are to conceive of the permanent possibility of rationally uncontrollable deviation?

III

Neither an inborn capacity for aggression nor an initial sense of self offers an appropriate expression for the question of how we are to conceive of the 'work of the negative' within the framework of intersubjectivism. The first conception is too empirically controversial to provide the basis for a serious objection to intersubjectivism. And besides, the assumption of an aggression drive would not necessarily force us to abandon the concept of recognition, but would only imply that we would, in addition, have to recognize an endogenous source of social hostility. By contrast, when it comes to the second conception – that is, the assumption of an antecedent experience-of-self – neither Henrich nor Stern, whose arguments lie at different levels, claims a structural agency (*Instanz*) of hostility in humans. On the contrary, they merely seek to demonstrate that the intersubjective encounter must be preceded, either conceptually or genetically, by a kind of elementary sense of self in order to explain the fact that individuals are capable of understanding themselves as addressees of affection or recognition. Ultimately, therefore, from the variety of theorems that Whitebook presents, only the psychoanalytical conception of early childhood delusions of omnipotence remains as a possible justification for his central presumption. As we saw above, however, there is significant tension between this classic thesis and the justifiable assumption that infants already possess an intuitive sense of self. For we cannot, on the one hand, speak of an initial unity between self and world and, on the other hand, claim the development of a 'core self' during this same phase. Nevertheless, a fantasy of omnipotence, anchored in early childhood and continuing to influence us throughout our lives, seems to be the underlying claim of Whitebook's argumentation. It clarifies the meaning of his digression on the *Phenomenology of Spirit*,[14] explains the genesis of the hostility that is seen as contradicting the process of recognition, and, finally, reveals what the idea of constitutive human irrationality is supposed to indicate.

In order to recount this thesis, we should employ a conceptual distinction that implicitly underlies Whitebook's essay, but is never justified explicitly. Although we can understand the claim that there is an antecedent form of elementary intuition-of-self as an indication of a constitutive 'asocial' dimension (*Asozialität*) in all subjectivity, because it attempts to retain an irreducible perspective of subjective experience as the opposite pole of intersubjectivity, the claim that we have a constant striving for omnipotence must be interpreted as an indication of an antisocial dimension in each subject, because this refers to tendencies of constant negation of social intersubjectivity. This distinction between an 'asocial' and 'antisocial' dimension marks the step that Whitebook must take, going beyond George Herbert Mead's thesis that the individualization of the subject represents an often conflict-filled process in which the tension between internalized intersubjectivity ('Me') and subjective feeling ('I') is resolved. Within every subject, there is not only a more or less articulable perspective of subjectivity representing the opposite pole of the intersubjective perspective, but also a constant impulse to deny or fight back against intersubjectivity, to the degree that the latter indicates the existence of independent others. This constitutive 'antisocial' dimension is what Whitebook seems to have in mind when he speaks of the 'work of the negative' as a theoretical desideratum of intersubjectivism.

Now, when it comes to the question of whether and how intersubjectivism can integrate the assumption of this kind of antisocial striving, every step is dependent upon a more precise clarification of the underlying concept of omnipotence. Here we have an open arena for combining theoretical speculation and clinical observation, which child development research is only beginning to explore. According to the research already available, it seems clear that we cannot so easily presuppose an initial state of total fusion between self and world. This denies us the possibility of viewing the unconscious striving for omnipotence as an almost natural trait of the subject stemming from the desire to compensate the inevitable realization of an independent reality. By contrast, not only clinical observation, but also crowd psychology and existential-phenomenological observation point to a deep-seated receptiveness to experiences of fusion with other people within each individual subject. The willingness to fall back behind an already attained boundary of identity (*Ich-Grenzen*) and enter into a state of fusion with others seems so widespread as to require an anthropological explanation.[15] In my view, a way out of this dilemma, which today appears to represent a scientific anomaly within psychoanalysis,[16] would be to assume that the early phase of infancy represents not a permanent state of fusion, but momentous *episodes* of fusion with primary objects. Although children are often capable of sensing a core self that is separate from the external world, they sporadically enter into a state of experience in which the actions of their primary caretakers appear as extensions of their own needs, to the degree that they can experience themselves as fused with their primary caretakers.[17] If we assume that these episodes are filled by the elation of pleasurable expansion/fusion on the part of the infant, then we are certainly justified in describing the gradual development of a sense of the independence of the other as a negative phase of separation/non-fusion. This does not occur suddenly and all at once;

rather, children gradually develop the affective certainty that their beloved primary objects possess an unalterable reality that must be tolerated.

Of course, this reinterpretation demands that we abandon a number of crucial psychoanalytical premises. Experiences of fusion now occupy only a small part of infants' world of experience; the dissolution of these experiences through an increased sense of independent reality is no longer so sudden and shocking; on the whole, the process loses the character of being a subsequent adaptation to an already existing perception of the separation between self and world. Although this segmented process of separation might cause displeasure, sorrow and pain, the experience of the independence of the primary caretaker is no longer perceived as a kind of external attack on the child's world of experience, and thus can hardly be viewed as traumatic. An additional change concerns our conception of the quality of merely partial states of fusion: because the latter no longer cover the entirety of infants' contact with the external world, but only temporal episodes of intensive interaction with their primary caretakers, it would be wrong to describe these experiences with the concept of 'omnipotence'. According to this new conception, children do not perceive the world as mere material at their disposal, but imagine themselves in certain situations to be fused with their primary caretaker. The proper expression for this state would therefore be a 'state of fusion'. The conception of a 'fantasy of omnipotence' is misleading, for what infants abandon by acquiring a sense of the independent reality of their primary caretakers is not a state of imagined omnipotence, but beloved objects occasionally experienced as fused with their own experience.[18]

At this point, however, there is a problem that Whitebook justifiably raises by criticizing my occasional use of the term 'intersubjectivity' to describe such early stages of fusion as a case of conceptual confusion. Only from the perspective of the observer, not from the perspective of the infant (or the primary caretaker), can we describe episodes of fusion with beloved objects as a process of interaction. If, by contrast, we take up the perspective of those involved, these states of fusion cannot be conceived of as a form of intersubjectivity, because the prerequisite of an encounter between two self-aware, independent subjects is lacking. But even this modification does little to alter the general thesis that we should only retain a small part of the classical assumption of a primary narcissism, an initial state of experienced omnipotence: the episodic occurrence of experiences of fusion. The beginning of the individual maturation process is thus determined not by a phase of ubiquitous fantasies of omnipotence, but by a stage in which a budding sense of the distinction between self and world (*Selbstabgrenzung*) is accompanied by experiences of fusion.

But the real difficulty concerns how we can build a bridge from this altered perspective to the speculative hypothesis that forms the innermost core of Whitebook's considerations – the concept of negativity. Is there among these changed premises some justified assumption that would suggest that we should ascribe to subjects an antisocial tendency or a need to fight back against the independent reality of the social, one that originates in early childhood? Within this altered framework, the concept of separation also takes on a new, much weaker interpretation, which no longer makes it the obvious key to determining the corresponding cause. If the experience of separation only consists in the gradual process whereby infants, under the pressure of an increasing perception of reality, are forced to abandon a state of fusion with their beloved objects, then this experience loses its shocking, traumatic character, which for psychoanalytical theory made it appear to be a cause for the lifelong existence of fantasies of omnipotence. Nevertheless, if humans have a constitutive receptivity to experiences of fusion, then these experiences must have their initial cause in the overwhelming experience of abandoning beloved objects, if such states of fusion are only episodes. How could we otherwise explain infants' apparent fears of separation when they are weaned, attempt to fall asleep or feel alone, if not by assuming that they are overwhelmed by their growing sense that their primary caretakers are independent and cannot be controlled? Infants' experiences of fusion in especially intense moments of being held must have awakened a psychological expectation of physical and mental security, which is then increasingly disappointed by their growing sense of reality; thus we can expect the reaction to be a tense unity of fear and pain, anger and sorrow. We then need to assume, in addition, that these expectations remain anchored in the subject beyond childhood, if we are to explain the remarkable fact that even mature adults react to separation with panic and a tendency to regress into a state of fusion. As if they had remained small children, even adults have affective difficulties recognizing the independence of beloved and desired subjects and thus accepting the fractured nature of intersubjectivity. Only in this way can we make sense of why 'transitional objects' (Winnicott) retain their highly significant function, beyond childhood and even into old age, of opening up a potential free-space between mere fantasy and objective reality, allowing us to cope with the pain of separation.[19]

Whether the life-long influence of early expectations of security can be described as the 'work of the negative' or merely as a largely unconscious need might be a question of scientific temperament. In any case, it does not seem to me to be wholly inappropriate to view this as an infinite source of antisociality, because each act of resistance to the independence and uncontrollability of the other, who thereby embodies sociality, is new. But it remains unclear to me why this motive should be antithetically opposed to intersubjectivism. Why should the idea of a life-long willingness for fusion contradict the concept of recognition? Is the fact that transitional objects serve to help us cope emotionally with our separation from primary objects, which we now recognize as being independent, not a clear indication of the inordinate significance of intersubjectivity? It is true that infants' early experiences of fusion do not have an intersubjective structure owing to the fact that they lack a sufficiently differentiated partner with whom a relationship would need to be formed; but, paradoxically, we can only grasp this early state by employing the concept of primary intersubjectivity. It is only by being held, cuddled and cared for that infants can experience fusion. Therefore, it would be right to grasp infants' sporadic experiences of fusion as the 'zero-point' of all experiences of recognition. As deep-seated feelings of security lost forever, they compel us to strive for those fractured forms of intersubjectivity that take on the form of mutual recognition between mature subjects.

Notes

I am indebted to Martin Dornes for various suggestions on this essay. I have also profited from discussions in the 'Psychoanalysis' working group at the Institute for Social Research, Frankfurt am Main, and wish to thank all the participants in our two-week session for their many diverse suggestions.

1   See Joel Whitebook, 'Mutual Recognition and the Work of the Negative', in William Rehg and James Bohman, eds, *Pluralism and the Pragmatic Turn: The Transformation of Critical Theory. Essays in Honor of Thomas McCarthy* (Cambridge, MA and London: MIT Press, 2001), pp. 257–91.

2 Theodor W. Adorno, 'Sociology and Psychology', *New Left Review*, nos 46 and 47 (November/December 1967 and January/February 1968), pp. 67–80, 79–97; Herbert Marcuse, 'Obsolescence of Psychoanalysis', in Douglas Kellner and Clayton Pierce, eds, *The Collected Papers of Herbert Marcuse: Philosophy, Psychoanalysis and Emancipation*, vol. 5 (London and New York: Routledge, 2011), pp. 109–21.

3 In the recent research on Hobbes, see Christine Chwaszcza, 'Anthropologie und Moralphilosophie im "Leviathan",' in Wolfgang Kersting, ed., *Thomas Hobbes, Leviathan (Reihe Klassiker Auslegen)* (Berlin: Akademie Verlag, 1996), pp. 83–108.

4 See Dieter Henrich, 'Self-Consciousness and Speculative Thinking', in David Klemm and Günter Zöller, eds, *Figuring the Self: Subject, Absolute and Others in Classical German Philosophy* (Albany: SUNY Press, 1997), pp. 99–133; Dieter Henrich, *Bewusstes Leben: Untersuchungen zum Verhältnis von Subjektivität und Metaphysik* (Stuttgart: Reklam, 1999).

5 Mark Sacks, *Objectivity and Insight* (Oxford: Oxford University Press, 2000), ch. 4.

6 See Martin Dornes, *Die Frühe Kindheit: Entwicklungspsychologie der ersten Lebensjahre* (Frankfurt/Main: Fischer, 1997), ch. 9.

7 See Donald W. Winnicott, 'The Use of an Object and Relating through Identifications', in *Playing and Reality* (New York: Tavistock Publications, 1971), pp. 115–27.

8 For an overview, see Martin Dornes, *Der kompetente Säugling: Die präverbale Entwicklung des Menschen* (Frankfurt/Main: Fischer, 1993), ch. 3.

9 Daniel N. Stern, *The Interpersonal World of the Infant* (New York: Basic Books, 1985).

10 For an overview, see Dornes, *Die Frühe Kindheit*, ch. 5.

11 Stern, *The Interpersonal World of the Infant*, p.70.

12 Ibid.

13 Lutz Wingert, 'Der Grund der Differenz: Subjektivität als ein Moment von Intersubjektivität', in Micha Brumlik and Hauke Brunkhorst, eds, *Gemeinschaft und Gerechtigkeit* (Frankfurt/Main: Fischer, 1993), pp. 290–305.

14 I do not go into the difference between Whitebook's and my own assessment of the role of the *Phenomonology of Spirit* within the theory of recognition. I continue to believe that the use of the concepts of recognition in the *Phenomenology* is not very clear and of little benefit. But I now have a much more positive view of the conception of recognition that underlies Hegel's *Philosophy of Right*.

See Chapter 2 in the present volume, as well as Axel Honneth, *Suffering from Indeterminacy: An Attempt at a Reactualization of Hegel's Philosophy of Right*, trans. Jack Ben-Levi (Amsterdam: Van Gorcum Ltd, 2000).

15 This is the direction taken by Matthias Baumgart in 'Psychoanalyse und Säuglingsuntersuchung: Versuch einer Integration unter Berücksichtigung methodischer Unterschiede', *Psyche*, vol. 45 (1991), pp. 780–809. We also find many rich descriptions of phenomena of self-transcendence in Hans Joas, *The Genesis of Values*, trans. Gregory Moore (Cambridge: Polity, 2000).

16 See Thomas S. Kuhn, *The Structure of Scientific Revolutions* (Chicago: University of Chicago Press, 1996), ch. VI.

17 Fred Pine, 'Infant Research, the Symbiotic Phase, and Clinical Work: A Case Study of a Concept', in *Drive, Ego, Object and Self: A Synthesis for Clinical Work* (New York: Basic Books, 1990), pp. 232–46. A marvellous overview can be found in Dornes, *Die Frühe Kindheit*, ch. 5.

18 Joachim Küchenhoff, 'Verlorenes Objekt, Trennung und Anerkennung', *Forum der Psychoanalyse*, vol. 15 (1999), pp. 189–203.

19 Tilmann Habermas, *Geliebte Objekte: Symbole und Instrumente der Identitätsbildung* (Frankfurt/Main: Suhrkamp, 1999), ch. 5.

14

Disempowering Reality:
Secular Forms of Consolation

As members of Western culture, when it comes to dealing with the heaviest blows of fate, we have all become naturalists. Even the most faithful Christians will hardly see death as a chance for redemption, but instead merely as the definitive endpoint of a natural process of organic decay. None of us sees in serious illness even a hint of a spiritual entity that is punishing us for our worldly misconduct. And when it comes to natural catastrophes that cost countless lives, even after a few hours we all have the necessary information about the causes. Whether we like it or not, whether we are religious or staunch atheists, there no longer seems to be any alternative to a naturalistic explanation for the causes of our suffering on earth. We suffer the same fate as all other natural creatures; at birth we are exposed to a life filled with risks; we are constantly threatened by organic illnesses; and at the end of life, death awaits us. All our advances in technology and medicine have in no way been able to change this feeling of being exposed to nature. With each therapeutic victory over illness, our knowledge of further physical dangers grows; every technically successful struggle against a natural catastrophe is quickly followed by an even more dangerous threat. There is no doubting Freud's prognosis that scientific enlightenment robs us of the compensation offered by religious faith and compels us to 'submit to the inevitable'.[1] We are exposed to the causal powers of nature without any prospect of compensation or redemption in the afterlife.

In light of this naturalism that we now almost take for granted, it is all the more astounding that we seem to tolerate and even welcome a number of practices and attitudes that do not at all harmonize with this worldview. None of us is confused when a person begins to converse with the tombstone of a recently deceased loved one. We all are touched by and approve of a friendly couple's efforts to maintain the bedroom of a lost child in order to preserve his or her home. And we are not shocked to see ourselves choked up at funerals, whose ritual procedures more or less implicitly presuppose the existence of an eternal soul. Naturalists that we are, we take part in various spiritual practices and adopt attitudes that are anything but naturalistic. Whether we retain a Christian faith or are staunch atheists, in certain moments of our lives we all seem to set aside our naturalistic certainties in order to remain in contact with those who have died, and even to feel ourselves in their presence. The strangest thing about these spiritual traces in our profane everyday life is the fact that not only those involved, but detached observers as well, take them to be entirely natural. Nobody points out the contradiction in efforts to communicate with the dead, and none of us draws attention to the discrepancy with our other everyday beliefs; rather, all seem to willingly assume that the one is reconcilable with the other. It is a bit like when caring parents support their children in treating some object like a living entity, even though they are aware of its pure materiality.

The fact that, despite such scientific disenchantment, the dead have preserved a peculiar kind of presence among the living has long been a topic of literature. James Joyce, for instance, described in his marvellous short story 'The Dead' how a woman's dead lover continues to be a conversational partner in her everyday life, even convincing her husband of the man's 'wayward and flickering existence'.[2] The further events progress, the more the otherwise clear lines between the kingdoms of the dead and the living seem to blur. The most touching instance is to be found in Joan Didion's recent autobiographical account of how she began, after the sudden death of her husband and without explicitly noticing it, to engage in virtually 'magical' practices in order to secure his continued existence. Here as well, the pull of the narrative results from the way the author allows us to observe how we approve, with growing sympathy, of a series of strange attitudes and measures that are entirely irreconcilable with our normal attitudes.[3] The question of how we explain our willingness to occasionally put aside our scientific worldview in the face of death and allow a 'dedifferentiation' (*Entgrenzung*) of our world becomes all the more urgent. Again, what we experience in such situations has little to do with the sudden return of basic religious faith. Hardly anyone will all of a sudden see themselves in God's protecting hands, and in general we do not believe in life after death. What we experience is instead the sudden chance to communicate with entities that, according to our naturalist presuppositions, we take to be part of a dead world. So how can we explain the fact that we allow ourselves to bracket or suspend the reliable subdivisions of our worldview?

At first, it seems certain that our willingness to adopt such attitudes relates to our need for consolation after the loss of a loved one or someone close to us. It is difficult for us to bear the fact that the dead are gone forever; we observe our own feelings of desperation and assume that others feel the same in similar situations. This might produce a secret bond of solidarity that allows those still living to refrain from applying customary standards of rationality and allow themselves ontological primitivizations, as if they were dealing with children. But is it really true that we view these peculiar attitudes and practices so therapeutically, as if we sought to give a necessary dose of consolation to the bereaved? Do we tolerate interaction with the dead as a category mistake because we know that the bereaved could not otherwise deal psychologically with their sorrow? Or is it that our observations are only rarely so detached, and that we instead often feel invited to share this communicative perspective, if only briefly? Of course, there are different degrees of this feeling, but when it comes to funerals or encounters with close friends who have lost a loved one, we often catch ourselves spontaneously adopting the perspective of the deceased and attempting to communicate with the dead, even if we ourselves are not among the bereaved. So have we also become infected? Do we need ontological illusion? Or is the ability to occasionally bracket out the differentiations of an enlightened worldview simply a part of being a mature individual?

It is only at first sight that Freud seemed to have a clear answer to all these questions. It is true that in *The Future of an Illusion*, our 'mental advances'[4] clearly lie in the gradual abandoning of all illusions that the natural world accommodates us, and in soberly accepting our painful helplessness in the face of nature. Here, modern, enlightened individuals accept the implications of a scientific worldview for the lifeworld, without ever contradicting it through cognitive dedifferentiation. But only three years later, in *Civilization and Its Discontents*, things look a bit different. Throughout the text, Freud struggles with the phenomena he describes, drawing on Romain Rolland, as 'oceanic feelings'.[5] At this point, Freud is still not entirely comfortable with assuming that such feelings are widespread, but at least he concedes the necessity of exploring their place in the individual's psyche. Soon he must realize that the ego of a healthy personality has just as few internal as external 'clear and sharp lines of demarcation'.[6] When someone is in love, for instance, 'the boundary between ego and object threatens to melt away'.[7] People in love feel joined to their partner and behave as if they act together from the same centre of action. But if such dedifferentiations are possible – that is, if psychologically healthy subjects are also aware of elements of self-transcendence – then, according to Freud, the key to explaining this phenomenon must be sought in the return of more primitive psychic states. In the early stage of development, children pass through a phase in which they feel 'fused' with real objects. Overcoming this stage leads to the construction of precisely those borders to the external world that, in the stage of maturity, appear to vanish in the aforementioned situations. Therefore, the only way to explain the dedifferentiation of the mature ego is to assume that a person has temporarily regressed to a previous stage of mental development. The explanation that Freud offers on the following pages clearly shows how much he struggles with the presumption that such regression could be a normal capacity of a mature, rational subject. Initially he refers to these states as 'disturbances'[8] of the ego, then he tries in vain to illustrate in spatial terms the possibility of preserving in our mind what has perished in reality, only to then point out that such mental regressions are 'rather the rule than the exception'.[9] Freud does not want to admit that enlightened, twentieth-century individuals allow themselves to regress behind an already attained threshold in which they recognize an independent outer world. Even when he turns to the issue of sorrow, he is astonished at how much we take for granted that we imagine the continued existence of those we love.[10]

Although in *Civilization and Its Discontents* Freud is aware of the anthropological necessity of finding 'palliative measures'[11] against our suffering in the face of the overpowering force of nature, he refuses to take the next step of accepting the fact of cognitive regression. His attachment to the scientific enlightenment prevents him from seeing the temporary bracketing of our ontological presuppositions as a chance to arrive at a controlled, reflective disburdening. Freud refused to recognize the fact that, even with our enlightened ideals, we could still want to let ourselves slip into the illusion that nature has a soul, and that the dead continue to live. In his view, rational enlightenment meant ridding oneself of all cognitive

regressions, but not in order to put them in the service of relax-
ing (*Entkrampfung*) our rationality. Within psychoanalysis, Donald
Winnicott was the first to break through this narrow-minded worldview. With his concept of transitional objects, Winnicott offers us
a conceptual tool that allows us to understand these spiritualist
sprinklings in our everyday life, which we do not hesitate to retain
alongside our basic naturalist conceptions.

For Winnicott, transitional objects are not only an 'ontological'
aid that small children use to deal with their frustration over their
recently recognized independence from the external world. Instead,
they also represent an instrument that adults use to fend off the
overwhelming pressure of reality by occasionally tearing down
ontological borders.[12] As we saw in Chapter 12, Winnicott maintains that small children can use all different kinds of materials in
their surroundings, such as the corner of a blanket, a teddy bear
or even a certain melody, as phenomena for constructing a 'transitional world' between inner experiences and objective reality. In
this 'intermediate' zone of experience, children temporarily bracket
their gradually germinating certainty of an independent, uncontrollable external world; by playfully using such affective objects, they
enter into a mental state in which the ontological borders between
internal and external reality are suspended. The fact that adults
support this kind of play with caring attention and corresponding
measures is an indication that even they have not entirely lost the
capacity for such transgressions. Winnicott is convinced that 'the
task of reality-acceptance is never completed, that no human being
is free from the strain of relating inner and outer reality'.[13] Therefore, even adults will occasionally fall back into a mental state in
which the borders to the outside world seem suspended, giving
rise to a kind of transitional ontological zone belonging neither to
our merely internal experiences nor to the sphere of objective facts.
Once we discover such an 'overlapping'[14] in these intermediate
spheres, Winnicott argues, a common world of transition develops,
about which none of us raises any questions. We have entered into a
state in which we fend off the intolerable weight of external reality
by playing with the possibility of a world that we can control and
force to obey our desires.

This intermediate world can now serve as a key for explaining
the many phenomena of our profane everyday life, which could
not be explained in terms of a rational, differentiated relation-to-
world. Winnicott uses this concept to give us access to an area of
cultural experience that derives essentially from such a bracketing

of external reality,[15] but if we did not apply his idea to other borderline areas of our world of experiences, we would be wasting the initial potential of his idea. The very fact that we, without any sense of confusion, observe how other people touch old, faded pictures in order to make contact with the people in the images might be a part of this intermediary zone. Another example is the fact that we take for granted that other people communicate quite intensively with their house pets. In each case, it does not seem to bother us that human subjects treat lifeless things or non-speaking beings as if they were like humans with whom they maintain vital communication. To correct such behaviour would seem inappropriate to us, because, contrary to our empirically proven beliefs, we assume the existence of an intermediary world that belongs neither to the zone of our inner experiences nor to the sphere of objective facts.[16] Together we presuppose a familiarity with such transgressions in which the pressure of the external world suddenly seems bracketed. We all need such moments of relief, be it to assure ourselves, counter-factually, of the closeness of loved ones who have passed, or to master our fears in the face of a world beyond our control.

In this zone of rationally tolerated metaphysics, we must also abandon the ontological primitivizations discussed above. In the face of that which is most dreadful, namely the death of those we love, we allow each other to truly play with the possibility that they remain among us. This is neither a merely internally experienced fantasy, nor an event in the world of external facts; rather, it is an ontological 'in-between' (*Dazwischen*) that does not require any further inquiry. Cognitive regression therefore serves an enlightened coping with life. Unlike Freud, we now know that the increase of our rational capacities depends on our ability to occasionally free ourselves from their requirements. Under the conditions of a universal acceptance of naturalism, consolation means nothing other than the acquired willingness to allow ourselves, with the acceptance of all involved, to slip back into a stage of our own existence at which it still helped to wish.

Notes

1   Sigmund Freud, 'Civilization and Its Discontents', in *The Standard Edition of the Complete Psychological Works of Sigmund Freud*, vol. XXI, ed. James Strachey (London: Hogarth Press, 2001), p. 86.

2 James Joyce, 'The Dead', in *Dubliners* (Oxford: Oxford University Press, 1967), p. 176.
3 Joan Didion, *The Year of Magical Thinking* (New York: Knopf, 2005).
4 Sigmund Freud, 'The Future of an Illusion', in *The Standard Edition*, vol. XXI, p. 11.
5 Freud, 'Civilization and Its Discontents', pp. 64–73.
6 Ibid., p. 66.
7 Ibid.
8 Ibid.
9 Ibid., p. 72.
10 Sigmund Freud, 'Mourning and Melancholia', in *The Standard Edition of the Complete Psychological Works of Sigmund Freud*, vol. XIV, ed. James Strachey (London: Hogarth Press, 2001), pp. 237–58.
11 Freud, 'Civilization and Its Discontents', p. 75.
12 Donald W. Winnicott, *Playing and Reality* (New York: Tavistock Publications, 1971).
13 Ibid., p.13.
14 Ibid., p. 14.
15 Ibid., pp. 128–39.
16 For other such examples, see the marvellous study by Tilmann Habermas, *Geliebte Objekte: Symbole und Instrumente der Identitätsbildung* (Frankfurt/Main: Suhrkamp, 1999).

Index